Where Teachers Thrive

Cast of Characters

SECOND-STAGE TEACHER (SST) STUDY (2008)

Ms. Dolan   Principal, **Deer Park** Middle School

Ms. Landry   Principal, **Lane** Elementary School

TEACHING IN CONTEXT STUDY (2010–2011)

Mr. Andrews   Principal, **Angelou** K–5 Elementary School

Mr. Gilmore   Principal, **Giovanni** K–5 Elementary School

Ms. Maxwell   Principal, **Morrison** K–8 School

Ms. Sterling   Principal, **Stowe** 6–8 Middle School

Ms. Thomas   Principal, **Thoreau** High School

Ms. Wheeler   Principal, **Whitman** Academy High School

SUCCESSFUL SCHOOLS STUDY (2014–2015)

Ms. Davila   Principal, **Dickinson** PreK–5 School

Ms. Forte   Principal, **Fitzgerald** PreK–5 School
(former turnaround school)

Ms. Forsythe   Assistant Principal, **Fitzgerald**

Mr. Hinds   Principal, **Hurston** K–8 School
(former turnaround school)

Ms. Honor   Assistant Principal, **Hurston**

Mr. Hanover   Director of Professional Development and Data Inquiry,
Hurston

Mr. Kain   Principal, **Kincaid** Charter 6–8 Middle School
(restart school)

Mr. Kaplan   Director, **Kincaid** Charter Management Organization

Ms. North   Principal, **Naylor** Charter K–8 School

Ms. Nelson   Codirector, **Naylor** Charter Management Organization

Ms. Rowland   Director, **Rodriguez** PreK–8 Charter School

Ms. Rega   Principal, **Rodriguez** K–4 Charter School

Mr. Ryan   Principal, **Rodriguez** 5–8 Charter School

Where Teachers Thrive

Organizing Schools for Success

Susan Moore Johnson

HARVARD EDUCATION PRESS
CAMBRIDGE, MASSACHUSETTS

Paperback ISBN 978-1-68253-358-1
Library Edition ISBN 978-1-68253-359-8

Library of Congress Cataloging-in-Publication Data

Names: Johnson, Susan Moore, author.
Title: Where teachers thrive : organizing schools for success / Susan Moore Johnson.
Description: Cambridge, Massachusetts : Harvard Education Press, [2019] | Includes bibliographical references and index.
Identifiers: LCCN 2019007151| ISBN 9781682533581 (pbk.) | ISBN 9781682533598 (library edition)
Subjects: LCSH: Teachers—Recruiting—United States. | Teachers—Selection and appointment—United States. | Teachers—Salaries, etc.—United States. | Teachers—Training of—United States. | School personnel management—United States. | School management and organization—United States.
Classification: LCC LB2832.2 .J64 2019 | DDC 371.102—dc23
LC record available at https://lccn.loc.gov/2019007151

Published by Harvard Education Press,
an imprint of the Harvard Education Publishing Group

Harvard Education Press
8 Story Street
Cambridge, MA 02138

Cover Design: Ciano Design
Cover Image: Miroslav Boskov/E+/Getty Images

The typefaces used in this book are Janson Text and Scala Sans.

Contents

To my dear grandkids,
who inspire and entertain me

Eli Johnson Asper
Leah Johnson Asper
Connor George Johnson
Lola June Johnson

Introduction

When we think about our own schooling, most of us remember a favorite teacher—someone who took us seriously, sparked our imagination, and taught us skills that gave us an unexpected sense of mastery, confidence, and independence. For me, it was William Dykins, my high school English teacher and speech coach, affectionately called "Dyke." I was fascinated by his clever talk and sophisticated knowledge about literature and life beyond the small midwestern suburb where I lived. He treated me kindly and influenced my life more than any other teacher. Those of us who care deeply about education remember our own schooling through memories of such teachers.

These vivid recollections of outstanding teachers often lead us to frame the problem of educational improvement very simply: How can we attract and retain more teachers like Mr. Dykins? This intuitive response was reinforced at the turn of the millennium when researchers concluded that the teacher is the most important school-level factor in students' learning.[1] Using *value-added methods* (VAMs) to analyze data sets that included both students' standardized test scores and the identity of their teachers, scholars produced estimates of each teacher's contribution to her students' learning. They found that teachers within a school often varied widely in their effectiveness—a few were outstanding, many were competent, and some were inadequate. In one teacher's class, students showed unexpected academic growth over a single school year, while those in the class of the teacher next door seemed to have made little, if any, progress. Recently, when economists analyzed school district data and tax records for more than a million students, they concluded that having teachers with high value-added scores leads, on average, to long-term positive consequences: higher income, more likely college attendance, and fewer adolescent pregnancies.[2]

In light of these findings, many policy makers took up the challenge of improving unsuccessful schools with a plan to increase their *human capital*—the sum total of their teachers' qualifications, skills, and professional habits. Rarely, if ever, has academic research had such an immediate and far-reaching impact on education policy, much of it focused on teachers in urban districts and schools. After 2000, "teacher quality" rapidly became the watchword of public education's reformers, analysts, and policy makers. The term identified not only the source of schooling's problems (weak teachers), but also the most promising lever for addressing it (replace those weak teachers with strong ones).[3] This theory of change was straightforward, if simplistic. Thus began nearly two decades of policies and practices intended to increase human capital in schools, one teacher at a time. Largely ignored were alternative strategies for reform, such as relying on teachers with the most expertise and experience to support the development of their less experienced or skilled peers. In the rush to fix schools, the schools themselves received scant attention.

This focus on the individual teacher gained momentum throughout the US. Some states reduced or removed preservice preparation requirements, often criticized as "barriers to entry" into teaching for "the best and the brightest" college graduates. The prime candidates for teaching often were bright, fresh, determined graduates with no education training or skills. Seldom acknowledged was the fact that teaching is complex work that requires hard-won knowledge and skill acquired over time in preparation programs and practice.

Districts and states in some parts of the country offered substantial signing bonuses to attract "high-quality" teachers, hoping they would revive failing schools. My own state of Massachusetts gained national attention by offering a $20,000 signing bonus "to encourage high achieving candidates to enter the profession who otherwise would not consider a career in teaching." Districts in other states offered smaller bonuses of $2,000 to $5,000.[4] As reliance on VAMs accelerated, many districts began to use students' standardized test scores to assess the effectiveness of individual teachers and then award bonuses to those whose students had the highest scores.[5]

In a move to reform schools by increasing human capital, the US Department of Education called for "turning around" chronically underperforming schools by replacing the principal and at least half of the current teachers. During the

Great Recession of 2008, states competing for Race to the Top funding acceded to the federal government's pressure to rigorously evaluate teachers, often annually, and to include student growth as a "significant factor" in a teacher's rating. Many new evaluation policies also enabled districts and schools to dismiss ineffective teachers more quickly than in the past.

However, nearly two decades after this intense and costly effort began, schools that serve low-income and high-poverty communities have not been reformed as many had hoped. Results from the 2018 National Assessment of Educational Progress (NAEP), often called "the nation's report card," were sobering. After seeing gradual improvement in NAEP scores in the early 2000s, analysts found that achievement had "flatlined" by 2018. The one bright spot was a continuing, gradual decline in racial and ethnic achievement gaps, which began in the 1970s and could not be attributed to recent policies.[6] Further, after an exhaustive evaluation, RAND analysts concluded that the Bill & Melinda Gates Foundation's six-year, $575 million intervention to improve human capital in three large urban school districts and four charter management organizations had failed to reach its goal of improving student achievement and graduation rates.[7]

What explains the failure of these widespread efforts to improve schools by increasing their human capital? I would argue that, although the researchers identified an important problem—the wide variation among teachers that left some students with ineffective ones—their strategies for explaining and fixing that problem were largely off the mark. Unquestionably, schools need smart, skilled, and committed teachers. However, by focusing on those individuals while ignoring the schools where they work, reformers failed to address a major source of the problem: the outdated, inefficient, compartmentalized school organization that rarely provides teachers with the resources and support they need to improve teaching and learning, both in their own classroom and schoolwide. By neglecting the school as a professional work environment for teachers, policy makers have placed all their bets on recruiting talented individuals, rewarding and retaining those who succeed, and dismissing those who fail. Yet a simple strategy of swapping out ineffective teachers for effective teachers has, in itself, shown no promise for achieving the kind of school improvement that students deserve.

Relying exclusively on efforts to improve human capital in this way rests on the shaky assumption that a teacher's success is independent of the school context in which he works, that a teacher who is effective in one school will be equally effective in any other. It is as if the features of schools that teachers regularly report matter to them—for example, the knowledge and skills of the principal, the effectiveness of schoolwide order and discipline, how time is used, whether they have a curriculum and what it is—have no influence on teachers' practice or their ability to successfully educate their students. According to this view, schools are little more than collections of classrooms, each housing a teacher and her students, who work together unaffected by others.

In this book, I argue that however important it is to attract knowledgeable, skilled, and dedicated individuals to teaching, whether they perform well and stay in their school will depend not only on who they are—their training, skills, and disposition—but also on whether their school supports their development and multiplies the strengths of their human capital throughout the school. In a traditional, compartmentalized school, an excellent teacher who works in isolation may bestow life-changing benefits on her students, but have no influence on the students assigned to less skilled or caring teachers nearby. This inequity is not only unacceptable and unwise, it is unnecessary. Through the case studies presented and discussed throughout this book, we can learn how educators purposefully work together to ensure that all students within a school learn and steadily develop.

EGG CRATE OR BEEHIVE?

Many teachers continue to work largely alone in their classrooms, and many schools still have essentially the same "egg-crate" structure first described by historian David Tyack and sociologist Dan Lortie over forty years ago.[8] But should they? In no other field is the basic organization of professional work as spare and rudimentary as in the school. Professionals working in other large-scale enterprises—for example, health management organizations, banks, and technology companies—are not left on their own to develop their skills, devise their strategies, and serve their clients as they see fit.

The egg-crate school is both a structural and an organizational metaphor. Not only are classrooms arranged on opposite sides of corridors, resembling the physical form of an egg crate, but teachers also are isolated within those classrooms, by both the walls and doors that encapsulate them. Tyack explains that when the US population moved to the cities in the 1800s and early 1900s, public education progressed from being a widely dispersed set of one-room schoolhouses to becoming multistoried buildings with age-graded classrooms organized like egg crates. Administrators who contended with rapid growth in enrollments found these to be practical and efficient structures, because as student populations grew, schools could grow with them, one classroom or corridor at a time.

When enrollments fell years later, administrators could conveniently downsize their school one classroom at a time. As long as teachers worked independently with their students, such fluctuations did not disrupt their instruction or their students' experience.

However convenient this structure might have been for administrators, it had organizational disadvantages for teachers. It impeded or discouraged their collaboration and development, which in turn limited students' opportunities to benefit from the school's full complement of its teachers' knowledge and skills. It assumed that a student's education is no more than the sum of his or her experiences with individual teachers in different classrooms. From the perspective of management, having self-sufficient instructional units worked well: when teachers' responsibilities were clear and distinct, administrators could ignore ways to create greater interdependence among teachers, such as shared curriculum development, peer observations, or collegial consultations about students' needs. Meanwhile, as Lortie explained, professional norms of privacy and self-reliance endured among teachers, reinforced in part by the very organizational structures in which they worked.

The egg crate had the unintended effect of stifling teachers' growth and limiting their schoolwide responsibility and influence. Within the routines and schedules of most schools, teachers had few opportunities or obligations to watch and learn from their colleagues' instruction or to systematically consider the learning needs of students who were not enrolled in their classes. Within this compartmentalized setup, most teachers were on their own to assess their teaching. Given these deeply rooted priorities and practices that increased isolation and self-reliance, it should be no surprise that teachers vary so widely in their effectiveness, even within the same school.

There have always been exceptions to the egg-crate model—schools or departments where teachers meet regularly, share resources and lessons, watch one another teach, and offer feedback. As a new high school English teacher in 1967, I was fortunate to be assigned to such a school and department. Quickly, I was included with teams of teachers who wrote curriculum together during the summer and then taught and refined it in the fall. We met often, both formally and informally, to check in with colleagues who taught similar courses or students and to discuss what worked well or how we might do better. Each of us had one unassigned period a day when we were not teaching and could plan our classes. Although that time was not deliberately scheduled to promote collaboration, we each had a desk in a common English workroom where two or three of us could confer when our planning periods happened to align. I'm sure that when I left that school nine years later, I was a much better teacher than when I arrived, due largely to my colleagues and the organization of our school.

When I returned to graduate school as a doctoral student, I mistakenly assumed that most teachers experienced their school much as I had—as a stimulating, inspiring environment where teachers collaborated regularly, holding high standards for themselves and each other. So I was surprised to learn from many of my classmates that the schools where they had taught functioned more like inert egg crates than the intense beehive I had inhabited. The collegial interaction that I had assumed was a given for most teachers turned out to be rare.

When teachers don't have frequent, well-organized opportunities to work alongside and learn from their colleagues, the school squanders the precious human resources that it has worked so hard to gather. Given an arid professional context, even promising novices and tested experts may decide to withdraw to the security of their classrooms or leave their school. The fundamental mistake that policy makers and administrators made in their focus on human capital was not that they wanted to have knowledgeable, skilled, and committed teachers, but that they imagined those teachers could succeed and be sustained without the school's ongoing investment in their learning, development, and joint efforts to better serve their students.

Although wide variability in teachers' effectiveness from classroom to classroom deserves attention, some variation is inevitable. In any school, at any time, certain teachers know more than others about particular subjects, have skills that others don't, and have more teaching experience, which research shows makes them on average more effective.[9] However, these assets often do not inhere in the same individuals. Given that diversity, school leaders could do much more to draw upon teachers' strengths throughout the organization in ways that enhance everyone's performance and the overall effectiveness of the school. Teachers could learn from watching their peers teach and collaborate on teams where they coordinate their instruction, improve their pedagogy, and review students' progress together. They could work with specialists and administrators to identify additional supports for individual students and develop common approaches to improve behavior. Together they could assume leadership at the grade level or by subject area to diagnose and address their school's challenges. Many possibilities exist, but meaningful change does not occur either swiftly or spontaneously. It requires the ongoing, deliberate effort by educators within the school to develop both a professional culture that is committed to improvement and systems of practices that stimulate and support it.

In 1988, James Coleman explained that an organization benefits when the human capital of individuals is increased and transformed by its social capital—the ongoing interactions of people in various roles. In this way, as teachers and administrators work together, a school's social capital can be said to increase its human capital.[10] Policy makers and practitioners need a dependable model for improving schools, with policies and practices to match—a model that acknowledges, supports, and promotes teachers' best performance not only within their classroom, but also across the school. Research conducted within schools can help us identify the components of that model, learn how it works in practice, and understand what it takes to enact, implement, and sustain it so that teachers and students thrive.

THE PROJECT ON THE NEXT GENERATION OF TEACHERS

For the past forty years, my research and teaching have been motivated by an intense interest in understanding, explaining, and improving the school as a workplace for teachers.[11]

In 1998, I joined with four doctoral students, Susan Kardos, David Kauffman, Ed Liu, and Heather Peske, to create the Project on the Next Generation of Teachers at the Harvard Graduate School of Education. We all had been teachers and shared an interest in strategies to improve teachers' work and their workplace. At the time, a large cohort of experienced teachers who had joined the profession in the late 1960s and made teaching a lifelong career were beginning to retire. They were being replaced by a new generation of teachers who were entering the profession in a labor market with many professional options that had not been available to women and to men of color of my generation when we entered teaching three decades earlier. By 1998 virtually all career options were open to anyone considering teaching, and administrators could no longer expect well-educated candidates to choose a teaching career by default, as many in my generation had done.

Our Study of Fifty New Teachers

Our initial research goal at the Project was to learn about this cohort of new teachers as they moved into schools. Who were they? Why were they entering teaching? What did they experience as novices? Would they remain at their schools and in teaching, as their predecessors had done? What factors influenced their career choices? A key decision that researchers make in designing a study is what the unit of analysis will be—that is, *who* or *what* it will focus on. The unit of analysis might be individuals, social groups, institutional groups, or organizations (such as schools or school districts). Given our research goal and the issues that interested us, the unit of analysis for our study was the individual teacher.

In an effort to answer our questions, we identified a sample of fifty first-year and second-year teachers in Massachusetts public schools. We intentionally selected a diverse group in order to learn about the full range of new teachers—individuals with different types of preparation, working in urban and suburban schools, and teaching different subjects in elementary, middle, and high schools. In addition, we sought to have racial, ethnic, and gender diversity in our sample, which was not easy to achieve at that time, when over 80 percent of US teachers were white women.

We deliberately chose teachers working in different types of schools, but we realized later that we didn't design the study to examine those schools. Although we interviewed many teachers while sitting in their classrooms, we also met with them in other settings, such as libraries or coffee shops, never setting foot inside their schools. We made no deliberate effort to investigate their work environment or to verify their description of it. In our interviews, we focused on teachers' personal experiences, with questions such as: "How did you decide to teach?" "How did you come to teach at this school?" "Please describe the type of support you've received as a new teacher, either within the school or the district." "What formal or informal contact do you have on a regular basis with other teachers?" "Do you have a curriculum for the subjects you're expected to teach?" In response to these questions and others, our participants told us again and again about their schools and what it was like to teach in them.

The primacy of the school

Eventually we realized the obvious: although there were notable similarities among the fifty teachers of this new generation, what mattered much more was what they experienced within their particular school. Those schools differed as work environments, even within the same district, and those differences mattered. Many of these new teachers had made a conditional commitment to teaching. They said that, if they achieved a "sense of success" in their work, they would probably stay, but if not, they would (and could) move on to a different school or turn to another career.[12] Their satisfaction with teaching was determined almost entirely by what happened at their school. If they were not assigned to courses that matched their areas of expertise, if they did not get support from their colleagues and principal, if they did not have an adequate curriculum, or if their students were disruptive, they might leave. Although state and district officials were making consequential decisions that substantially affected their work, such as setting licensing requirements or pay levels, what mattered most to those teachers occurred day to day in their school.

Surprising rates of turnover

We tracked these fifty new teachers over four years and by the end of our study, we documented troubling rates of turnover among them. Approximately one-third of our fifty teachers remained in their original school, one-third had changed schools, and one-third had left public school teaching. In our 2004 book *Finders and Keepers*, we describe the experiences of ten representative teachers and analyze their career decisions.[13] Because we had selected the teachers we studied deliberately rather than randomly and all our participants taught in Massachusetts public schools, we could not generalize what we learned to other teachers or locations. However, we did find that the proportions of "stayers," "movers," and "leavers" in our sample were similar to those being reported nationally.[14] At about the same time, Richard Ingersoll and Thomas Smith also identified high rates of turnover in their analysis of national data from the Schools and Staffing Survey and the Teacher Follow-up Survey, leading them to aptly characterize the teaching career for novices as a "revolving door."[15]

We then wanted to know more about how new teachers in other states experienced their work. Did the problems that our fifty new Massachusetts teachers identified in their work hold true for others? And so we surveyed random samples of first-year and second-year teachers in different states about three key experiences: how they were hired, how they interacted with colleagues, and whether they had the curriculum they needed.[16] In large part, we found that the experiences of the teachers we surveyed were similar to those we had interviewed. Many had been hired hastily and late, found their relationships with assigned mentors paltry and disappointing, and reported that they often lacked the curriculum and materials they needed to teach.

Because the unit of analysis for these additional surveys was again the individual, we never learned what we needed to know about those teachers' schools. We did, however, identify notable differences between teachers' experiences in schools serving low-income and high-income communities. New teachers in low-income schools were less likely than their counterparts in high-income schools to experience timely and informative hiring, to benefit from mentoring and support from experienced colleagues, and to have a complete but flexible curriculum that was aligned with state standards.

CONTEXT MATTERS

Recognizing that school context was potentially more important than we had initially acknowledged, Matthew Kraft, John Papay, and I studied the relationship between the teachers' work environment and both their satisfaction and their students' performance.[17] We analyzed two large data sets. The first was a statewide online survey (MassTeLLS) that asked teachers detailed questions about their work environment. For example, keeping their school in mind, teachers were asked to report how much they agreed or disagreed with statements such as: "The faculty has an effective process for making group decisions to solve problems," "Teachers have sufficient instructional time to meet the needs of all students," "The school leadership consistently enforces rules for student conduct," and "Teachers receive feedback that can help them improve teaching."[18] The second data set in that study included information about students' performance on the state's annual test, the Massachusetts Comprehensive Assessment System (MCAS), using a measure of student achievement growth (student growth percentile, or SGP) reported by the state. For this study, our unit of analysis was the school.

When we compared schools that served similar proportions of low-income and minority students, we found that teachers whose schools received overall high marks on the TeLLS survey reported that they were more satisfied with their work and planned to stay longer than teachers in schools that received low marks. In low-income schools that teachers rated highly, few said that they intended to leave, while in others that received low ratings overall, many did. This seemed particularly important because it suggested that when teachers left their low-income schools, they were not leaving because of the students in those schools, as some researchers had suggested, but because they found their work environment unsatisfactory.[19] The factors that mattered most to the teachers surveyed were social and organizational—the principal's leadership, relationships with colleagues, and the culture of the school, including discipline. Further, and equally important, when we compared schools that were demographically similar, we found higher rates of student growth in schools rated more favorably by their teachers.[20] It appeared that what was good for teachers was also good for their students.

Our research and similar studies by other scholars suggest that students and teachers could substantially benefit by improving the school as a workplace for teachers.[21] Providing a strong and supportive work environment is likely to enable teachers to succeed with their students and thus to retain more teachers. Some critics contend that efforts to reduce turnover among teachers are misguided because evidence suggests that, although the average teacher improves steadily during his first few years in the classroom, his progress levels off after three to five years.[22] However, other studies find that more experienced teachers are on average more successful than less experienced teachers and, therefore, worth retaining.[23] Proponents of reducing turnover value not only teachers' instructional effectiveness, but also the organizational stability that comes with having a staff of experienced teachers—stability that can support efforts to increase a school's overall instructional capacity and success.

Policy makers and district officials often ignore the fact that teacher turnover within schools is costly, both financially and organizationally. When a school or district must repeatedly hire new teachers to fill vacancies, it incurs steep expenses (in both dollars and time) as it recruits, selects, employs, and provides both induction and professional development for new entrants. In their detailed 2006 study of the Boston Public Schools, Sarah Birkeland and Rachel Curtis found that, in a single year, the cost for the turnover of 194 first-year through third-year teachers was $3.3 million.[24] Turnover also exacts organizational costs. Elaine Allensworth and colleagues identified "a range of organizational consequences" of turnover in the Chicago schools they studied, "such as discontinuity in professional development, shortages in key subjects, and loss of teacher leadership."[25] Matthew Ronfeldt, Susanna Loeb, and James Wyckoff analyzed data from the New York City Schools and found that students' academic achievement fell when high rates of teacher turnover occurred at their grade level within the school, even if their own teacher was unaffected. This suggests that losing current teachers may compromise instructional capacity by disrupting the school's systems for curriculum and instruction.[26]

Over the first ten years of our Project, we found that retention was a powerful, though certainly not infallible, indicator of a school's success. Teachers were inclined to stay in schools where they and their colleagues had the resources, systems, and support they needed to serve students well—both individually and as a group. Yet, because we had not studied schools themselves, we couldn't yet explain in any detail what factors differentiate positive, sustaining work environments that serve teachers and students well from unproductive, demoralizing ones that shortchange both. We wondered what practices distinguish one school, where collaboration among teachers is intermittent, superficial, and unsatisfactory, from another, where teachers work together steadily and purposefully to plan instruction and review their students' progress. How do teacher leaders in one school gain the skills and respect they need to improve instruction across grade levels, while teachers in another school ignore what happens in other classrooms, keep their heads down, and comply minimally with whatever the principal requires? How is time managed in a school where teachers get their work done and still enjoy a life outside of it, while in another school, the demands of the job are so overwhelming or mind-numbing that teachers plan to leave?

OUR FOCUS ON LOW-INCOME SCHOOLS

Our subsequent case studies at the Project focused on teachers working in low-income, urban schools, which historically have been systematically shortchanged by city and district officials.[27] Clearly, other schools, such as those serving Native American students and poor, rural communities, also have been neglected and deserve both sustained attention and the resources needed for improvement. Further, we know that schools serving wealthier and whiter student populations also have shortcomings that should be addressed. We don't assume that our findings about teachers' experiences in low-income, urban schools will apply in all settings, but we are convinced that many of the basic principles we found—the importance of collaboration, ongoing support for teachers' development, encouragement for teacher leadership, practices that contribute to greater schoolwide coherence, and professional norms that encourage everyone to steadily get better at what they do—are relevant to all schools.

Compared with schools in middle-income and high-income communities, schools that are located in low-income, urban communities are more likely to be assigned the least experienced teachers and administrators, to have the worst facilities, and to have the highest rates of turnover among teachers and principals. Their students are more likely to repeatedly experience racism, violence, homelessness, and a severe lack of access to medical and social services. On average, these students depend more on their school and teachers for their learning than do students in higher-wealth communities.[28] Given these challenges, it is no surprise that low-income, urban schools are also among the poorest performing schools in the nation. However, as we learned by analyzing data from the TeLLS survey and students' performance on the MCAS, some low-income urban schools do provide positive work environments for their teachers, enabling them to serve their students well. If we can explain how this works, then policy makers, administrators, and teachers themselves will know much more about how to improve students' learning in many types of schools and communities.

Massachusetts as a State Context

The multisite case studies featured here were conducted in Massachusetts. Interviewing nearly four hundred educators in twenty-six schools takes a great deal of time and, given teachers' tight schedules, requires repeated visits to a school. Because we lived and worked in Massachusetts, we could conduct the intensive, ongoing data collection that this kind of research requires. Also, there was an advantage to watching how schools functioned within the same state environment and observing how policies and practices within that context evolved over time. Although it certainly would have been worthwhile to duplicate these studies in different states, the expense and time required to do so were well beyond our budget.

State education agencies across the US vary widely in size, influence, and priorities, all of which affect what happens in schools. Given that variation, there would have been no merit in studying districts in some hypothetically "typical" state. We realized that the lessons we might learn from these school-based studies would be tied to specific practices, not average or typical ones. Massachusetts schools are funded by a mix of state and local property taxes. With a history of local control, state education officials in Massachusetts exercise less control over its districts and schools than those in many other states. However, the state is notable for its investment in public education and the success of its schools. Currently, it ranks first in the nation on various measures of educational performance, including the NAEP. This does not mean that all of its schools are effective, but that, compared with other states, more schools in Massachusetts are more effective. Therefore, because our goal was to identify best practices in challenging urban settings, studying schools in Massachusetts promised to yield valuable lessons.

THE FEATURED CASE STUDIES

In the chapters that follow, I draw directly and indirectly on many studies, including those we have conducted at the Project as well as those conducted by other researchers. However, I focus on findings from three major studies that we carried out in low-income urban schools between 2008 and 2015. Each study is described in detail in the appendix. Our unit of analysis for each of these studies was teachers within schools. Rather than trying to learn about the teachers' work environment indirectly by talking with one or two individuals, we visited those schools and interviewed diverse samples of teachers, administrators, and staff who worked there. The three multisite case studies that provide the core data for this book are summarized next.

Second-Stage Teachers in Urban Schools

The Second-Stage Teacher (SST) study, conducted in 2008, focused on teachers in the second stage of their career (years four through ten). We designed it to chronologically follow our earlier study of novice teachers, who would have been SSTs by 2008. We were especially interested in learning how these SSTs experienced professional learning opportunities, curriculum, accountability, and instructional coaching in their low-income schools.

We used a nested design so that we could learn about individual teachers working within their school context, situated within a district. We interviewed eighty-five teachers in fourteen schools located in three underperforming urban Massachusetts districts. Based on student performance and demographics, most of the schools we selected were similar to others in the district. All but one school had been sanctioned by state officials for failing to make Adequate Yearly Progress (AYP) on the MCAS, under the federal No Child Left Behind Act of 2001 (NCLB). Here I draw on findings from two schools in the same district, Lane Elementary School and Deer Park Middle School. (See table I.1 for descriptive data about these and other schools in our three studies.)

Teaching in Context

We conducted the Teaching in Context study in 2010–2011 in the Walker City School District (WCSD), a large, urban school district in Massachusetts that the state had rated as underperforming. The metropolitan area surrounding Walker City enjoyed a strong economy, a very high proportion of college graduates among its citizens, and many colleges and universities that prepared new teachers.

Based on our earlier study of school context, we carefully selected a diverse group of six elementary and secondary schools that varied on two dimensions: student growth on the MCAS and teachers' satisfaction with their work environment as reported by the TeLLS survey. All six schools in our sample enrolled large numbers of students of color who lived in low-income or high-poverty communities.

In this study, we sought to understand the instructional and organizational challenges that teachers in each school faced and the practices their schools

Table I.1 Three major studies

School	Principal	Grades	Teachers	Student enrollment	Low income	Students of color	Student growth percentile, ELA	Student growth percentile, math
				SECOND-STAGE TEACHER STUDY				
Lane Elementary	Ms. Landry	K–6	19	350	81%	79%	62	70
Deer Park Middle	Ms. Dolan	7–8	34	580	84%	70%	63	49
				TEACHING IN CONTEXT STUDY				
Angelou Elementary	Mr. Andrews	K–5	55	700	90%	95%	35	50
Giovanni Elementary	Mr. Gilmore	K–5	45	450	95%	90%	55	60
Morrison K–8	Ms. Maxwell	K–8	27	400	95%	95%	45	20
Stowe Middle	Ms. Sterling	6–8	50	700	90%	95%	45	45
Thoreau High	Ms. Thomas	9–12	69	900	80%	95%	50	55
Whitman Academy High	Ms. Wheeler	9–12	24	250	85%	95%	60	65
				SUCCESSFUL SCHOOLS STUDY				
Dickinson Elementary	Ms. Davila	PreK–5	30	400	76%	91%	60	83
Fitzgerald Elementary	Ms. Forte	PreK–5	35	390	85%	98%	63	63
Hurston K–8	Mr. Hinds	K–8	65	800	75%	99%	58	58
Kincaid Charter Middle	Mr. Kain	6–8	40	475	88%	90%	56	85
Naylor Charter K–8	Ms. North	K–8	37	500	82%	99%	55	58
Rodriguez Charter PreK–8	Ms. Rega Mr. Ryan	PreK–4 5–8	45	420	72%	83%	68	65

adopted to deal with them in the context of accountability. These practices included teacher teams, instructional coaching, discipline and supports for students, and opportunities for teacher leadership. We interviewed twelve administrators and eighty-three novice, second-stage, and veteran teachers.

Teaching in Successful Schools

The Successful Schools study, conducted in 2014–2015, focused on teachers' experiences in six elementary and middle schools serving students from low-income and high-poverty communities within Walker City. Notably, all had received commendation from Massachusetts officials with a rating of Level 1, the highest in the state's accountability system. These schools were both successful academically and well regarded publicly. The sample included three district schools and three state charter schools.

Two of the district schools had earlier been placed in turnaround by the state, while the third had performed well for many years. Two of the charter schools were well established, having been created under the state's charter law ten and twenty years earlier. The third charter school was selected to restart a failing middle school in WCSD. Therefore, both in the past and at the time of our study, these six schools operated in different policy environments, which imposed diverse requirements and granted them varying levels of autonomy.[29]

In this study of teachers' experiences in successful schools, we sought to understand the systems and practices that shaped teachers' work. We interviewed ninety-seven teachers, seventeen administrators, twenty nonteaching staff, and eight teachers-in-training. We deliberately chose teachers who had different levels of experience and taught a varied selection of grades and subjects. Our goal in this study was to understand, compare, and describe practices used by these successful schools for hiring, evaluating, supporting, and retaining teachers, while also comparing practices among the district and charter schools in this sample.

RECONCILING THE TENSION BETWEEN PEOPLE AND SYSTEMS

As we explored how to improve schooling by improving the teacher's workplace, two themes repeatedly emerged, often in tension with each other. The first is the reality that public education is a thoroughly human enterprise from its core in the classroom to its boundaries in the district office or state legislature. Students' learning needs, teachers' skills and preferences, staff members' background and commitment, parents' priorities, administrators' leadership, and policy makers' sense of responsibility to their constituents all play a role in this enterprise. The fact is that schools can never be reformed while ignoring these actors' various needs and preferences.[30]

The second theme is the importance of having orderly, sensible systems for doing the work of schooling. When individual differences are not only recognized but given full sway, schooling becomes personalized and rewarding for some, but arbitrary, capricious, and inequitable for many others. Systems and practices can provide valuable supports that guide teachers in deciding what and how to teach, allocating their time, and judging what works in their classroom. However, teachers often distrust systems that are imposed by policy makers, district officials, external experts, or principals, because they threaten to reduce or eliminate the professional discretion that teachers need to do their work well. Such systems might include teacher-proof curricula and pacing guides, zero-tolerance discipline requirements, test-prep regimens, or computerized templates for reports, record keeping, and grading. In many teachers' experience, these kinds of mandated practices too often discount the people who must use them and suppress good practice by prohibiting variation, discouraging innovation, barring adaptation, and penalizing independent thinking. Therefore, unless a school's systems are chosen, adapted, and well understood by those who will use them, they are likely to trigger skepticism and resistance from the start.

However, good systems that are adopted with good reason can enhance good practice. Atul Gawande richly illustrates how this works in medicine, where "extreme complexity is the rule for almost everyone." He likens the complex problems of saving lives and restoring health to those of "raising a child. . . .Their outcomes remain uncertain. Yet we all know it's possible to raise a child well." Gawande explains that when many individuals participate in solving complex problems, as they do in effective health care, everyone involved does not exercise individual autonomy. In fact, he calls autonomy "a disaster. It produces only a cacophony of incompatible decisions and overlooked errors." However, neither does the answer rest in unquestioning compliance with an externally imposed system, which cannot address all the conditions and complications that emerge. Instead, he explains, "the philosophy is that you push the power of decision-making out to the periphery and away from the center. You give people the room to adapt, based on their experience and expertise. All you ask is that they talk to one another and take responsibility. That is what works."[31]

These basic principles hold for educators engaged in the "extreme complexity" of improving urban schools, where teachers and administrators continue to search for how best to educate their students. The cases discussed in these chapters reveal this ongoing tension between the people and the systems meant to guide or regulate them. In many schools, policy makers and administrators have tried to impose structures and practices that demand compliance and produce predictable outcomes, only to discover that those outcomes are meager. In part, this occurs when the required systems and those who oversee them disregard the realities and potential of the teachers who are expected to implement them. They all too often divert teachers' attention and waste their energy because they fail to address the school's real challenges or the teachers' real needs. In other cases, however, teachers contribute to diagnosing problems, adapting practices, and devising systems that enhance their ability to do their work well. In doing so, these schools successfully reconcile the tension between people and systems so that they are mutually reinforcing. As educators adapt, improve, and strengthen these social systems to meet their students' needs, they also rely on them for guidance and support. From their experiences we can learn not only what works, but also how and why it works.

HOW TO READ THIS BOOK

The chapters in this book are thematic, each addressing a different challenge in the teachers' work environment. Examples from the three case studies just introduced run through those chapters. Therefore, you will find descriptions and analyses of practices from a single school in several chapters and, over the course of the book, you will come to know many schools. I have provided a Cast of Characters for the three studies as well as table I.1 to summarize basic information about the fourteen schools discussed here. You'll notice that the pseudonyms for the fourteen schools and their principals, directors, and other administrators all begin with the same letter, which is meant to make your reading easier. Even though the many teachers we interviewed for these studies are the focus of this book, I have not identified them individually with pseudonyms because having so many names would complicate reading.

The chapters that follow are organized thematically, but they need not be read sequentially. Instead, each is part of a whole and together they address key features of the teacher's work environment, which ultimately shapes the students' learning environment. Each chapter presents a challenge and explores how various schools in our studies dealt with it, as well as how teachers experienced and assessed their school's approach. I highlight both problematic and promising practices because it is important to understand not only what to do, but also what *not* to do; both offer valuable lessons for policy makers, administrators, and teachers.

Chapter 1, "Making a Match in Hiring," focuses on the basic human capital challenge of hiring teachers. It highlights the importance of making a good match between a job candidate and a school. Hiring in many schools continues to be late, rushed, and "information-poor." However, effective, "information-rich" hiring ensures not only that a prospective teacher has a good preview of what it will be like to work in the school, but also that she can demonstrate her teaching and exchange important information with prospective colleagues.[32] Such opportunities increase the likelihood that, from the start, a new teacher will be known and supported by her colleagues.

Chapter 2, "Deciding What and How to Teach," focuses on the choices that teachers make about curriculum and instruction, especially in the context of state standards and accountability. This is a continuous challenge for teachers, especially if the state's curricular frameworks and performance standards do not align well with the materials they have, their assigned curriculum, or their school's instructional goals. Here we see how teachers choose, develop, and teach one or more subjects, given the demands of standardized testing and accountability. Although district officials may select the curriculum, it is at the school where teachers and administrators explore and enact new instructional strategies to address their students' learning needs. When schools support those efforts with resources and coaching, they can augment instructional capacity schoolwide.

Chapter 3, "The Potential of Teacher Teams," focuses on teachers' working relationships with their colleagues and the promise of teams to integrate and advance their joint efforts. Although teachers have long reported that peers are their greatest source of support, the physical and professional isolation that they experience in many schools often limits access to their colleagues' expertise and advice. When teacher teams are organized to address both individual and school-wide needs, the collaboration they provide can benefit the participating teachers, their students, and others within the school.

Chapter 4, "Who Addresses Students' Needs and Conduct?" focuses on the students themselves, for if their teachers are to succeed in their work, then students must learn and perform well. However, students introduce uncertainty into teachers' work, because of both their academic and personal experiences and needs. This is especially true in low-income, urban communities, where many students live in challenging environments and schools have repeatedly failed to deliver what their students need. The teachers we interviewed raised concerns about student discipline and order; the academic, social, and psychological supports required to address students' needs; and strategies for engaging parents and families to support their children's education. This chapter compares two types of schools—those that take on broad responsibility for serving students and families and those that confine their attention to what happens within the school.

Chapter 5, "Using Evaluation to Improve Instruction," focuses on the role of supervision and evaluation in helping teachers to improve their instruction. Classrooms may protect teachers' privacy, but a closed classroom door also deprives those teachers of opportunities to learn more about their own instruction and that of their peers. Teachers widely view traditional professional development as being far removed from their classroom and, therefore, providing virtually no feedback about how they teach. This chapter examines exemplary practices in teacher supervision and evaluation, which offer the kind of feedback and coaching that teachers welcome and learn from.

Chapter 6, "When Teachers Lead," explores the leadership that teachers exercise, both as faculty members who guide school improvement and as teacher leaders with specialized roles. All teachers can influence change in their school, whether by supporting and contributing to others' ideas and initiatives, resisting them, or advancing their own proposals for improvement. Much depends on whether the principal encourages teacher leadership or tries to suppress it. As the experiences of several schools show, when principals and teacher leaders join together to improve a school, they can make remarkable progress.

The final two chapters deal with two resources that make it possible for teachers to effectively do their work. Chapter 7, "Making the Most of Teachers' Time," focuses on what is arguably the scarcest resource of all in schools—time. Teachers spend many more hours each week preparing to teach than their formal workday requires. Much of that work is invisible to policy makers, but essential for effective instruction. Decisions about how teachers' time is allocated have a far-reaching effect on what a school can achieve. Recent initiatives to create common planning time for teachers and extended learning time for students have introduced new opportunities and benefits for teachers and students. Both have promise, but only if they are well implemented.

Finally, chapter 8, "What Pay Means to Teachers," examines teachers' pay by exploring its purpose, what it means to teachers, and whether teaching is an affordable profession. Public school teachers' pay is usually set at the state or district level, often through collective bargaining, while charter schools and charter management organizations (CMOs) independently decide how and how much their teachers are paid. Here we learn from the experiences of teachers working in schools and districts that variously rely on a traditional salary scale, award merit pay bonuses, or provide career ladders.

In the conclusion I summarize the key findings of the book. I review the importance of teachers' leadership in school improvement and the principal's role in making that leadership not only possible, but likely. I highlight systems and practices that are widely acknowledged to be effective as well as those that continue to be debated and developed. I suggest what policy makers and district officials can do to enhance the quality of teachers and teaching. Finally, I explain how teachers and principals within schools can use what we learned from these case studies to improve their own schools as work environments.

Although each of these chapters addresses a distinct topic, the practices they explore often are entwined and interdependent within the schools. However, in tracking those relationships, I do not mean that school improvement is an all-or-nothing process. Having one practice work well makes it easier to improve another. For example, a good hiring system establishes early support for a new teacher among his colleagues. Curriculum that is coordinated across the school can ensure that no student gets lost or left behind. If a school has strong teams, then teachers will not have to depend entirely on their principal for feedback and instructional advice. If teachers can exercise influence throughout the school and in formal positions as teacher leaders, then the school's systems and practices can be better adapted to fit its needs. If teachers are paid a fair wage, then the demands of teaching will be less daunting and the school's progress more sustainable. It is through such interactions and coordinated efforts that a school builds capacity, as teachers and principals learn to work together productively on behalf of their students.

CHAPTER ONE

Making a Match in Hiring

Hiring a teacher is arguably the most important decision a school administrator makes. Done well, hiring can open the way for a school to succeed in its primary responsibility of educating students. Done poorly, it leaves students wasting precious time as they endure weak instruction and schools spending scarce resources to compensate for their mistake. Yet many districts and schools approach hiring as little more than an employment transaction by which a school appoints a teacher to fill a vacancy. This bureaucratic stance assumes that schools are generally the same and that one credentialed teacher is as good as another, what The New Teacher Project (TNTP) calls "the widget effect."[1]

Alternatively, hiring can be viewed as a process of mutual selection between a prospective teacher and a school. Those who see hiring this way recognize that teachers vary widely in their interests, knowledge, practices, and experience, while schools differ markedly in how they educate their students, as well as what they can offer and will expect from the teachers they hire.

In the early 2000s, after researchers documented that some teachers are much more effective than others in the same school, many scholars and reformers focused fiercely on the promise of recruiting and selecting a "high-quality" teacher for every classroom. Influenced by studies suggesting that teachers with higher SAT scores are more effective, scholars reported that schools often did not hire the candidates with the highest test scores for positions, leading them to conclude that schools didn't choose the best teachers they could.[2] Such analysts apparently ignored other valuable assets that teachers might offer, such as having subject matter expertise, knowing how to clearly explain complex ideas within a content area, understanding how children learn, or having experience implementing a specific curriculum or pedagogical approach.

Also, these scholars centered their attention solely on the candidate who might be hired, not the school where she might work. Historically, focusing on an individual's qualifications rather than the match between the individual and the school was consistent with established practice in most large school districts, where central office administrators rather than principals hired teachers. Traditionally, job candidates submitted applications to the district office. There, personnel administrators screened them to verify that candidates were properly licensed, conducted interviews, made job offers, and assigned newly hired teachers to vacancies in schools throughout the district. This centralized process may have been adequate when most schools offered similar programs and a qualified secondary English teacher could be expected to function effectively in any of a district's high schools. However, as schools have increasingly offered specialized academic programs while also being held accountable for performance under policies such as NCLB, responsibility for hiring has gradually shifted from central administrators to principals.[3]

Meanwhile, evidence grows that all teachers—even those of "high quality"— will not succeed in every school and that all schools are not appropriate for every teacher.[4] Fit matters. But how does this process of matchmaking work in school districts long accustomed to screening, hiring, and assigning teachers centrally? What do teachers and schools seek to achieve in a good match, and what do they actually do to ensure it? Our recent case studies in twelve schools that enrolled students from low-income and high-poverty urban communities offer both insight into the challenges of school-based hiring and models for effective practice.

MATCH AND WHY IT MATTERS

The concept of match in hiring makes intuitive sense and is commonly considered in other fields. Ideally, a candidate should accept a job that aligns with his skills and experience in a school that embodies his values and beliefs. At the same time, a school should hire teachers who are committed to its mission, have the knowledge and skills to advance its programs, and are prepared to work in ways that will support its staff and students. Credentials such as degrees, licenses, and test scores can inform selection, but they never tell the whole story. In fact, teachers who have similar paper credentials often differ widely in practice. For example, some prefer to instruct students from the front of the classroom using a traditional curriculum, while others engage students in studying real-world problems that generate findings with practical implications.

Similarly, schools increasingly have distinct goals and serve different groups of students, a change that has been fueled, in part, by the growth and prominence of charter schools. Schools vary in how they assign students and schedule instructional time; some call for teaching in ninety-minute blocks, while others rely on computers and online instruction throughout the school. In some schools, classes are tracked, while in others students are grouped heterogeneously. Some schools have a detailed code of behavior and a "no excuses" policy for violations, while others encourage self-expression and promote informal relationships among students and teachers. A thorough, informative hiring process provides opportunities for the candidate and the school to explore what the prospective teacher seeks and can offer as well as what the school expects and can provide.[5]

A FRAMEWORK FOR UNDERSTANDING AND ASSESSING HIRING

Edward Liu developed a framework for explaining key differences between centralized, bureaucratic hiring and school-based, information-rich hiring, based on our research about new teachers' experience with hiring (see figure 1.1).[6]

It is helpful to consider teacher hiring on two dimensions. The first focuses on where hiring decisions occur—that is, whether most of the hiring process happens centrally at the district office or locally at the school. The second focuses on the amount and quality of information that is available and exchanged during the hiring process.

Figure 1.1 Types of hiring systems

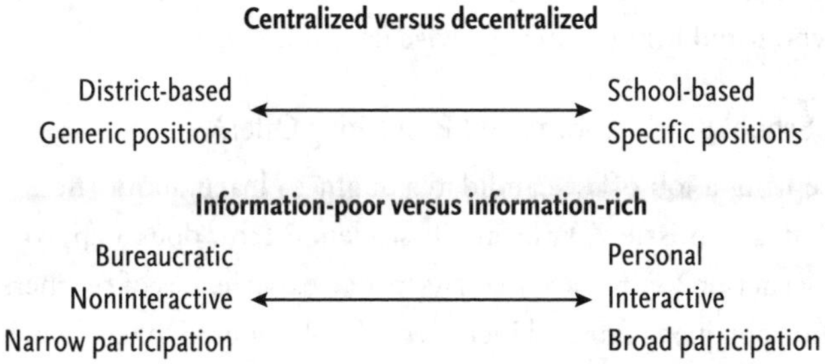

Centralized versus decentralized

| District-based | ←———————————→ | School-based |
| Generic positions | | Specific positions |

Information-poor versus information-rich

Bureaucratic		Personal
Noninteractive	←———————————→	Interactive
Narrow participation		Broad participation

Source: Edward Liu, *Information-Rich, Information-Poor: New Teachers' Experiences of Hiring in Four States* (Ed.D diss., Harvard University, Cambridge, Massachusetts, 2004).

Traditionally, most teacher hiring was centralized and "information-poor," in that it provided neither the candidate nor the school with much information about the other. Typically such hiring focused on a review of the candidate's paper credentials and an interview or two. Those who hired prospective teachers didn't watch them teach, and the candidates had no opportunity to visit the school where they might work to see it in action.

In contrast, school-based hiring is potentially "information-rich" because it can promote a worthwhile exchange about whether a candidate's skills, interests, and needs align with a school's mission, programs, and expectations. Hiring that is school-based makes it possible for principals and their staff to recruit and select teachers who are qualified for specific, rather than generic, positions—for example, a teacher who focuses on current issues in politics and government rather than one generally prepared to teach social studies, or a teacher trained in progressive pedagogy rather than direct instruction. Also, conducting hiring at the school site rather than the central office creates opportunities for broad participation by administrators, teachers, and students, thus increasing what a candidate can learn about the school he might join and the position he might hold. Through various school-based activities—touring the school, conversing informally with teachers and students, observing a class or two, doing a demonstration lesson, and participating with teachers in a team meeting—the candidate and those in the school can assess whether there is a match, all before a contract is offered or accepted.

Importantly, just because hiring is school-based does not mean that it will be interactive or information-rich. In fact, what is technically a school-based decision actually may be based only on a principal's cursory review of credentials or a brief interview with a candidate who talks enthusiastically about his rapport with students. A job offer that follows a single conversation might relieve a candidate's anxiety about finding a job, but it can never ensure that either the teacher or the principal who hired him has made a wise decision.

What Does School-Based, Information-Rich Hiring Offer?

Before accepting a job offer, candidates ought to learn about their prospective school. What is its mission? Who are its students? How does it approach curriculum and instruction? What are the day-to-day experiences of teachers who work there? Is the principal a fair and inclusive school leader? Do teachers have a hand in guiding the school's improvement? Are parents involved and supportive? It is in the applicant's interest to investigate such questions, even if hiring policies and practices make that difficult to do.

Similarly, other educators at the school have important questions for candidates that formal applications seldom answer. Do they understand the needs of the school's students? Do they have the commitment and skills required to teach those students well? Will they collaborate effectively with colleagues? Do they use formative assessments of students' learning to inform their teaching, and if so, what kind? Do they accept feedback and are they committed to improving their practice? Unless a hiring system attends to both what the individual candidate can offer and what the school needs and can provide, neither the teacher nor the school—nor ultimately its students—will be well served.

When hiring is hasty, impersonal, and uninformative, achieving a good match between a school and a candidate is, at best, accidental. New teachers who secure a job without actively choosing their school are likely to be isolated, disappointed, and far less effective than they could have been had they participated in a more informative process. Meanwhile, those in the school may be disappointed when they have to compensate for the shortcomings of a new teacher who arrives unaware of the school's strengths and needs, unfamiliar with its curriculum and routines, and therefore less likely to achieve success with students. If hiring is both timely and informative, the teacher will have accepted a job based on a good preview of who her students and colleagues will be—a preview that research suggests can increase employees' resilience in the face of difficult circumstances and setbacks.[7] Meanwhile, if a new teacher's colleagues participate in hiring her, they will know her strengths, anticipate her needs, and be far more likely to feel invested in having her succeed. As a result, students will experience a more integrated and coherent program as they move from her class to others in the school. Most people think of hiring as a preliminary step to becoming a teacher, rather than what it really ought to be—a crucial first stage in an ongoing professional relationship between the teacher and her school.

How Does School-Based Hiring Work in a Large Urban District?

School-based, information-rich hiring makes good sense, but how does it work, especially in the context of a large district where hiring long has been highly centralized? What makes it possible for principals to hire the right teachers for their school? What challenges and obstacles do they face? What promising practices do they adopt? We found answers to these questions in two studies we conducted between 2010 and 2015 in Walker City. The first, Teaching in Context, included teachers and administrators in six WCSD schools with different levels of student performance and teacher satisfaction. Principals could hire their own teachers, although some found the process difficult to implement. We learned from them about both the challenges they faced and the promising practices they adopted. The second study, Successful Schools, included teachers and administrators in six district and charter schools located in Walker City, all of which had received a Level 1 rating by the state. These schools all relied on remarkably similar, robust, school-based hiring practices, which can serve as a model for other schools.

Looking over time at these schools' approaches to hiring, we saw how changes in district policy influenced whether and how schools could conduct information-rich hiring. However, we also learned that simply having the opportunity to hire their own teachers yields little or no benefit to schools unless they have the capacity to do so well.

HIRING IN WCSD

Metropolitan Walker City is home to many colleges, universities, and nonprofit organizations that offer an array of teacher preparation programs; therefore, the schools we studied had ready access to a large pool of licensed teachers actively seeking jobs. Although no overall teacher shortage existed during the 2010–2015 period when we conducted these studies, schools still had difficulty hiring well-qualified teachers in certain fields, such as foreign languages, middle school science, and special education.

Before 2000, hiring in WCSD was highly centralized. Then, through collective bargaining and changes in central office policies, the district took a number of steps to improve and decentralize the process. Principals gained the authority to hire candidates once district officials had screened them. Senior teachers were no longer permitted to "bump" junior teachers from their position, which had long pushed hiring into the summer when many strong candidates already had accepted jobs in other districts.[8] WCSD also adopted an accelerated timetable that allowed schools to consider all candidates—new applicants as well as current teachers seeking to transfer—in a single round of hiring beginning in April. This timetable allowed the schools to better compete with suburban districts for the same pool of candidates. However, considering new candidates in April required either that 60 percent of the staff voted to approve early postings or that the positions carried an additional stipend of $2,500 for special responsibilities.

Overall, we found that by 2010, hiring within WCSD was much more school-based than it had been in 2000. Nevertheless, it remained an uncertain, unsatisfactory process, often falling far short of the information-rich exchange and matchmaking that we envisioned in our framework. Because of late budget approval, unexpected enrollment changes, and last-minute resignations, transfers, or retirements, hiring continued to be delayed and then rushed, often not completed until after school started, which John Papay and Matthew Kraft have found carries costs not only for teachers, but also for their students.[9] Just before school opened, district officials sometimes notified principals that their school was being assigned a "must place" tenured teacher, who had lost his position due to program changes and failed to find another. Principals never were optimistic about the promise of such forced assignments.

LESSONS FROM TEACHING IN CONTEXT

The principals in our Teaching in Context study had few, if any, models to guide their hiring and often devised their approach on the fly in response to last-minute changes or opportunities. Meanwhile, candidates—especially those who were unfamiliar with WCSD schools—were left to contend with a highly unpredictable process for finding a job in the district. This section describes the efforts of the schools in this study to make well-informed hiring decisions despite these challenges, and the lessons we can draw from their experience.

Connecting with Candidates Required Initiative and Inventiveness

After WCSD's central office administrators screened candidates' applications in 2010, they made them available to principals on an internal website, while also giving candidates access to a list of vacancies. It was then up to principals and candidates to find one another. Applicants could contact principals about openings and principals could scour the website for promising applicants. Teachers who were familiar with WCSD schools might contact the principal of a school that interested them and request an interview. Meanwhile, however, the applications of candidates who lacked inside information about the schools often sat on the internal website, waiting to be discovered. Sometimes they were, but in many cases candidates heard nothing more.

Not all principals understood the demands of the new online system, and many were unprepared to respond. For example, in 2011, Mr. Andrews, a relatively new principal at Angelou Elementary School, said that during the prior spring he "had lots of applicants contacting [him] about jobs, but [he] wasn't sure how the district's online clearance system worked." By June, he realized that he was expected to review applications online and recruit candidates, but because he was late to the game, he had lost many promising teachers to other schools. Rather than consulting the website, he then relied on professional connections within the district to find candidates. Of the two teachers he hired in August, he said one "turned out to be good," but the other had been "a mistake."

Other, more experienced, principals had hoped to complete all hiring by June so that new teachers could prepare for their assigned classes and participate in their school's professional development during the summer. However, they discovered that this sensible goal often was unattainable. For example, when we asked Ms. Maxwell of Morrison K–8 School whether all her new teachers had been hired by the end of June, she responded, "That was our hope. . . . Our hope last year was to try to get everything done before summer so that [the new teachers] would know what the professional development is for the summer and we can all start at the same time. But it did not happen." In fact, late in the summer Morrison's director of curriculum and several teachers were recruited to staff a new turnaround school, leaving key positions vacant. Looking back later that year, Morrison's administrators expressed doubt that they had made the best possible choices while under intense pressure to fill those positions.

Similarly, Ms. Thomas at Thoreau High School recalled that, although she had no openings in the spring of 2010, everything suddenly changed in July, when four teachers who were scheduled to transfer to Thoreau decided to take positions at new turnaround schools, leaving Ms. Thomas to find replacements in a hurry. At about the same time, the district instituted a new program for Spanish-speaking students at Thoreau, requiring the principal to hire five additional teachers. Finally, as she had expected, three veteran teachers formalized their retirements during the summer, so she needed to recruit their replacements. Ultimately, Ms. Thomas had to hire twelve new teachers during July and August. She recalled: "I hired them. It was very last-minute, but I hired them." Reportedly, such late changes and rushed hiring scenarios were common in WCSD that year.

Initiating and Planning School Visits Paid Off

Teachers, too, told of having to be resourceful and persistent in finding a school once the district office approved their application. A teacher who had recently been hired by Giovanni Elementary School said that, as a candidate, he had "pretty much applied anywhere [in the district] that had openings." He recalled going to a hiring fair, where he could sign up to meet various principals, each in a separate room. But those interviews didn't give him what he wanted to know: "It's just you and the principal, so you don't really get an understanding [of the school] at all." Therefore, he began to arrange visits to schools so that he could get a good look at the students and teachers. He reflected on his experience:

When you are around [the schools], at least you see [what they're like]. [In some], it seems like everybody is focused and on task. And as you are walking through the hall, it appears that kids are listening. [At other schools] you'll see them running through the halls—doing whatever, and the teachers are just standing there. Here [at Giovanni] it seemed like teachers were more kind of proactive. When I came through, another teacher was talking to a class that wasn't even hers. So, you kind of already sense that they are going to help each other out.

Opportunities for candidates to meet with potential colleagues also varied from school to school among the six WCSD schools. According to the teachers union contract, Walker City principals were obliged to involve current teachers in the hiring process through the first round of hiring, although principals ultimately had the final say in who received a job offer. Two of the schools we studied that year had standing hiring committees. Two others sometimes assembled current teachers in response to specific vacancies so that they could interview prospective colleagues for their department or grade level.

Thoreau High School had a standing hiring committee composed of teachers and administrators, and Ms. Thomas decided whether to convene it for specific openings. During the summer of 2010 when twelve teachers had to be hired, the committee met to consider applicants for the first three positions. However, by August, when nine teachers had yet to be hired, Ms. Thomas recalled, "I just was like, 'I'm not even going to try. I'll just try to get the best people I can.'" Because it was summer, she wasn't obliged to convene the committee and the members wouldn't have been obliged to attend. The pressure of time might have explained her unilateral decisions, but several teachers claimed that she never took the hiring committee seriously and they objected strongly to being asked their opinion, only to have it ignored. One complained, "I'm 100 percent sure that the final decision rests with [the principal]. So if she wants you, that's it, and if she doesn't, that's it. . . . What is this sham of a process, where we're all going to sit and interview Mr. Jones and Ms. Smith and the next thing you know, it doesn't even matter?"

Prospective teachers learned a great deal from those visits and meetings. A teacher at Giovanni Elementary recalled that she participated in several interviews at other schools before accepting her current job: "I went to other places. I tried to [imagine] myself in those schools and I felt like I was pushing it, even though I had great interviews." While at those schools, she wondered, "Well, can I do this? Can I be in this population with this group of kids? Does that make sense?" At Giovanni, she was impressed by having "a whole team of teachers" join her meeting with the principal: "So I was being interviewed by a group. There was a reading-literacy person, a first-grade teacher, and a math coach. So all these people were together making sure that the person they're interviewing will be a right match for the school in all areas. . . . So not just from the principal's point of view."

Once she joined the school, she realized that "these teachers have a say [in hiring]. I think that's good to see that it's not ruled by one person or decided by one person. There are many perspectives."

Giovanni was the only school of the six we studied that year where prospective colleagues routinely participated in candidates' interviews. As the principal, Mr. Gilmore, explained, "When we're hiring for first grade, the other first-grade teacher would sit on the committee. . . . This year, we got lucky when we got to hire the ESL [English as a Second Language] teacher. All the teachers that would be working with the ESL teacher were sitting in on the interview."

Meetings with prospective colleagues have potential benefits for all parties. If newly hired teachers are interviewed by current teachers, they're far less likely to be isolated and uninformed when they begin their job, increasing their chance to succeed with their students. Even though a principal's independent decision to hire a teacher might be well informed, failing to solicit and seriously consider current teachers' views can have negative consequences down the line. After all, once a new teacher begins his job, he usually must depend day to day on colleagues for guidance and support. Those who participated in the hiring process will be much more inclined to welcome and advise him about routine practices, such as how to order supplies or conduct recess, as well as share pedagogical information and insights about the curriculum, past practices at their grade level, and students who are likely to need extra support. As time passes, experienced teachers may begin to solicit their new colleague's views and suggestions, thus enriching the school with alternative perspectives, knowledge, and skills.

Therefore, actively and genuinely including teachers in the hiring process can substantially influence whether the school's current teachers will be invested in their new colleague's success. We know that being isolated and foundering alone in the classroom can cause a teacher to disengage or leave teaching.[10] Over time, a school that steadily loses teachers may find itself perpetually coping with costly turnover. One Thoreau High School teacher recalled:

> A few years back, it seemed like every year we were hiring the same number [of teachers]. . . . In September we'd come back to our staff meetings [and the principal

would say], "We've just hired twelve new teachers." What happened to the thirteen teachers that were hired last year? It was a revolving door. Of course, not all of them, I assume, were quitting the profession. Some went back to school. There were a lot of reasons. But I know for sure some didn't even make it to November. It was just like, "I can't do this."

A robust hiring process that is well informed by administrators and teachers can minimize such instability, even in very challenging schools.

Watching Candidates Teach Could Be Decisive

Although most educators would agree that it's wise to confirm that job candidates can effectively do the work they're being considered for, remarkably few new teachers are observed teaching before they're hired. Of the 374 new teachers that Liu surveyed in Florida, Michigan, and Massachusetts, only 13 percent of those who taught in low-income schools had been asked to do a demonstration lesson as part of their hiring. Although these low rates may in part have been a consequence of late hiring, it's worth noting that only 22 percent of teachers hired by high-income schools—where hiring was more likely to be finished by the end of June—reported having done teaching demonstrations during the hiring process.[11] Thus, when Liu conducted his survey in 2004, a large majority of principals apparently did not view demonstration lessons as an essential step in hiring.

Of the WCSD schools we studied in 2010–2011, only Morrison K–8 included observations as part of its hiring process and, even there, it was a relatively new and undeveloped practice. Some principals pride themselves on being able to discern a teacher's promise and predict her future performance based on a single interview. However, those who insist on watching a candidate teach before offering a job sometimes come face-to-face with the mistake they might have made if they had relied entirely on a single interview and their intuition. Morrison's Ms. Maxwell explained, "This year we made sure that we *tried* to have each person that we interviewed come in and do a classroom demonstration. . . . Some people did an excellent job talking and then when it came to the classroom—awful!"

Having a Farm Team Provided Backup

One of the greatest demands these principals faced was maintaining contact with a pool of strong candidates so that they could move quickly when vacancies occurred. Many reported finding the district's online system cumbersome and incomplete and, as a result, relied on informal referrals and recommendations from either their own teachers or from principals in other schools, as Mr. Andrews did at Angelou Elementary. Or, they responded in the moment to candidates who stopped by the school to drop off a résumé or check about openings. None of these informal approaches proved to be reliable over time.

However, in an effort to have a strong pool of candidates whenever vacancies occurred, two principals had built a private pipeline or "farm team" for their school by establishing an ongoing relationship with one or more teacher preparation programs. For example, when a vacancy opened at Stowe Middle School, Ms. Sterling relied on candidates she had observed closely when they served at Stowe as full-time residents in the local teacher preparation program. Sterling said that not only had she "seen that teacher through the year," but the teacher had "gotten to know the culture of the school. It's just much better to have somebody who knows the culture of the school." One new teacher at Stowe had moved directly from being a resident teacher one year to becoming a full-time teacher the next, after her mentor teacher left the district: "I was teaching the exact same subject, same curriculum, and same classroom. Working with the same team and everything."

Similarly, Ms. Wheeler at Whitman Academy High School relied on what she described as a "firm partnership" with a local university program that engaged teachers in year-long student teaching placements. It was those candidates she looked to when openings occurred. A department head at Whitman explained, "The majority of teachers [here] used to be my interns." One recently hired teacher had been impressed with Whitman's students when she was employed by the university-based program that partnered with the school: "I'd never seen kids so proud of their school in my life and I thought, 'I have to be part of that'. . . . I really wanted to teach there." She couldn't arrange to do her student teaching at Whitman, but she did teach summer school there. "At the very, very end of August, [Ms. Wheeler] called me and said, 'We just found out we have an English teacher position. You need to be [special education] certified, which I know you're not, but we'll put you through the process. You have until noon to let me know if you want the job.'" Unlike last-minute job offers that are informed by no more than a single interview, a well-seasoned and carefully vetted candidate from a school's farm team can ensure a good match. This was, as one Whitman teacher said, her school's "go-to" process for hiring and the principal's way of coping with sudden enrollment changes and delayed postings.

Therefore, each of these WCSD schools relied on at least one school-based hiring practice. All principals interviewed candidates, leveraging online resources and professional networks to identify and connect with them. Several hosted interested candidates for site visits. One routinely included teachers and administrators on their interview teams. Another required candidates to teach a demonstration lesson while members of the hiring committee observed. Two had created informal farm teams composed of potential candidates who had completed student teaching or served as teaching residents in the school. In each case, these practices were initiated by the principal in an effort to make well-informed hiring decisions. However, these were not practices adopted by all schools. They were the exception, not the norm.

BEST PRACTICES OF SUCCESSFUL SCHOOLS

Three years later, when we studied successful district and charter schools in Walker City, we hoped to identify best practices. Given the variety of these settings, we were surprised to find very similar hiring practices from school to school.

Although these successful schools all served low-income or high-poverty communities, only Dickinson Elementary School (preK–5) was a traditional district school that was obliged to follow WCSD policies and practices, which had changed again in 2014. Schools were no longer limited in any way by current teachers' transfer requests, but were free to select the best internal or external candidate for any opening. With the approval of 60 percent of staff or with an appended $2,500 stipend, the school could post positions in March, a month earlier than before, enabling it to better compete with suburban districts for the most promising candidates. And the central office no longer required schools to accept a "must place" tenured teacher who failed to find another position after hers was eliminated. Instead, displaced teachers who weren't hired by another school joined a pool of unassigned teachers who then became available as substitutes or assumed special responsibilities. Finally, WCSD's Office of Human Capital had created what Dickinson's Ms. Davila called an "amazing website" that made it possible for candidates to apply for positions at specific schools, while schools could manage applications for their positions through a customized portal.

Two other district schools, Hurston K–8 and Fitzgerald Elementary (preK–5), could exercise even more freedom than Dickinson. While their schools were in turnaround, Principals Hinds and Forte had complete autonomy to hire, fire, and transfer teachers. When the schools emerged from turnaround, both principals arranged to retain much of that autonomy. When it opened in 2003, Hurston had been a school with special status in WCSD and it reverted to that status once it emerged from turnaround. Mr. Hinds, like his predecessors, had the right to hire new teachers, dismiss nontenured teachers who failed to meet the school's standards, and transfer tenured teachers out of Hurston. After exiting turnaround, Fitzgerald successfully applied to become a Massachusetts Innovation School within the state, which gave Ms. Forte the authority to freely hire teachers at any time. However, she could not transfer teachers once they were on her staff.

Among the three charter schools in Walker City, Kincaid Middle School had been selected to restart a failing WCSD middle school and Mr. Kain had full autonomy to hire and fire teachers. Naylor Charter School (K–8) and Rodriguez Charter School (preK–8), which had been established under the state's charter school law ten and twenty years earlier, respectively, had no obligations to WCSD, despite being located within district boundaries. They could hire any teacher who met basic qualifications and passed the state teachers' test. And they could fire teachers at will.

Given the increased autonomy that all of these schools had in hiring, we had the opportunity to see what successful schools do when they can design their own hiring process. Demographically similar students attended these schools, but the schools themselves differed in curriculum and pedagogy, their expectations for students and families, their academic calendars and daily schedules, and their prevailing culture. Therefore, we expected to also find that hiring practices varied substantially from site to site. Across the sample, however, approaches to hiring were remarkably consistent.

Every principal viewed hiring as a powerful lever for improvement and, therefore, committed considerable time and other resources to ensure that it was done well. All conceived of hiring as a two-way process between the candidate and the school. Everyone involved paid close attention to the individual applicants in an effort to learn what they might offer students and their fellow teachers. But they also wanted the individuals they selected to have a good chance to succeed and contribute to their school's improvement. Therefore, hiring was an educative process not only for those at the hiring school, but also for the candidate. It was designed to ensure that teachers who accepted a job offer would already be enthusiastic about their school's mission, know their obligations as members of the faculty, understand the assistance they could expect, and quickly become engaged with their colleagues in providing a coherent, effective program for students. Together, these schools' experiences illustrate how school-based, information-rich hiring can and does work. We'll look first at the components of their hiring system and then consider the hiring process in action.

Making Fit a Priority

Principals in all six schools believed that their school would not be the right place for every teacher—even for an individual who stood out on paper as an outstanding candidate. None thought hiring was successful if it simply filled a vacancy with an objectively well-qualified teacher. Instead, the principals sought teachers who would quickly fit in and help improve the school. Ms. Rowland, director of Rodriguez Charter School, captured this widely shared perspective when she described her applicant pool: "[S]ome are a good fit for Rodriguez. Others are great teachers, but we are not perfect for them and they are not perfect for us." Moreover, beyond making fit a priority in hiring, the principals of these schools were very clear on the dimensions of fit that mattered. They looked for a candidate's match with their school's mission, core practices, professional norms, pedagogy, and expectations for collaboration and development.

Mission fit was essential

As schools assessed fit on candidates' applications, the most important factor was whether they were aligned with the school's mission. Each of these schools served students from high-poverty communities and they expected their teachers to be genuinely committed to ensuring those students' success. Teachers at Naylor and Kincaid Charter Schools repeatedly spoke about their school's commitment to "closing the achievement gap." Ms. Forte at Fitzgerald Elementary School said that her school's mission was one of "social justice" and that she and her teachers knew that "this school is altering the course of these kids' lives." She told candidates, "We're on a mission and, if you don't see yourself as fitting in here, we welcome you to go somewhere else." Her primary concern was whether candidates shared the "belief system" needed to achieve Fitzgerald's mission: "Did they think that children who are African American or Latino and poor could learn?" Mr. Hinds, whose K–8 school also had been in turnaround, pointed to the importance of Hurston's teachers having a "fundamental belief" in all students' ability to succeed, even if those students did not "have a track record of success." Once teachers were hired, Hinds wanted to be sure that he wouldn't have to convince them that "this could be done." He made a commitment to "supporting them in how" it would be done.

Endorsing the school's practices counted

Second, principals and teachers assessed whether a candidate endorsed the practices their school relied on to achieve its mission. For example, Ms. Davila at

Dickinson Elementary School said she wanted to probe a candidate's belief about "the way to make a difference." At several schools, implementing a uniform behavior system was viewed as fundamental to maintaining the school's steady focus on learning. For example, teachers at Kincaid Middle Charter School were expected to endorse a "no excuses mentality," defined in documents as a belief that "regardless of circumstances . . . there is no reason why a student cannot be successful in school and why a teacher cannot achieve meaningful results with his or her students." Mr. Kain explained that, if a student failed to turn in homework, "we do not want to hear excuses about why it's missing. Instead, we want to see the homework completed and we don't want the homework to be missing in the future."

By contrast, Ms. Rowland at Rodriguez Elementary School said, "We're not a 'no excuses' charter school. That's not what we believe in . . . You need to believe that you're here to serve all the kids who walk through the door and you need to believe that they can and will succeed. You need to believe that we're not giving up on kids and that it may sometimes take heroic efforts, but we're going to work with kids and families to have them succeed."

Similarly, Ms. Forte spoke explicitly with candidates about the "intensity" of teaching children who grow up in poverty: "The biggest challenge is that [our students] don't have their basic needs met. [They] don't have a lot of social and emotional support." Consequently, she explained, students must have "a lot of their needs met by their classroom teachers."

Professional norms and practices mattered

Third, schools sought teachers who would be committed to their professional norms and pedagogical practices. For example, teaching at Fitzgerald and Rodriguez was, as one administrator said, "very demanding academically," in part because teachers were expected to develop complex, project-based learning experiences for students. Therefore, it was important for candidates to know this in advance. At Hurston and Dickinson, the arts were a priority because, as Ms. Davila explained, a strong arts program was key to providing Dickinson's students with an education comparable to what their suburban peers experience. As a result, the arts were taught in separate enrichment classes and integrated into regular classes.

Although administrators recognized the need to convince candidates that their school would be a desirable place to work, they viewed it as necessary to, as one said, "be up front about the challenges." Rodriguez's K–4 principal, Ms. Rega, spoke candidly with applicants about what she called the school's "work ethic." Teachers, she said, were "never satisfied—we want every child to succeed. . . . There are teachers who stay until 6:00, 7:00, 8:00 at night. There are teachers who come early. There are teachers who have [their own] kids and go home and [continue to] work." Similarly, Naylor's principal, Ms. North, explained to applicants that they would be expected to "work really long hours . . . creating curriculum from scratch . . . staying after school tutoring . . . calling parents on their way home." Mr. Kain said that, in considering candidates for Kincaid, he weighed them on the "will-skill" dimension: "We try to limit as many low-will hires as we can, because that is the thing that we've found we cannot change or don't have the patience to change."

Expectations for ongoing development and collaboration were explicit

Finally, schools assessed candidates' alignment with their norms for development and ongoing collaboration with colleagues. Did they exhibit an unflinching determination to improve their instruction? As we will see in chapter 4, supervisors in all these schools regularly observed instruction and provided feedback to teachers, who then were expected to make changes in subsequent classes. Applicants who seemed self-satisfied were viewed with skepticism, while those displaying a confident "growth mindset" were seen to have promise.[12] As an administrator at Hurston said, teachers had to "be willing to constantly reassess, reinvent, and really be creative."

Also, teachers at these schools were expected to collaborate frequently with others, as coteachers, members of teams, and participants in schoolwide professional development. Because this kind of interdependence is not the norm in most egg-crate schools, those who hired teachers had to devise ways to discern whether candidates would actually value such interaction. This meant not simply being satisfied when candidates gave lip service to collaboration during an interview, but instead providing opportunities, such as attending a grade-level team meeting with prospective colleagues and demonstrating that they truly wanted to learn from and with others.

Investing Resources in the Recruitment and Hiring Process

To achieve fit in each of these areas, the schools committed substantial resources to simultaneously learn about candidates and inform them about their school and how it worked. Implementing the steps of their process—recruiting and screening a strong, diverse pool of candidates; arranging school visits for candidates where they could see the school in action and talk with administrators and teachers; interviewing candidates along with current teachers; and organizing a demonstration lesson with a follow-up debrief with the principal—was not left to chance.

Recruiting a diverse pool of candidates from various sources

These schools had access to different pools of candidates. Administrators at the district schools (Dickinson, Fitzgerald, and Hurston) could search for candidates on the WCSD internal website. Meanwhile, applicants who met the district's educational and licensing requirements had access to posted school openings and could contact a school directly. Although some large school districts conduct ambitious recruitment programs, WCSD did not, possibly because of the strong, local labor market. Therefore, these schools went beyond the district's applicant list and recruited candidates from other sources, including regional job fairs, Teach for America's job board, and online employment services such as School Spring. They ran their own advertisements in community newspapers and even posted vacancies on websites, including Idealist and Craigslist.

Current WCSD teachers who sought to transfer also applied on the district's website. One Hurston administrator reported that improvements in the district's hiring process had substantially increased the number of applicants for his school's openings. Ms. Forte at Fitzgerald said she, too, appreciated being able to "look at all of the candidates who applied to the system . . . for example . . . I need a sixth-grade math teacher. Only thirteen people applied to *my* sixth-grade job, but 168 applied to the district." With the new website, she could "just open up every one of those résumés and personally recruit promising candidates."

The three charter schools—Naylor, Rodriguez, and Kincaid—relied on their CMO's "talent staff," whose sole responsibility was to recruit and screen promising candidates for positions in their schools. Rodriguez and Naylor each employed one talent staff member, while Kincaid was supported by a team serving several network schools. These talent staff consulted with principals about their needs and then arranged for them to meet promising candidates who had been recruited and screened.

Two of the charter schools had their own internal farm team composed of a small number of teachers-in-training (TTs), who served for a year as teaching assistants and substitutes while learning more about teaching. They earned approximately two-thirds of a beginning teacher's salary at Naylor and a full beginning salary on the WCSD scale at Kincaid. TTs who did well could reasonably expect to be hired as full-time teachers the following year, although often they were asked to step up and fill vacancies that occurred during their first year as a TT. Hurston maintained an active partnership with Citizen Schools, a national nonprofit organization that partners with US middle schools in low-income communities. Its staff, who ran an extended day program for Hurston's students, included recent college graduates, many aspiring to be teachers. They gained valuable experience tutoring and organizing enrichment opportunities for students after classes ended each day, and some assisted in classes during the regular school day. Hurston occasionally hired very promising members of the Citizen Schools staff for regular teaching positions. Fitzgerald also had an established relationship with a university-based teacher preparation program and recruited some of its most successful student teachers. Nonetheless, all these recruitment efforts generated fewer strong candidates than the schools needed, including candidates of color.

Indeed, attracting candidates of color was one of the most important and difficult recruitment challenges these schools faced. Because the large majority of their students were classified as students of color (ranging from 83 percent at Rodriguez to 99 percent at Hurston and Naylor), many teachers and administrators in these schools strongly believed that, for the sake of developing self-esteem and community among their students, they needed to have a more diverse teaching staff. In addition, research also suggests that students learn more when their teachers are of the same race or ethnicity.[13] However, 80 percent of current US teachers are white, and far fewer college students of color currently aspire to become teachers now that all professional fields are open to them.

Mr. Ryan explained that Rodriguez "look[s] very hard" for candidates of color, but receives very few inquiries or applications from them. In response, the school was developing localized strategies, such as visiting churches in the neighborhood to inform members of the community they served about staff openings. In addition, the school's teachers of color were actively involved as personal emissaries in Rodriguez's campaign to increase its diversity by identifying promising candidates of color. Naylor made an effort to hire TTs of color, who initially were members of their farm team but could eventually move up to full-time teaching positions. Recruiters from Kincaid and Naylor visited Morehouse College and Howard University, both historically black institutions, and then hosted visits so that applicants could see the school, talk with students, and meet current teachers of color on their staff. Recruiting faculty of color was somewhat less difficult at Hurston and Fitzgerald because the district already employed many black and Latino teachers and, therefore, some candidates of color could more easily envision working in those schools than in the charter schools.

Although researchers have called recruitment in public schools "passive and provincial," administrators in these schools understood that good hiring necessarily depends on successful recruitment and, therefore, it deserved their active attention and effort.[14] None relied on a single source or limited their recruiting efforts to a single season. They often commented on how small the pool of strong candidates was and, through their responses, suggested that they were actively competing with other schools in our study for similar or the same applicants.

Screening candidates carefully

At the district schools—Dickinson, Fitzgerald, and Hurston—administrators carefully reviewed résumés, which they received directly from candidates or retrieved from the district's online dashboard. They then contacted promising applicants to arrange interviews and school visits. Given all their other responsibilities and the need to coordinate hiring with the district office, this was inevitably a time-consuming and sometimes fragmented effort. At the charter schools—Kincaid, Naylor, and Rodriguez—talent staff managed all steps of the recruitment and hiring process and were responsible for screening all applicants.

Schools then prescreened candidates further. Once principals of the district schools and talent staff of the charter schools reviewed applicants' submitted materials—a résumé, cover letter, and sometimes a teaching portfolio including videos—they decided which candidates deserved further consideration. The charter schools first screened promising candidates by phone or online using a structured interview protocol designed to reveal whether a candidate was genuinely interested in their school and committed to its mission. At Rodriguez, Mr. Ryan explained, "It's kind of a test to see how much you want to work here. If you're sending your résumé to a thousand places and we [say] 'Now do a little more work' and you do that work, it's showing that you want it." Kincaid's talent team posed scripted questions and assessed all candidates' responses on a five-point scale; those who scored three to five points advanced to a school-based interview. A Naylor network administrator who conducted all screening interviews for its three schools explained that they "never take a chance on mission alignment," which she assessed by asking candidates why they wanted to teach at Naylor: "If they don't have a good answer, that's a big red flag. If they don't mention the achievement gap, if they don't ever discuss urban kids and that all students need good teaching—not just rich, white kids—they are rejected." She also said that Naylor eliminated candidates whose attitude toward students was "deficit-based, not respect-based," as well as "any people with savior complexes, who think that they're here to save our kids and there's something wrong with them."

Similarly, district principals reviewed candidates with the needs of their school in mind. Fitzgerald's principal, Ms. Forte, looked for evidence of a candidate's successful teaching experience because, she explained, "my students can't afford a lost year." At Dickinson, Ms. Davila looked for teachers with experience at other local schools that effectively served low-income students, preferring candidates who had attended district schools themselves. Because the district's online system made it easy for candidates to apply to many schools, Davila looked for evidence that a prospective teacher already knew about her school and "really wants to work here." She also scanned résumés for specific skills. For example, in hiring a new literacy interventionist, she sought a teacher who had been trained in a specific reading technique and "ha[d] taught first grade." Several schools favored candidates who had successfully completed their two-year commitment to Teach for America and wanted to continue their teaching in a low-income school that was well organized. Administrators at Rodriguez sought applicants who would bring the benefits of "interesting experiences," such as living abroad or working in an unusual setting, and they, too, favored candidates with urban teaching experience.

Organizing school visits and interviews

Promising applicants then were invited to visit the school while it was in session so that they could see the facility, observe the students, and experience the school's professional culture. These principals believed that candidates needed to have a good preview of the work ahead if they were to make a well-informed decision that would last. For their part, candidates appreciated the openness and candor that a well-organized school visit conveyed.

All schools arranged for candidates to meet not only with the principal, but also with teachers. A current teacher at Dickinson said that when she was hired, Ms. Davila invited her prospective grade-team colleagues to participate in the interview because, as she told them, "you're the ones who are going to have to work with [her]." A teacher at Kincaid, who recalled having been isolated in her prior school, was amazed to hear administrators and teachers discuss a vision for the school during her interview. She thought that their vision "might [actually] come true," especially when "it was pretty clear that [teachers] would have a hand in it."

Those conducting the interview tailored questions to both the candidate and the position to be filled. Ms. Honor, the assistant principal at Hurston, explained her approach: "If they're [in literacy], I might ask [how they teach] tone and mood. . . . If it's math, 'How do you get kids to not just do fractions, but understand fractions? What does that look like? How do you make it come alive for them? . . . What's a difficult concept that you've cracked—that you have figured out how to present to kids and engage kids in and get them to master it?'"

Principals also continued to press candidates about their commitment to the school's mission and their readiness to enforce its expectations for discipline. For example, Kincaid's Mr. Kain explained that he often probed a candidate's readiness for Kincaid's no-excuses norm by posing a scenario with a difficult dilemma: "You see a student on Friday afternoon walking down the hall. They're getting ready to leave and their shirt is untucked. What do you do?" He said that he found their responses revealing: "If, philosophically, you might say something in that moment—'I don't think students should ever have to have their shirt tucked in'— then you're not going to really like [the fact] that they have to raise their hands [in class] . . . or that we require them to sit up without their hands on their face." Although the school's strict discipline code might deter some candidates, others found it attractive. One current teacher said that the interview convinced her that she could "slip right into the culture" of the school and teach, rather than having to establish her own expectations for student behavior.

At other schools, administrators sought to learn more about candidates' approaches to curriculum design. Ms. Honor, Hurston's assistant principal, who said she would ask a candidate in literacy how to teach tone and mood, explained that she listened carefully for details in the candidates' responses. In her view a strong literacy candidate would not say, "I use this textbook," but would present a more nuanced approach, such as "If I want to grow the reading, writing, and speaking of my English language learners, then these are the key components of my classroom I need to have. I'm going to pull from this material and that material." Current teachers at these schools recalled appreciating that they were asked to speak in detail about their approach to curriculum and instruction during the hiring process. Such questions generated excitement among candidates about eventually working with informed colleagues who reflected thoughtfully on their work.

At Dickinson, Ms. Davila said she found it "cumbersome" to ask a specific set of questions in every interview, as the district required. She recalled one candidate who said he already knew all the interview questions because "they're the same questions wherever you go." So she supplemented the required list with "little questions" that allowed her to "go with [her] gut" and probe candidates' commitment to working in partnership with families or their awareness of the "family feel" of the school's professional environment.

Requiring a teaching demonstration and a debrief

Although most schools continue to offer teachers a position based on a successful interview, these schools insisted on first watching a candidate teach. As one Fitzgerald administrator explained, "You can have the most fabulous answers in an interview, but if you can't stand up in front of the class and build positive relationships with [our] students . . . it's not going to be a good fit." Arranging for demonstration lessons could be difficult, but everyone agreed that these classroom auditions were telling and often decisive. As Hurston's Mr. Hinds said, "With demos, you can tell really quickly" whether a candidate deserves to be hired. He recalled visiting one applicant's class in a school slated for closure: "As soon as we walked in the room, I knew, I was like, 'I want this woman . . . every kid should have this . . . teacher.' Just remarkable."

Similarly, at Dickinson, which had only recently begun to require demonstration lessons, a teacher on the hiring committee compared the instruction of two finalists for a position. He found one applicant's lesson "rudimentary," and said, "I wanted to pull my hair out" after the teacher took ten to fifteen minutes getting the students settled and ready to listen. In contrast, the second applicant "did classroom management . . . in about a minute" and got quickly to her lesson.

> By the end of the class, [the candidate] had taught them about pantomime. She had the kids paint, with their bodies, this picture of being at a baseball game. She put one kid in a pose and it was obvious that the kid was about to hit a baseball and then she said, "Now, who could add something to this picture?" One kid ran up [and started] selling hot dogs. Another person was cheering in the stands. Another person was an umpire. Another was fielding. It was incredible.

The principals had different preferences for whether the class participating in the demonstration lesson should be the candidate's current class or one at the hiring school. In addition to being convenient, having the candidate teach in the hiring school allowed teachers and administrators to see whether he could quickly develop rapport with their school's students. However, other administrators agreed with Mr. Hinds, who preferred to see the "relationships that [candidates] have with the kids that [they've] been working with all year." Because arranging demonstration lessons introduced many logistical problems, especially if the candidate lived out of state, Naylor's Ms. North asked candidates to submit a video of their teaching and to "tilt the camera so that I can see the kids." In a few cases, administrators traveled long distances to watch a candidate at work in her own setting.

Several administrators explained that the candidate's reflections after the lesson sometimes were more revealing than the lesson itself, because it was then that they could see how she responded to feedback and could judge whether she was intent on improving. Ms. Forte said she listened for whether applicants took personal responsibility for shortcomings in the lesson or subtly blamed students. She described listening during the debrief conference for whether a candidate who had difficulty "catching students' attention" said, "I wish I had put nametags on the kids" or "Oh, the kids moved around a lot on the rug." Forte was amazed at how often candidates "tr[ied] to fight" when she offered constructive criticism. Like other principals in this study, she believed that "if [candidates] can't take any hard feedback," teaching at her school would "not go so well."

A few current teachers who had participated in a post-lesson debrief as applicants said that the experience convinced them that they wanted to teach at that school. An early-career teacher at Naylor said he "loved the process" because it provided "a great preview of what it would be like to work here." After he had joined the school, he realized that his demonstration debrief, which had been conducted online, "was exactly the same tone and intent as my [current] weekly debriefs with my principal after she observes me." Instead of "feeling like they were looking for canned answers, we really got into the nitty-gritty of the lesson." He said he received "a lot of helpful ideas about how to improve the specific lesson that I had sent them." He recalled being "shocked" but impressed by comments about "how informal I was in the classroom" when "I thought it was the strictest and most efficient class."

CONCLUSION

This group of successful schools was remarkable in that each had developed a multistep recruitment and hiring approach that engaged educators throughout the school in meeting and assessing candidates. They began the process with clear agreement about their school's mission, culture, and practices. New teachers were hired to contribute to and improve the school, not just to fill vacancies. Therefore, although the principal typically made the final hiring decisions, those were informed and influenced by others. Timely, two-way, information-rich hiring was not left to chance in these schools. Like others we had studied in the past, these successful urban schools sometimes contended with the challenge of having to hire a replacement on short notice, such as when a current teacher unexpectedly resigned late in the summer or even mid-year. However, because the schools conducted hiring carefully and teachers felt personally responsible to their school and their students, that happened less often than in schools that were less successful in retaining their teachers.

Unquestionably, these schools benefited from having autonomy to recruit and hire teachers. The charter schools had been granted autonomy by the state. The district schools had gradually gained autonomy; Dickinson did so as a traditional school working under WCSD policies that decentralized hiring over time; Hurston reverted to having the special status it had enjoyed since its opening; and Fitzgerald enjoyed autonomy as a state-authorized Innovation School.

In addition, crucial changes in the WCSD teachers union contract and related district policies enabled principals to actively recruit and hire teachers without being snagged by bureaucratic requirements that slowed them down or limited their options. It might be tempting to attribute the successful hiring processes at Dickinson, Hurston, and Fitzgerald to these changes in district policy, especially the increase in autonomy available to schools, but that would probably be mistaken. No doubt, such changes were essential so that schools could create and implement hiring practices that worked for them. However, while policies can remove obstacles and streamline procedures, ultimately it is up to school-level administrators and staff to use that potential on behalf of their school, as these principals did. Their success can serve as a model for other schools where administrators may not yet have realized the opportunities they have in hiring.

The experiences of these schools also document how labor-intensive the process of successful hiring is. As we saw, each of the charter schools benefited from additional assistance by their CMO's talent staff. Although WCSD's central office had created a new website that allowed schools to review and recruit many more candidates than those who applied to them directly, the district's recruitment efforts were less extensive and ambitious than they might have been. With the processes for posting jobs now streamlined and the barriers to implementing mutual selection removed, district officials could turn their attention to more ambitious recruitment, with the needs of individual schools in mind.

Education reformers who contend that schools should hire individual teachers based primarily on measures of intelligence and mastery of content might doubt whether the investment these schools made in achieving a good match were worth the time and resources they required. However, the administrators and teachers we interviewed were convinced that inquiring deeply about candidates' alignment with the school's mission and professional norms, their views about low-income students' needs, and their instructional knowledge and expertise all paid off. As Mr. Ryan, 5–8 principal at Rodriguez, said, "Good hiring matters. If you hire well and you're explicit beforehand, you don't need to fire people." And if candidates understand "the kind of teacher" who is successful and satisfied at the school, "they'll just know" whether the environment is right for them. Those who benefit from a good preview are far more likely to begin their teaching well informed about the challenges they face, as well as the supports they can count on from colleagues and superiors. Unlike teachers whose path to a job—especially a first job—is rushed, haphazard, and ill informed, they are more likely to achieve the success with their students that they had hoped for when they chose to teach.

Having examined the steps and benefits of information-rich hiring, we move on in chapter 2 to consider how teachers decide what to teach, given the demands of standards-based accountability.

CHAPTER TWO

Deciding What and How to Teach

ONE OF THE MOST DAUNTING AND PERPLEXING responsibilities that US teachers face is deciding what to teach and how to teach it. Parents and citizens might reasonably expect districts and schools to provide teachers with a curriculum detailing the topics they should cover; the concepts and skills their students should master; a general schedule that guides them in charting their progress; and materials, including texts and other media, they can use for instruction. Unfortunately, in many schools today teachers lack these essential resources.

When we interviewed first- and second-year teachers in 1998, we were stunned to learn how few of them had anything resembling a complete curriculum for the subjects they were assigned to teach. Except for a few who taught in high performing suburban schools, these novices faced—often alone—what we called the "curriculum void."[1] One of the most memorable was first-year teacher Amy, who said that she had "no set curriculum" for social studies: "No one has ever told me anything I am supposed to cover. They kind of just said, 'Here's the books.' And even the books, I didn't know where they were. I had to ask for them. . . . No one has ever told me anything that I had to cover. No one has actually given me the [local district] curriculum. . . . No one has ever told me, 'You need to teach that.'"

So what did Amy do? Like many of the novices we interviewed, she "just kind of made it up on [her] own."

Teachers in many other countries, such as France, the UK, South Korea, New Zealand, and South Africa, don't face this predicament. Instead, they rely on a well-established national curriculum that lays out the course of study for all schools, including the subjects to be covered in every grade and the sequence of topics, concepts, and skills to be taught each year. These national curricula vary widely in length and specificity, from the detailed French curriculum that prescribes daily lessons for every teacher in all subjects, to the spare Japanese curriculum that lists the standards to be met and topics to be covered but allows teachers to decide how to approach each lesson.[2]

In the US we have no national curriculum, largely due to our history of local control. The Constitution formally reserves for the states responsibility for public education. In turn, many states have handed off to local districts and schools decisions about curriculum—including the learning standards (what students should know and be able to do), the courses to be taught, and the content of those courses. Practically speaking, districts and schools also implicitly have delegated those decisions to teachers. As a result, the US curriculum historically has developed from the classroom out, its content and pedagogy being determined largely by individual teachers' interests and beliefs.[3]

That was my experience in 1967 when I began teaching English in a large suburban high school. Before classes started, I received a three-ring notebook with a short curriculum on heroes and heroism, which several experienced teachers had written during a summer workshop. I was encouraged to use it in my ninth-grade "standard" English classes as I taught classic and contemporary literature, from *Julius Caesar* to *The Pearl*. Having majored in English literature, I felt confident teaching literary concepts, such as character development and point of view, but I still was grateful to have day-to-day lessons suggesting what I might actually *do* in class. I liked having that basic curriculum to fall back on, but I also welcomed the freedom to take the class where I wanted.

Although I was convinced my students were having a worthwhile experience, what I actually taught was not closely aligned with what my colleagues taught. No one talked about the standards that my students should meet at the end of my course, although I'm confident we each had some in mind. I listened to my colleagues for clues about what really mattered and I occasionally watched them teach. Except for a few formal observations by my department head, no one monitored my teaching, and I alone decided whether my students were learning what they should.

Throughout the twentieth century, US teachers largely decided on their own, as I did, what to teach, when to teach it, and how to teach it.[4] This often led to a haphazard patchwork of topics and skills that varied widely, even from classroom to classroom within a school. Not surprisingly, students who were ostensibly studying in the same program might move from course to course and grade to grade, learning dissimilar content and acquiring different skills.

Teachers often had access to textbooks that were prepared by commercial publishers and approved by local school boards. Although these volumes were formal and sequential, teachers still chose whether, when, and how to use the units, lessons, and assignments they provided. Few textbooks directly addressed the fundamental question of what students should be learning. Teachers usually inferred that answer from the textbooks' lists of topics to be covered, recommended texts, and sample assignments, study questions, problem sets, or essay questions. Students were promoted and eventually graduated because their teachers judged that they had successfully completed their courses. Except in specialized programs, such as Advanced Placement, no standardized tests or formal review assessed whether students had mastered essential skills and competencies.

Teachers who relied on textbooks, even minimally, could think that they were meeting their obligation to teach the curriculum, just as education officials could believe that their schools were providing comprehensive and coherent instruction for their students. In reality, however, textbooks provided only a semblance of order and continuity in an otherwise atomized professional environment, where teachers were left alone to decide what and how to teach.[5] In effect, textbooks preserved teachers' autonomy while perpetuating their isolation.

POLICY MAKERS INTERVENE WITH A "HORSE TRADE"

In the 1980s, however, education analysts began to realize that policy makers, the public, and educators themselves had a false sense of confidence about students' learning. *A Nation at Risk*, which alerted US citizens to a "rising tide of mediocrity in public education," urged policy makers to arrest decline in the nation's schools by setting standards about what students should learn and then testing them to assess whether teachers had effectively taught what they were supposed to.[6] Importantly, these reformers viewed the problem our society faced as one of ensuring that teachers comply with their expectations, rather than developing their capacity to teach well, which was arguably the more important and fundamental challenge.

Although the authors of *A Nation at Risk* viewed the crisis in education as a national emergency, state and federal policy makers widely opposed moves to adopt a national curriculum. In response, a group of governors launched the standards-based accountability movement in the 1990s by proposing a "horse trade." The states would grant school districts autonomy in deciding what and how to teach in exchange for adopting instructional standards and assessing students' learning.[7]

At the time, few educators realized that these accountability policies—first enacted in the 1990s by various states and later fortified by the federal government in NCLB—would indirectly, but undeniably, affect what and how teachers taught. As the horse trade signaled, accountability policies preserved traditions of local control by not imposing a curriculum. However, by setting standards and requiring annual tests in core subjects, policy makers substantially restricted teachers' freedom to decide what and how to teach.

Yet teachers still had scant guidance from school officials about what to teach. The new laws and regulations riveted teachers' attention to their students' test scores. And as schools became increasingly responsible for ensuring that all students progressed steadily toward proficiency, accountability grew as an urgent organizational concern, especially in schools serving low-income and high-poverty communities, where many students failed the state tests.

In response, some districts and schools adopted "teacher-proof" curricula, which were packaged and sold by commercial publishers. These included day-by-day lessons with word-for-word scripts that teachers were required to read aloud in class.[8] Because such scripted curricula were grounded in research and driven by experts' views about the best way to teach reading, proponents believed that students would learn to read, if only all teachers would fully and faithfully implement the program. Scripted curricula were thought to compensate for many teachers' lack of knowledge about how to teach reading—and some *did* improve their students' reading skills—but the approach did little to build teachers' capacity to diagnose and respond to students' individual differences and learning needs. Enthusiasm for scripted curricula waned when teachers vehemently objected to their detailed requirements and it became obvious how difficult and controversial it would be to create comparable daily lessons in all other subjects.

Teachers Contend with State Standards and Tests

In 1998, when we began our study of new teachers, Massachusetts was one of a number of states that had enacted a new accountability policy. In what was locally called "the Grand Bargain," Massachusetts policy makers granted substantial increases in state aid to districts in exchange for establishing an accountability system that coupled state-based instructional learning standards with a high-stakes standardized test.

The first set of standards were approved in 1993, and in 1998 the state administered the Massachusetts Comprehensive Assessment System (MCAS) statewide to all students in selected grades (third, eighth, and tenth) and subjects (English language arts [ELA], math, and science). Compared with other states' early assessments, the MCAS was and continues to be viewed as a high-level, demanding test.[9] State education officials could review individual students' scores and judge whether they, their class, their grade, or their school were learning what they were supposed to learn. Further, they could hold schools and teachers accountable if their students failed. Public reporting of MCAS scores compelled schools to take the standards seriously and, in high performing communities, real estate agents often used them to sell houses.

Although state test results captured local administrators' attention, the teachers' need for a curriculum and materials often was overlooked. State learning standards clearly specified skills and competencies that students should master in each grade or course. But teachers still needed much more, including guides that explained how to build the required skills and competencies; materials, texts, and textbooks that included stories, essays, and explanations they could use during instruction; and model units or lesson plans illustrating how students might acquire the competencies by participating in a discussion or lab experiment, watching a demonstration, completing a reading, or listening to a lecture. For example, a history teacher might know that his students would be expected to draw inferences from artifacts, yet have no idea what content to use in teaching them how to do so.

When we interviewed new teachers in 1998, nearly two-fifths of them had been assigned to teach tested subjects and grades, suggesting that more experienced teachers preferred to avoid responsibility for the new standards by teaching in untested grades. Most of these novices were anxious about whether they could adequately prepare students for the tests ahead. Yet one-fifth of them reported having no curriculum or approved textbook in at least one of their core subjects (English, math, science, or social studies), and those who did often said that the materials aligned poorly with the new state standards. Many teachers felt, as one said, "lost at sea," trying to reconcile the state standards with whatever curriculum or texts they had available or could piece together.[10]

Participants in our study often were bewildered by the range of topics they were expected to cover as specified by the state's curriculum frameworks. Robert, who taught history at a suburban high school, called the standards "mindbogglingly comprehensive and vague." Amanda, whose elementary school stressed the importance of test scores, wondered what she could possibly do to meet the state's broad social studies requirements for first grade. She said that she was supposed to teach "all the way from the Ice Age with hunters and nomads coming over the land bridge, to Vikings and explorers, Native Americans, [the] first three colonies, all thirteen in the colonization, and then the revolution into how we became America. The list goes on."

Amanda knew that she wasn't expected to teach every topic in detail, but no one told her how to choose or which topics deserved priority. When these teachers found no guidance from their textbooks, colleagues, or supervisors, they often said that they analyzed questions on prior state tests and then inferred what they should teach. It was a time-consuming, sketchy strategy that gave them little confidence.

These Massachusetts teachers were not unusual in contending with such uncertainty. David Kauffman surveyed a random sample of 295 second-year elementary teachers in Massachusetts, North Carolina, and Washington and found that they had similar concerns about their lack of access to curriculum materials. Second-year elementary school teachers in both high-income and low-income schools reported having insufficient curricular support in all major subjects. Teachers reported the most severe lack of guidance in social studies (69 percent) and science (56 percent), which were generally not tested subjects. However, even in tested subjects, teachers reported having inadequate support in ELA (32 percent) and math (20 percent). Notably, teachers in low-income schools reported receiving more curricular support in language arts than those in high-income schools.[11]

NCLB Intensifies Policy Makers' Pressure on Schools and Teaching

Although accountability policies in many states heightened teachers' attention to state standards, it was the federal NCLB act that fundamentally transformed how they and their schools responded. The law required states to establish accountability systems that included curriculum standards, annual tests, public reports of test scores, and a means for identifying schools that failed to progress. Students were to be tested annually in grades 3 through 8 and in one grade of high school. The curriculum in many states remained unspecified, but the targets that schools were required to meet and the sanctions they faced if they failed became explicit.

The problem that the policy makers addressed continued to be one of teachers' compliance with requirements rather than their capacity to teach well, and schools had no playbook for how to get from where they were to where they needed to be. That would have called for helping teachers learn how to use curriculum materials to engage students in learning activities so that they would master the required skills and competencies specified by the learning standards. For most schools, that was a very tall order.

NCLB required that schools achieve Adequate Yearly Progress (AYP) on state assessments so that all students nationwide would achieve proficiency by 2013–2014. One of NCLB's most important, consequential demands was, that in assessing whether a school met AYP, it required that all subgroups of forty students or more—including those learning English, those with disabilities, and those from racial and ethnic minority groups—had to show steady, sufficient progress toward meeting proficiency. Initially, teachers were motivated to take the tests seriously out of fear that their school might be publicly censured if they failed. But when many states, including Massachusetts, made students' graduation or promotion contingent on passing those tests, teachers became alarmed that their students might be unfairly penalized. The policy had succeeded in seizing teachers' attention and eliciting their compliance with local requirements, including conducting test-prep classes for students. However, in many cases, neither the state nor their district gave them sufficient support as they decided what and how to teach.

State Officials Assess the Schools' Performance

In 2006, Massachusetts adopted policies to address the shortcomings of districts and schools that repeatedly failed to meet AYP targets in math or ELA. Its regulations called for those underperforming schools to receive one of three ratings— "identified for improvement," "corrective action," or "restructuring"—each of which carried sanctions. The state's message to districts, schools, and teachers was stern and firm: if a school in any of these categories did not make demonstrative improvement after twenty-four months, the commissioner could designate it "chronically underperforming" and subject to takeover.

SECOND-STAGE TEACHERS: DIVERGENT RESPONSES TO STATE SANCTIONS

In 2008 my colleagues and I studied the experiences of eighty-five second-stage teachers (SSTs), who had four to ten years of experience and were teaching in one of fourteen schools located in three low performing urban school districts. (See the appendix for a full description of the SST study.) At the time, nearly half of Massachusetts schools had been sanctioned with one of three negative ratings, and state officials had begun to impose new requirements and frequent

monitoring on the schools they judged to be the least successful. We chose to focus on SSTs because they had worked in the context of accountability throughout
their career and, having achieved a level of competence in their teaching, could
offer an informed perspective on recent changes in state oversight and how it influenced what and how they taught.

The schools we studied responded differently to the state's efforts to improve
students' learning. In a very few, teachers and administrators worked collaboratively to improve instruction schoolwide, based on their shared understanding
of how to teach the district's approved curriculum. Most, however, remained
disorganized and instructionally fragmented.[12] Two schools located in the same
urban district, Lane Elementary and Deer Park Middle School, illustrate these
differences.

Lane Elementary School: Shared Practices, Instructional Leadership, and Resolve

Lane Elementary School, which enrolled 350 low-income students, was "identified for improvement" by the state and required to develop a school improvement
plan. Ms. Landry, the principal, was a knowledgeable and skilled administrator, respected as an expert teacher in her own right. She and Lane's teachers
worked together to define the school's challenges and to address them with instructional practices that they agreed were promising. Lane adopted an improvement plan featuring three key components—common planning time for teachers,
a full-inclusion coteaching model to accommodate the needs of special education
students, and differentiated instruction based on ongoing analysis of student performance data. Although Ms. Landry made most school-level decisions about
curriculum and pedagogy, teachers widely endorsed them because they respected
and valued her instructional expertise and judgment. A sixth-grade teacher suc-
cinctly characterized the practices included in the school improvement plan as
"the way we run the school."

Teachers responded well to Ms. Landry's leadership and the professional culture she fostered. As one special education teacher explained: "She really feels
that these children deserve everything anyone else would have and that our job
is to be here to give 110 percent." She went on to clarify her point: "I mean that
in a positive way. . . I don't want to sound like you've got to get in there and drill,
drill. . . . It's just that everybody needs to be on board." Ms. Landry visited classes
often, engaging with both students and teachers. A fourth-grade teacher said,
"When you're teaching, she'll come over and she might kneel next to a kid and
[ask], 'What are you working on now? What is the objective here?'" This teacher

said she felt proud when her students could answer the principal's questions. Professional norms encouraged teachers to collaborate about their work, rather than hide their pedagogical successes and failures.

All of the teachers we interviewed at Lane spoke about being, as one said, "faithful" to the district curricula and state standards, while adapting instruction to meet their students' needs. The district had adopted *Everyday Math*, a student-centered math curriculum meant to engage students in learning and using fundamental concepts. The district also had selected a basal reading series that included excerpts of stories and nonfiction texts, sequenced by difficulty. Neither of these was a scripted curriculum meant to tightly prescribe instruction. However, the district had created pacing guides to ensure steady progress so that all students would experience continuity if they moved to another school within the district.

It was Ms. Landry who specified the teachers' pedagogy. She expected them to create "learning centers" within their classroom that focused on a specific task or text with small groups of students. As one teacher of a combined fifth- and sixth-grade class explained, having learning centers "works at this school . . . I never have more than five or six kids in front of me, working in a small group. [Others] are working independently." Her fourth-grade colleague explained that she always divided her class into "three groups—an independent group, a teacher-directed group, and a partner group—that rotate during the class." A fifth-grade colleague initially was skeptical about using learning centers, but came to fully support them. "It's just about trying to move everybody forward . . . so that when [students] leave here, they have those strong strategies that stay with them. So, do I have to [teach with learning centers]? I do what she tells me, but she wouldn't have to [tell me]. It's just the way we do it here." A teacher of English language learners (ELLs) said that "there is no choice in the matter" of learning centers, but she went on to observe that teachers were not simply complying with Ms. Landry's expectation, but were making the practice work "for the good of the children." Teachers deeply trusted Ms. Landry's expertise. As the fourth-grade teacher quipped, "If [she] told me kids learn better if you write in orange crayon, I'd write in orange crayon."

Lane's teachers also tracked and analyzed various types of data about their students and, along with colleagues and their school's instructional coaches, reviewed how students were responding and progressing. Based on that analysis, they adjusted their teaching and provided extra support to students who needed it. Lane maintained a data wall that displayed an ongoing record of each student's baseline test scores in September and subsequent scores on interim assessments.

The fourth-grade teacher said that this allowed her to see "exactly where [students] were when they entered and where they are when they're leaving." The teachers, she said, had come to "look at the bigger picture . . . where they were and how far they've gone."

This ongoing record of performance served as the basis for analysis and informed action. During the school year, teachers worked with peers and coaches to analyze how well individual students understood the concepts on the tests. A sixth-grade teacher stressed that this analysis was for the students' sake: "I feel accountable to them. Not to a principal or to the school. . . . I need to make sure that I give the students what they need in order to be successful." She explained further: "We have five different types of math on the math MCAS, so I look at each kind and say, 'Well, which kid is having a hard time here? Which one is having a hard time there?'" She thought it was the principal's responsibility to hold teachers accountable for understanding students' needs, although two teachers expressed dissatisfaction with the unavoidable fact that test scores had become so important. A teacher of ELLs observed, "Results—good, bad, or indifferent—teaching now is driven by test scores. And unfortunately, we measure growth [and] success by test scores."

Lane had two instructional coaches—one in ELA and one in math—who helped teachers become more proficient in using learning centers and finding additional materials to address the needs of individual students. One sixth-grade teacher called the coaches a "good investment" and described them as "people who are really willing to get in there." When she asked for support, the literacy coach was quick to respond: "She's pulled [for] me academic articles, sample lesson plans, books, anything she can think of." Similarly, she said the mathematics coach "mapped out with us our whole *Everyday Math* series, both fifth and sixth [grades] . . . with these Excel sheets to refer to. I always have something new in my box from them to use."

Lane's teachers said that collaborating with their colleagues was both expected and worthwhile. A special education teacher who cotaught fifth- and sixth-grade inclusion classes had been reassigned from second grade, which meant that she had to learn an entirely new curriculum. She found this a challenge, but said that because she could rely on her colleagues, "I never feel like I'm swimming upstream." She explained further, "In this building there's lots of support. Anytime you need anything, whether you have a question, even if you think it's a real silly question, there are plenty of people who are willing to talk to you, to walk you through it."

Each week, teachers submitted lesson plans to Ms. Landry, who reviewed them to ensure that the teachers were following the district's required curriculum and pacing guides. The fifth-grade teacher said, "Everyone does it," but acknowledged that the pacing guide took out "a little bit of the flexibility and some of those fun units that you made as a student teacher about whales and penguins and the continents. That freedom to teach those things is just gone." However, relinquishing the flexibility she once had was a price she accepted for the sake of her students, her colleagues, and her school. Teachers who disagreed and tried to go their own way didn't stay long at Lane, where Ms. Landry gently but firmly discouraged practices that diverged from the school's improvement plan.

Deer Park Middle School: Contested Policies, Weak Leadership, and Disparate Practices

Whereas Lane Elementary was striking in the extent of teachers' collaboration and consensus about instructional practices, little such agreement existed among those we interviewed at Deer Park Middle School, except about one point—that they must raise test scores. Teachers at this school of 580 seventh- and eighth-grade students generally felt under siege by state officials and believed that only higher test scores mattered and could ease the pressure of accountability.

In 2005, state officials judged Deer Park to be "chronically underperforming," based on evidence that "substantial numbers of students attending the school [were] not attaining minimum levels of literacy and mathematical competency by the end of eighth grade." Officials placed the school in "restructuring," having concluded that Deer Park's "students would be best served by active state/ local collaboration."[13] An external state-appointed team of experts conducted an extensive review, including classroom observations and interviews to assess practices at Deer Park. Their findings, which one teacher called "offensive," stressed the need to improve how reading, English, and math were being taught. In response, the school developed an improvement plan that called for teachers to rely on the state's learning standards, develop lesson plans with clear objectives, and create unit assessments across classes. Further, it set a goal of reducing student failure rates by 20 percent.

When we visited Deer Park three years after that report was issued, it was clear that teachers there had responded very differently than their counterparts at Lane. Some practices that were recommended or imposed by the state were similar to those adopted at Lane, such as analyzing student data, hiring instructional coaches, and discouraging teacher-centered instruction. To the extent that

Deer Park teachers had a shared goal, however, it was not to expand students' knowledge and understanding, but to improve their test-taking skills. Teachers hoped that achieving success in that task would prove that their students were, in fact, learning.

A reading teacher said that state officials visited Deer Park frequently to monitor their progress and give their principal, Ms. Dolan, feedback and direction. Administrators then centered their attention on teachers of tested subjects, whose students' test scores would determine the school's eventual AYP standing. An English teacher said that the principal and other administrators then "tell us what we should be doing and what we shouldn't." For example, teachers' lessons had to follow a format that included ten minutes of reflection at the end of each class, an expectation that one teacher said had "filter[ed] down" from the state visits.

Nothing in the interviews suggested that Ms. Dolan was committed to increasing teachers' instructional strength and capacity. Instead, teachers said that the one common goal was to improve test scores. An English teacher complained, "They're telling us what to do. . . . We definitely teach to the test." Although Deer Park's teachers complied with the state's priorities as interpreted by Ms. Dolan, none expressed confidence in their principal's professional judgment.

Under the state's new requirements and Deer Park's school improvement plan, teachers were expected to stop lecturing, increase students' participation in group work, and augment students' independence as learners. However, teachers weren't sure how each of those goals related to their subject or what they should do. A relatively new teacher, who had completed her preparation in a graduate program, was surprised that many of her peers, including some "old-time teachers," didn't include standards and objectives in their lesson plans. One science teacher, who had been department head when science was first included in MCAS, recalled: "I kept saying, 'You have to teach to the standards.' And other teachers just kind of laughed and shrugged it off. When I would go in and do observations or when I was reading lesson plans, I would say, 'Why are you teaching oceanography? That's not even in the standards.' And I would get, 'Well, I like it. I like teaching that.'"

Initially, teachers didn't realize that the state would impose consequences for ignoring the standards, but as the English teacher we interviewed observed, "Accountability changed all that." As at Lane, Deer Park teachers had support from instructional coaches in ELA and math, and those coaches both helped them develop lessons that aligned with the standards and explained how their teachers' instruction might lead to students' success on the MCAS. Teachers repeatedly offered praise for their coaches' skills and expressed appreciation for their support.

By 2008, some Deer Park teachers were collaborating to use common curriculum frameworks and assessments, looking to data for guidance as they decided how to successfully approach both their classes and individual students, and planning more engaging learning activities to replace their lectures. Although teachers suggested that coordinating their instruction was difficult, some thought that working together was gradually paying off. Still, their descriptions suggested that it was easier to improve students' test-taking skills—how to analyze questions, exclude incorrect responses on a multiple-choice question, and write open responses that would produce high scores—than it was to successfully teach the content of their course.

Two science teachers described their contrasting approaches to aligning content, standards, and test questions. One said she routinely began with MCAS questions: "I use the old MCAS exams that are available on the [Department of Education] website as a teaching tool all year long. . . . I don't think it's such a bad thing." The science tests that she prepared also provided her students with test practice: "Every time I give them a test, I want the questions that go along with it to look like the MCAS questions."

Her colleague, who described himself as "an absolute enthusiast for science," used a different approach. He planned lessons by focusing first on the content and the relevant standard, then deciding how best to help his students grasp the scientific principle embedded in both by engaging them in active learning with lab experiments and demonstrations. For example, he taught the concept of density by comparing six different liquids: "Do you know that Coke floats because of the sugar, [while Diet Coke doesn't]? So, density is my thing." He knew the science standards well and was very familiar with the structure and questions on the MCAS science test. "There are more questions on density on the MCAS than anything else. More open responses. My kids know density backwards and forwards." He was not guided by those test questions, though. Instead, his north star was the content of science. He encouraged his colleagues to teach content well, convinced that if they did, good test scores would follow. For most teachers, however, the structure of test questions became the content that mattered.

The state had mandated that Deer Park's teachers meet weekly during common planning time. Teachers appreciated this opportunity to exchange ideas and discuss alternative teaching strategies, but found that they didn't have the time they needed to systematically develop and align their approaches. One told about her team's discussing "this whole thing about having the kids work in groups. It's been a nightmare this week. How do we do it?" Several other teachers described getting ideas for class activities from their peers. However, according to the teachers' accounts, these weekly opportunities to collaborate largely focused on exchanging suggestions that would pay off in higher test scores rather than improved student learning.

According to two teachers, Ms. Dolan wanted to show state officials that the school was making progress, even if the students were not. A science teacher told of disagreeing with Ms. Dolan's decision to promote six students who passed English and math, but failed other subjects, including science, social studies, and reading. "She's going to move them on anyways. As long as they pass those two subjects, the other[s] don't matter." If Ms. Dolan did not promote them, the teacher explained, the school would not meet its improvement goal of decreasing student failure rates by 20 percent. The principal's decision convinced this teacher that truly improving learning for students mattered far less than demonstrating that the school could meet the goals in its improvement plan, even when they were not truly met.

What Explains the Differences Between Lane and Deer Park?

One might reasonably argue that the teachers' experiences in these two schools differed due to the state's accountability decisions. Lane had been only modestly sanctioned by being labeled "intended for improvement" and therefore both Ms. Landry and her teachers had more freedom to decide how to approach the challenges they faced. In contrast, Deer Park had been severely reprimanded by being put in "restructuring," which triggered an external review and report. As a result, Ms. Dolan and her teachers were much more constrained in assessing and responding to their school's needs.

District officials set curriculum policy for both schools. However, it was up to the principal and teachers to take charge of implementing that curriculum. Lane did so with shared, carefully coordinated and monitored instructional practices, which were most apparent in the schoolwide use of learning centers. However, teachers at Deer Park never engaged in a schoolwide effort to address students' learning needs. Deer Park's teachers did not resist the new requirements, nor did they cling to professional autonomy. Instead, they largely did what they were told, focusing defensively on improving test scores, which most in the school had come to equate with learning.

Because we didn't interview the principal, we don't know if Ms. Dolan objected to the state's intervention and prescription. However, none of the teachers told us that she had a different diagnosis or alternative approach in mind. When she decided to promote students who failed to meet the school's requirements, she seemed far more concerned about how the state would review the school than whether students actually were learning. Interviews with Deer Park teachers also did not suggest that Ms. Dolan exercised meaningful instructional leadership or worked to develop a collaborative culture of learning among her teachers. Clearly, scheduling common planning time, in itself, was not enough.

In contrast, teachers at Lane accepted and endorsed Ms. Landry's expertise because they witnessed it in action when she visited classes, talked with students, and explained how teachers could use the practices she expected. She believed that the challenge of improving Lane depended on developing collective capacity, not extracting compliance from individual teachers. Staff were hired at Lane either because they already knew the school and wanted to teach there or because Ms. Landry had recruited them. As a result, a good match existed from the start between the school's approach to improvement and the teachers' priorities. Still, teachers retained considerable autonomy in how they taught and, if they disagreed with Ms. Landry, they felt that they could influence her decisions. As one teacher said, Ms. Landry "listens. I definitely feel heard." No teachers we interviewed at Deer Park expressed such appreciation or respect for their principal and, if they mentioned Ms. Dolan, they did so neutrally or critically. She was largely viewed as a conduit for district and state requirements and threats.

Also, with the support of instructional coaches, Lane's teachers learned how to use various types of data—not only formal test results—to diagnose and support their students' needs. Meanwhile, Deer Park teachers met to examine standardized test scores in order to identify curricular topics that required more attention, test-taking skills that could be sharpened, and specific students who could be targeted for tutoring so that the school's overall standing would rise. Coaches at Deer Park were well regarded by teachers, but they didn't seem central to the school's strategy for improving student learning, if indeed such a strategy existed.

Over the past three decades, prominent scholars have documented the important role that collaborative norms and practices play in fostering internally coherent, effective schools.[14] Our work builds on their findings. By comparing Lane and Deer Park, we can see how the organizational features of these two schools— their leadership, norms, systems, and processes—combined to define teachers' approaches to curriculum and instruction in the context of external accountability. These cases suggest that what matters is not whether teachers have access to materials, timelines, and texts—although those are necessary—but whether their school as an organization supports their learning, promotes their collaboration, and guides them in using curriculum resources effectively on behalf of their students.[15] Building capacity among teachers is the ultimate goal and challenge.

TEACHING IN CONTEXT: CONTINUING CHALLENGES AMID CHANGE

When we conducted our Teaching in Context study in WCSD schools two years later, we found many teachers contending with much the same uncertainty about what and how to teach. In part, this resulted from continuing challenges faced by both teachers and administrators about whether and how to improve curriculum and instruction schoolwide in the context of accountability.

For example, when we studied Angelou Elementary School in 2011, the state had already placed it in "corrective action." In response, administrators and teachers on the school's redesign committee decided to address the fact that teachers had no consistent curriculum or approach to instruction. A committee of teachers and administrators wrote a school improvement plan that required teachers to use only curriculum approved by the district. Teachers who agreed that this was necessary welcomed the change, describing the benefits of collaborating with their peers as they taught the same units and classes and followed the pacing guides. Reportedly, many but hardly all teachers complied. Like many other failing urban schools, Angelou lacked processes for building instructional capacity among teachers. Without those, progress might be made in isolated classrooms, grades, or subjects, but schoolwide improvement was nearly impossible to achieve. The stakes were high at Angelou and, in response, many teachers said that they were working intensely to coordinate their teaching. However, the effort was insufficient and came too late. Within a year, the state had taken over the school and designated a local charter network to restart it.

The policy context for teachers in 2010–2011 had changed since 1998 when we first studied new teachers. Notably, Massachusetts had not substantially revised the MCAS since it was first administered in 1998. However, in 2010, the state adopted the Common Core State Standards (CCSS) and updated its standards for student learning. Subsequently, state officials revised the MCAS twice to incorporate those new standards. Although those revisions arguably were needed and carefully considered, some schools and their teachers experienced the changes as sudden and difficult to respond to.

In 2010, schools that had succeeded in implementing a curriculum that aligned with the original state standards found that they had to reconsider that curriculum with the CCSS (and eventually an updated MCAS) in mind.[16] Many of the new standards were consistent with earlier ones, but some required schools and teachers to adopt new curriculum and pedagogy. For example, revised ELA standards called for students to become proficient in reading and analyzing non-fiction texts as well as writing convincing arguments about issues. Math standards required that they understand and explain how they solved problems, which meant that teachers had to focus less on teaching algorithms that students could use to get the right answer and more on conveying the underlying principles of mathematics.

SUCCESSFUL SCHOOLS: CREATING CURRICULUM TO MEET THE STANDARDS

In our Successful Schools study in 2014–2015, we were surprised to find that educators at four of the six schools had concluded that the available curricula did not meet their students' needs. Therefore, they developed their own, which proved to be an enormous undertaking.

For example, Kincaid Charter Middle School explicitly did not use textbooks, but instead expected teachers to work together to develop curriculum in a process they called "backwards planning." Teachers began by drawing topics and questions from interim assessments, which they then used to create units and lesson plans they all would teach. A sixth-grade teacher said she believed it was "a principle of the school" not to use textbooks. Instead, teachers provided students with packets of materials that they developed and assembled for each unit. Often, due to changes in standards, assessments, or evidence of their students' performance, Kincaid's math and ELA teachers found themselves starting over to develop a new curriculum each year.

A sixth-grade social studies teacher who had been at Kincaid three years said that until the current semester he had never been able to teach a curriculum twice. He was excited to finally have "a platform" that he could "reteach and re-fine" rather than "starting from scratch" and "guessing." However, earlier that week, he had learned that for the next academic year, social studies teachers would have to integrate ELA standards into their curriculum. There was, he said, "a very real possibility that we'll be starting from scratch [again]." Although he recognized the potential benefits of the revisions, he doubted that this practice was sustainable. Given that it took "anywhere between three to five hours" to write each lesson, he asked, "If you have a teacher that literally hasn't slept, what type of lesson are they producing?" Theoretically, teachers could use those lessons again because they were saved to a dropbox. However, this teacher rejected that possibility: "We're talking about thousands upon thousands of lessons that will never be looked at again. . . .This is almost the electronic version of a wastebasket. It's really disheartening."

In contrast, Kincaid's science teachers relied on a curriculum that was originally developed by one of the founding teachers and subsequently refined and repeated each semester so that it had been taught eight times. Both the teacher who wrote the curriculum and her colleague who was new to the school that year expressed confidence that students benefited from experiencing lessons that were repeated and improved over time.

These contrasting experiences at Kincaid illustrate the demands that the school placed on teachers to develop original curriculum and continuously update it, especially in tested subjects. Teachers at Hurston K–8 and Naylor Charter School also engaged teachers in ongoing curriculum development, although Hurston worked toward achieving stability more than Naylor did. Notably, teachers at both schools endorsed their school's practice.

Developing a Curriculum to Last at Hurston K–8

In 2010, when the state consigned Hurston to turnaround status due to chronically low student performance, all students were below grade level. In 2015, a teacher recalled "literally, all of them [were below grade level] at that point, but some of them were more significantly below grade level." He said that the idea behind their reform was to "create a curriculum that was going to catch them up."

In the spring before Hurston reopened as a turnaround school, a newly hired second-grade teacher tried to learn more about what he should teach. He recalled that there was "no reading or writing curriculum in place. . . . That was worrisome to me . . . because I didn't really know what the rules were for teaching reading and writing. It didn't seem like there were any." He described initially cobbling together various approaches with the materials that he could find in and around his classroom:

> I leaned a lot on basal curriculums. I got a little bit from *Reading Street*, even though it wasn't the school curriculum. I got a little bit from Lucy Calkins, which was useful. Reading never really panned out until this year [2014–2015]. [In the meantime, my grade-level] colleagues were using a blend of things. Some of them were using a hybrid of *Reading Street*, *Reading Workshop*, . . . and *Balanced Literacy*.[17] It was never clear to me what we were supposed to be doing, or if there was even any kind of rule or strategy in place.

He explained that initially the school "hadn't really adopted anything. There was this idea that autonomy would be best for the school because there was faith that the teachers who were working here would be really effective at doing what they thought was best." Although he said he had "really wanted to believe that, it wasn't necessarily always true."

Subsequently, he and his colleagues met as a team during common planning time and used the CCSS to "craft ten months of reading units through genre." He reflected, "It didn't really matter to me if [the CCSS] were good or not. The positive side of them that I saw was that they gave us a reason to actually come up with a curriculum." He said that the new standards "became a really useful lever for me. Because whenever there was pushback about 'Well, why do we have to do that? We've always been autonomous,' the answer was always, 'Well, we're not meeting the Common Core Standards.'"

Similarly, a sixth-grade ELA teacher with eight years of experience described how he and his grade-level colleagues used their meeting time to create a new literacy curriculum:

> We initially were using the old state frameworks and have transitioned the curriculum to the Common Core. We've developed units together by going over the standards, grouping them, and selecting our own texts and creating our own thematic units that are driven by those standards. [Then every spring] we look at what we did. We look at where we feel like we need to go and where we felt like, in the previous year, we didn't hit on a particular standard very well or where we didn't have a particularly good text for a unit. We try to rebuild it to get it better next year.

He went on to explain that he and his colleagues would not want to be "dictated to about what was taught when" and they appreciated the fact that they were not expected to proceed lockstep. However, his team agreed that they should choose where to focus their attention. They decided that assessments, most of which they created, "would be the commonality." Individual teachers chose different texts, but as this teacher explained, they were all using the same standards and "giving the same assessment at the end." He also saw the value of having a "vertically aligned curriculum, where we can have some confidence as to what's happening in sixth grade, seventh grade, and eighth grade, so we're not reinventing the wheel each fall."

Similarly, an experienced science teacher at Hurston who facilitated her subject-based team said that she and her colleagues achieved a sense of shared responsibility by linking curriculum and assessment. "We built accountability with each other that we were all going to bring our data and report our data out and then make decisions about reteaching or reassessing based on that data." She said that by going through that two-year process the teachers eventually agreed on "what we were going to teach, when we were going to teach, when we were going to assess."

Hurston's principal, Mr. Hinds, reflected on the schoolwide accomplishments of a collaborative planning process for teaching writing:

> [L]ast year, we finally tackled systematically what we are doing for writing [across all the grades]. And I think that's been part of what's been so hard [about being] a teacher here. As we've built [the curriculum], there have been years where [we were] constantly analyzing the data and making decisions. Whereas now we have a curriculum. We've developed a roadmap of units for writing and now reading [and defined] the standards that have to be mastered. Here's how we're going to assess it in a performance assessment.

Various teachers at Hurston recounted how traditional expectations of professional privacy gradually gave way to candid exchanges as they monitored and analyzed data together. They still valued autonomy, but it was the team's professional autonomy rather than individual freedom that mattered to them. When a teacher and her colleagues created action plans based on their interim test results, they posted them in a Google Doc, which team members and administrators reviewed closely. She said, "We're able to view each other's action plans and pull each other's resources, if needed or if wanted."

Therefore, across Hurston, teachers and administrators deliberately and intently used a wide range of data to inform and improve their curriculum and instruction—what, when, and how they taught topics and lessons. No one ignored the practical necessity of students' scoring well on the state tests, but teachers deliberately put curriculum and instruction first, constantly trying to improve their own practice not simply to protect their school's standing, but more importantly, to ensure that their students were learning what they should.

Continuously Creating Curriculum at Naylor Charter Elementary School

Teachers at Naylor Charter School shared responsibility for planning units and lessons. Although the school was building a resource bank with all units and lessons that were taught, Naylor's teachers, like Kincaid's, were constantly creating new material rather than adapting what had been used in the past. Naylor's administrators broadly defined the curriculum based on the Massachusetts learning standards, and then a team of teachers from either a grade level or subject area proposed a set of units, which administrators reviewed and responded to. Once these were approved, individual teachers took responsibility for developing a set of lessons in a single subject, which other teachers at the grade level would then critique, revise, and use to teach their classes.

A fourth-grade teacher said that after she and her team members had taught the same lesson plan, they took time to assess it: "'How did it work in your room?' 'What do you think about this?' 'How could we change it?' We're constantly evaluating what the students need and whether or not we thought it was rigorous enough." Although teachers appreciated the benefits of collaborative planning, it was not easy or quick work and teachers occasionally mentioned that a weak team member could stall their progress or hamper their success. However, surprisingly few of the many individuals we interviewed lacked confidence in their colleagues, largely due to the school's thorough hiring process, which reassured teachers that their colleagues would be, as one said, "rock solid." The teachers' long workday (9.25 hours) allocated adequate time for them to plan units and review lesson plans, although, as we will see in chapter 7, most teachers' lesson planning occurred in the evenings or on weekends.

Naylor sought to hire teachers who were prepared to use data to inform their instruction. One teacher explained: "We just believe in data. . . . We use it a lot to assess where kids are weak and where they need to improve more. It just informs our teaching. . . . It informs how we plan curriculum. It informs everything. If we are interviewing people who are not experienced at using data or maybe even have some opinions against it, [or] don't really like the idea of it, that might be a problem."

The small CMO to which Naylor belonged developed its own interim assessments for core academic subjects at each grade, aligning them with the standards of the Common Core and format of the MCAS questions. Soon after each interim test, teachers received detailed reports about the performance of each child in each class on each problem, including correlations between the assessment items and particular learning standards.

Teachers and administrators then met to analyze the results, consider how well students understood content they had recently taught, and develop plans for moving forward. This centralized process guided instructional teams in making changes. For example, a math teacher explained that in analyzing assessment data his team had identified a type of probability problem that repeatedly "destroyed our kids" in quizzes and tests. He said that his team's response needed to be twofold: "There was content [we missed] and there was also the way we delivered it that needed to be changed." They proceeded to address both.

Instructional practices were far more uniform across classes at Naylor than at Hurston. For example, all reading classes were organized around "a debatable question." As one eighth-grade teacher explained, students were expected to "gather evidence from the text to support their answer to the framed question." She said that she and her partner could choose any text, "as long as it's rigorous and at grade level or above grade level." For example, in teaching *Animal Farm*, the teachers asked their students to discuss, "How does Orwell use Napoleon to say something about greed?" She said that the classes themselves then "feature[d] mostly kids talking."

Curriculum and instruction at Hurston and Naylor were informed by teachers' systematically analyzing their students' performance on formal interim tests and teacher-made assessments, including unit tests and frequent "exit tickets" at the end of class to check on what students had learned. In both schools, the process of curriculum development was ongoing, with regular time scheduled for teachers to reflect on and refine their instruction. However, Hurston's administrators and teachers said that they were moving toward a stable but flexible curriculum, whereas Naylor was establishing some shared pedagogical practices while also encouraging teachers to respond continuously to test results as they decided what and how to teach.

Negotiating the Tension Between Autonomy and Control at Fitzgerald Elementary

Very few teachers in these successful schools complained about having lost the right to decide what and how to teach. Most wanted to have a well-designed, coherent but flexible curriculum that they could use to effectively teach students as they moved through the school from class to class and grade to grade.

An ELA teacher at Hurston expressed satisfaction that he and his colleagues could select texts to effectively teach the skills embedded in the ELA standards. He pointed out that, despite the attention to test scores within the district and school, "I have never once been told that on this day I should be doing this. I feel a lot of pressure, but I have been able to maintain my integrity as a teacher." A colleague concurred, noting that Hurston administrators showed "respect for the autonomy and the independence of teachers." However, those administrators also expected that teachers' major decisions about curriculum would be made in concert with colleagues, not independently.

Resistance to uniform requirements

Some teachers in our study, however, did object to the constraints that developing, refining, and teaching a shared curriculum placed on their freedom to teach as they thought best. At Fitzgerald Elementary School, which, like Hurston K–8, had been placed in turnaround in 2010 and successfully emerged at Level 1 three years later, teachers participated regularly with colleagues to analyze data and plan lessons, although many did so with less equanimity and satisfaction than those at Naylor Charter.

Fitzgerald's principal, Ms. Forte, was respected for her expertise in literacy and her fierce commitment to students' learning, but some teachers thought that she prescribed and monitored their practices too closely. It was Ms. Forte, not the team members, who decided which teachers would write a team's lessons for each subject, based on what she knew about their teaching. She required all teachers to use the same detailed template to plan lessons, which called for learning objectives, relevant state standards, activating background knowledge, materials to be used, learning activities, three higher-order questions for discussion, featured vocabulary, opportunities for practice, assessment, and closure. By Thursday, teachers were required to submit lesson drafts for the following week to their supervisor, who might or might not provide feedback.

Once a Fitzgerald team had reviewed and refined a lesson, all members were expected to teach it simultaneously. Although one teacher claimed that nobody used those lessons, others said they did and might be reprimanded if they failed to do so. To illustrate this point, a first-year teacher said that Ms. Forte stopped by her colleague's class and found that she was not using the lesson that the team had agreed on. Immediately after class, the teacher received a note saying, "Please come see me at the end of the day." When she did, Ms. Forte asked her to explain why she wasn't teaching the team's lesson. In describing this event, her colleague suggested that such intense oversight drove some teachers further into the privacy of their classrooms: "I've heard of other people saying, 'When my door is shut, my door is shut,' and they do whatever they want."

Every month, teachers at Fitzgerald prepared packets of data to be reviewed by their supervisor (the principal, assistant principal, or instructional coach). One said that these had to include "our running record sheet, which shows every single student and their level. We have to turn in our math data grid, which [includes] all of our unit tests with the kids' scores." Further, he was required to submit his homework log and monthly writing folders for three students, identified at the start of the year as performing at different levels—"tier one, tier two, and tier three"—along with their weekly responses to open-ended prompts in math and reading. Another teacher said that her supervisor would "look through" the data and provide comments such as "I see that so-and-so hasn't really moved in running records. What are we doing to support that?"

A few Fitzgerald teachers reported exercising considerable autonomy in their day-to-day teaching, despite close monitoring. One said that he "never look[ed] at the reading plans" because he had to adjust to his students' needs. "A lot of teams, from what I've known, don't look at each other's plans really at all." He did, however, use the shared lesson plans for writing because he had no other curriculum to follow. Other teachers, though, had grown to appreciate and rely on the required plans. One said that she and her colleagues "just laughed" when Ms. Forte first distributed the template. "We ignored it." However, "she pushed it on us the next year and said, 'This is what we're going to do.' We griped and we cried, but we did it as we were griping. In the end, it pays off." In her view, she and her peers were developing pedagogical skills and promoting higher-order thinking among their students.

Other teachers complained that the principal's broader instructional expectations were not open to negotiation. For example, a team of primary teachers were not permitted to use learning centers in their teaching—the very technique that Ms. Landry required all teachers at Lane to use. One Fitzgerald team member recalled trying to convince Ms. Forte to give them more flexibility: "Let Leticia create the centers. She has a lot of great ideas. She comes from a background of differentiated [instruction]. Her school was very successful. She's shown you her data from her old school." But the principal agreed only to allow teachers to use learning centers for one activity—word sorts. "That was the end of it."

Principals' use of their authority

By comparing teachers' responses at Hurston and Fitzgerald, we can see important differences in how much control the principals of these two schools exercised. Although teachers expressed considerable respect for both and took their expectations seriously, Mr. Hinds granted teams more discretion in curricular decisions and gave individual teachers more leeway in adapting the curriculum as they taught, while Ms. Forte closely specified what teams should and could do and monitored compliance by reviewing lesson plans and stopping by unannounced to observe individual classes.

These differences exemplify school leaders' ongoing efforts to find the right balance between the interests and capabilities of the people responsible for teaching and the systems the school develops to guide what they do. While teachers at Hurston seemed to feel empowered and motivated by the responsibilities they and their teams exercised, some at Fitzgerald resented the intrusion and suggested that their professional judgment was being trampled. Reportedly, several teachers had left Fitzgerald in response to Ms. Forte's tight management, and a few others currently were job hunting.

Embedding Deeper Learning in Curriculum at Rodriguez Charter K–8 and Fitzgerald Elementary

When failing schools start to rebuild their curriculum in response to state standards, teachers and data teams sometimes review test results and then create discrete units or lessons to "fill the gaps" in students' learning. Although that may be an effective tactic in specific situations, a sound curriculum—the kind that you would want your own child to experience—should do much more than methodically piece together segments of content and skills.

Rodriguez Charter School, which served four hundred elementary and middle school students, was well respected for its success in educating low-income students in Walker City. The school consistently achieved high test scores and received high ratings from the state. Its founding principal had hired teachers who could embed content and skills in engaging, interdisciplinary experiences that would pique students' curiosity, foster their creativity, generate respectful interactions, and instill responsibility. Teachers at Rodriguez had long been encouraged to follow their professional instincts in teaching. One recalled the founder saying, "I don't care how you get there, just get there."

A new teacher at Rodriguez might have access to materials used by his predecessor, but Ms. Rega, the principal of the K–4 school, explained, "We don't really have a lot of curriculum that is written to hand to people. We meet the standards. We have resources. We have some curriculum that is like a backbone that they can hang stuff on." Unlike the other successful schools we studied, Rodriguez teachers didn't meet regularly to analyze data or plan common lessons. Although novices faced what one teacher called "a very steep learning curve," she and her colleagues prized their autonomy: "You feel like [you're] your own boss in your classroom." She elaborated: "I love the flexibility of being able to think about what I've done in the past and work off that. Say, 'Well, that didn't work. Let me try this.' Or 'Okay,

I really like that. Now I'm going to add this to it.' Or 'Hmmm, this group of kids is really [struggling]. I'm going to have to change it up and do this.'"

Nevertheless, once the state adopted the CCSS in 2010, they realized that they, too, had to respond to the new requirements. Although Rodriguez was a charter school, its teachers couldn't ignore students' standardized test scores. One explained that the school's board of directors "wants to see that our MCAS results are good" and that expectation "trickles down" to the teachers. For the first time, the school had begun to adopt common expectations and practices for all students, such as how to annotate texts.

In response to the MCAS, Rodriguez teachers also began to teach some topics they otherwise might have skipped. An ELA teacher described how results from an interim assessment prompted her to review what she taught. "I say to myself, 'Gee, did we talk about onomatopoeia this year yet, when I've been doing poetry? No, I don't think I have. Does it always come up on the test? Yeah, it usually does. I'd better bring that in.'" The school administered the same quarterly interim assessments used by Hurston and Fitzgerald, although elementary teachers at Rodriguez said that Ms. Rowland, their director, did not expect those results to drive their curriculum. One teacher recalled Ms. Rowland saying: "Don't just teach something because you think you have to teach it, because of [the interim assessments]. [Instead], let's figure it out."

Rodriguez also had begun to require teachers to create and teach three or four thematic units each year, which offered what they called "rich and structured" learning experiences. Ms. Rowland explained, "Our middle school felt quite structured and our lower school felt quite rich." The new units specified learning outcomes, while being "incredibly memorable and incredibly engaging, and incredibly rich." For example, a middle school teacher of English and social studies had created an extensive unit she called "Hero or Not." Students read primary and secondary sources about explorers, including Cortez, Pizarro, and Columbus, and studied art depicting them. They then debated whether each was a hero. Teams of students were assigned to take the pro or con side in the debate and to create a visual representation of their argument. It was, she explained, "really, really hard work for them." These units coupled the school's prior focus on interdisciplinary learning with "the best parts of data-informed instruction and adherence to the curriculum standards."

For teachers at Rodriguez, curriculum remained highly personalized. However, the school had begun to devote one professional development session each month to having teachers explain a rich and structured unit they were planning and solicit feedback from their peers. In addition, administrators visited classes and photographed activities as these lessons were taught, distributing pictures by email several times a week. Teachers welcomed the chance to see the curriculum in action and these activities started to loosely knit together Rodriguez's highly varied instructional program.

The year before we began our Successful Schools study, Fitzgerald also had introduced more open-ended interdisciplinary units for each grade, called "Journeys of Learning." Each lasted about three months and complemented the tightly defined disciplinary units and lessons that teachers continued to prepare and share. At the conclusion of each grade's Journey, the teachers and students prepared a final product to distribute inside and outside the school. Administrators supported them by arranging speakers, performances, and field trips that enriched their learning, while specialists offered support to students who were creating PowerPoint slides or choosing music to accompany their presentation. When we visited during the second year of this study, grade-level teachers had chosen a wide variety of topics for their Journeys, including puppets, the rain forest, energy, and social justice. One second-grade teacher, whose students had participated in the rain forest unit, said that earlier that day she asked students to draw an animal they remembered. "José came to me and he said, 'I drew a toucan. He's on a tree, but there's an epiphyte on it.' I was like, 'Oh, my gosh. He remembered the word *epiphyte*!'"

CONCLUSION

State curriculum policies, with their standards, assessments, and attendant sanctions, substantially circumscribed and directed the decisions these Massachusetts educators made about what and how to teach. By targeting school-level performance, the policies gradually shifted responsibility for curriculum and instruction from individual teachers within their classroom to groups of colleagues at their grade level, department, and ultimately to the school, where performance was assessed. However, this shift of responsibility did not occur in all schools. Because many viewed the policies as being grounded in assumptions about teachers' resistance and noncompliance, some schools responded by imposing tight control on teachers' instructional practice, while others stalled out with minimal responses, such as tutoring for students who sat "on the bubble" between failing and passing the test.

Yet, when a school's administrators and teachers addressed the challenge of accountability as one of developing the teachers' capacity rather than exacting their compliance, the potential for real progress became apparent. In schools such as Lane, Hurston, Naylor, and Fitzgerald, where teachers met regularly to review their students' performance, assess their own instruction, and plan subsequent units and lessons, the challenge of deciding what and how to teach no longer remained either the prerogative or the burden of individual teachers. But neither was it taken out of their hands and reassigned to supervisors or external experts. Instead, teachers engaged regularly with peers to define a curriculum that was coherent not only within a single class or course, but also throughout the school.

These cases suggest that success in developing and implementing a curriculum *with* teachers, rather than *for* or *despite* them, depends first and foremost on the school's having a principal or other key administrators who deeply understand teaching and learning, have an organizational perspective on change, and possess strong, collaborative leadership skills. As these cases illustrate, such principals engage teachers in thoughtful reflection, ongoing collaboration, and a creative search for new strategies that will meet their students' learning needs. The examples presented here focus on teachers developing entirely new curriculum in response to CCSS and their students' needs. However, most of these educators didn't think that was necessary to do in every subject, because in some, such as math, they could use a well-regarded curriculum that already was aligned with the new standards. Most teachers and administrators did not see value in continuously developing original units or lessons, a time-consuming process that many referred to as "reinventing the wheel." Instead, they saw promise in building on prior accomplishments and preserving model units and lessons online so that they would be refined and reused. However, they also realized that, as the standards and assessments changed, they too would have to revisit earlier decisions and adjust both their curriculum and pedagogy.

Important questions remain about the level of autonomy individual teachers should retain as they teach either an adopted curriculum or one they develop collaboratively at grade levels or schoolwide. Because teachers also are expected to differentiate instruction in response to individual students' needs, they must retain some discretion to adjust their practice, whether that involves choosing alternative texts or substituting a discussion question in a shared lesson plan. Also unresolved are questions about whether and how to integrate teaching content and skills with broader experiences that give students opportunities to be creative, examine their values, and reflect on the world they live in. Such questions were being explored collaboratively by Fitzgerald teachers as they developed interdisciplinary Journeys of Learning and by Rodriguez teachers as they created "rich and structured" curricular units.

Given how complex and demanding the process of developing and implementing a curriculum can be, it's reasonable to ask how much instructional capacity a school must already have in order to seriously undertake this work. Clearly, it's important to have some teachers who bring to the process an understanding of the basics—how to approach and use learning standards; how to choose relevant, rich content through which to teach those standards; how to map out instructional units for a month, a semester, or a school year; how to plan daily lessons that actively engage students in the process of learning; and how to continuously assess what students understand and what they have yet to learn. Teachers who have worked closely with capable, experienced teachers during their preservice student teaching or apprenticeship will have a basic understanding of this work. However, the many teachers who have been licensed with scant clinical experience will have to acquire, practice, and develop such skills with the support of administrators, instructional coaches, and experienced colleagues.

Therefore, it is important for schools to continue building individual teachers' competence, while simultaneously moving this process of curriculum development and implementation beyond the classroom into the larger units of the school—its grade levels, subject departments, and clusters—where teachers can collaborate with colleagues as they assume collective responsibility for what and how they teach. That collaboration is the subject of the next chapter.

CHAPTER THREE

The Potential of Teacher Teams

For over fifty years teachers have reported that "cooperative and competent colleagues" are one of the most important sources of support in their work.[1] In interviewing hundreds of teachers over thirty-five years, I've often heard them say that they welcome their peers' encouragement when they're contending with a difficult class or facing a challenging student, and they appreciate their reassurance when things go wrong. Teachers solicit a colleague's advice about how best to handle a parent's complaint or respond to what they see as unreasonable demands by their principal. They're grateful to borrow a peer's good idea or adapt a lesson plan for their own use. Such valued interactions often occur during informal conversations over a hurried lunch or in the parking lot after school, around the edges of their "real" work. Sometimes two colleagues who teach the same grade or subject might plan their classes together, but until recently close and ongoing collaboration among teachers was not a common practice that schools in the US encouraged or systematically facilitated.

Over the past two decades, however, collaboration among teachers has gradually been on the rise.[2] Initially, this development was spurred by the entry of a new generation of teachers who had different expectations for their work than their predecessors. Growing up, they regularly teamed with others, whether they were competing on the soccer field or completing projects in class. When they began teaching, they anticipated similar, interdependent relationships with other teachers and were dismayed when those didn't materialize. For example, in 1998 we interviewed Esther, who began teaching in an urban high school after an early career in the space industry, where she enjoyed the excitement of being part of a team. Later she was surprised to discover that she was expected to be self-reliant as a teacher: "Here, it's pretty much, 'There's your classroom, here's your book. Good luck.'" For her and many others we interviewed at that time, going it alone was simply the way it was, especially in urban schools.

That isolation and lack of support contributed to unprecedented turnover rates as many new teachers precipitously left their schools and teaching.[3] In response, many states and districts instituted induction programs that provided personal mentoring for new teachers, in the hope that professional guidance by a more experienced peer would ease a novice's entry into teaching. However, mentoring turned out to be far less successful than reformers had expected.

In studying new teachers in Massachusetts, we found that novices were more satisfied with their work when they interacted regularly with colleagues as members of grade-level teams or departments than when they met intermittently with an assigned mentor.[4] In her 2002 survey of new teachers in four states, Susan Kardos found that shortcomings of mentoring were generally due to several factors: mismatches between novices and mentors, mentors' lack of training for their role, and insufficient time for meetings or classroom observations. Few new teachers reported talking regularly with their mentors about core activities of teaching.[5]

However, even at its best, mentoring fell short. Steven Glazerman and his colleagues at Mathematica Policy Research conducted a randomized experiment to assess the value of fully implemented mentoring programs. After two years, he compared the participating teachers with others in a control group who received no more than the regular supports that their school usually provided, and he found that mentoring improved neither teacher retention nor student performance.[6]

Mentoring suffers from a more fundamental problem than inadequate implementation. It is rarely integrated with the ongoing work of the school, instead typically being appended to an otherwise compartmentalized school organization.[7] No mentor can provide all that a new teacher needs as she learns her job and settles into her school. Mentoring was conceived and largely has been implemented as a short-term partnership intended to scaffold an individual teacher's entry into her classroom. It was not conceived as an enduring structure designed to promote and sustain collaboration among teachers throughout the school.

Even today in schools where teachers welcome new colleagues with offers of help, their invitations are not likely to extend into the classroom, where the real work of teaching and learning happens. A novice who hopes to discover how an experienced colleague efficiently settles her fourth-grade class at the beginning of the day or how a middle school ELA teacher orchestrates a rich and engaging discussion about a challenging text may have to make do with a secondhand explanation or, as one new teacher recently did, watch from outside the classroom door.

Colleagues may teach in adjoining classrooms but have no access to each other's lesson plans, strategies, or insights. As a result, valuable professional knowledge is lost or remains trapped in the memories, filing cabinets, and laptops of individual teachers. When such isolating practices persist, teachers not only lack access to their colleagues' ideas and examples, which might benefit their students, but also have no systematic way to influence others' instruction. Even when two peers regularly collaborate at lunch, during prep periods, or on a shared commute to and from school, their interactions are, at best, semiprivate. And, although they may talk openly and at length about their teaching, they may never watch one another teach. It's one thing to talk about teaching and quite another to observe and experience it. In such cases, valuable opportunities for organizational learning, which could fuel schoolwide improvement, are systematically sidelined in a distressing waste of professional resources.

Often invisible, but surprisingly inviolable, classroom boundaries continue to separate teachers from their colleagues.[8] Professionals who work in far more interdependent organizations, such as effective HMOs or businesses, would be puzzled by teachers' willingness to settle for such isolation and secondhand learning, which rarely obliges them to alter their own instruction in response to others' decisions and practices.

WHAT DISCOURAGES MEANINGFUL COLLABORATION IN SCHOOLS?

Research clearly documents that students learn more in schools where their teachers collaborate regularly.[9] Why, then, has it been so difficult to promote and sustain ongoing teaming and peer observation among teachers? Three factors—the architecture of schools, teachers' professional norms, and how teachers' time is scheduled—all contribute to the problem.

The School's Architecture

The egg-crate design and structure of schools discussed earlier, by which separate classrooms are arranged along the sides of the corridors, clearly has some influence on teachers' interaction. A product of the "cellular growth" of schools over time, classrooms provide a haven from interruption and commotion as students and teachers move to and from the library, gym, playground, restrooms, offices, and classrooms throughout the day.[10] When a teacher closes her classroom door, she not only ensures that instruction and discussions can proceed in relative calm and quiet, but also protects herself and her class from curious and potentially intrusive passersby. Closed classroom doors send clear signals to interested peers that they are unwelcome.

Teachers' Professional Norms

In his classic 1975 study of teachers and teaching, Dan Lortie first identified the powerful role that professional norms, including a teacher's right to privacy, play in shaping teachers' work with their peers: "Collegial norms can be said to arbitrate tension between [teachers'] quest for individual autonomy and the desire for collegial assistance."[11] He concluded that the classroom is at the center of teachers' energy and attention because it is there that they gain the "psychic rewards" of their work.[12] Subsequently, Judith Warren Little explained how this "persistence of privacy" is "sustained by the very organization of teaching work."[13]

In 2008, my colleagues and I again were reminded of the tenacity of teachers' expectations for privacy and egalitarianism when we studied teacher leaders who were formally appointed to roles such as instructional coach, department head, or professional developer. We found that, although these teacher leaders were supposed to influence their colleagues' practice, they were constrained in what they could do. Some of their colleagues refused to allow them to enter their classroom and others were reluctant to consider their advice, especially when they had less teaching experience.[14] Although change is under way, in many schools these professional norms continue to serve as powerful brakes on ambitious efforts to inform and improve instructional practice.

Limits on Teachers' Time

Another school feature that reinforces teachers' self-reliance and fortifies their isolation is a schedule that maximizes the use of teachers' time so that their students—not their colleagues—get the full benefit of their expertise. Arguably, from a teacher's perspective, the scarcest resource in schools is time, which we'll examine closely in chapter 7. Except for lunch, which often is thirty minutes or less, a teacher's time during the school day is divided three ways. First there is instructional time, when the teacher is assigned to teach her assigned students. Second is administrative duty time, when she is scheduled to assume tasks such as supervising bus arrivals and departures, recess, hallways, restrooms, or study areas. Third is preparation time, when she can plan and prepare for class, grade papers, confer with parents, meet individually with students needing extra help, or, if it's convenient, collaborate with colleagues. At best, most teachers have fifty to sixty minutes each day for all these activities, and many have less.

Therefore, if teachers want to meet with colleagues, they have to do so during their limited preparation time, over lunch, or after school, although that time is often reserved for faculty meetings and professional development. Until recently, teachers who tried to meet with their peers during preparation periods—the time left after classes, courses, and administrative duties were scheduled—were often stymied because those periods were scattered throughout the day, not deliberately arranged so that teachers sharing the same courses or students could meet regularly.

Given physical boundaries, countervailing norms, and scarce time, teachers who persisted in meeting with peers would have to be motivated by a clear and compelling purpose. What would it take to raise teachers' sights beyond their own classroom so that they could realize the benefits that collaborative, collegial work might yield for them and their school? Surprisingly, school-based accountability policies, such as NCLB, appear to have done just that.

COLLABORATING FOR ACCOUNTABILITY

Since 2000, state and federal policy makers' efforts to hold schools and school districts accountable for students' performance have had both positive and negative effects, many of them unintended. On the negative side, standardized tests narrowed the curriculum—what's tested is what's taught—and in some cases promoted gaming or even led to cheating by administrators and teachers as they tried to protect their schools from bad publicity and formal state sanctions.[15] On the positive side, though, because NCLB required schools to account for the performance in tested subjects of all subgroups of students—including students with disabilities, English language learners, and students from underrepresented racial and ethnic groups—accountability has ensured that many students who long were ignored are at last being taught, at least in math and language arts.

School administrators—especially those whose schools served students from high-poverty communities—quickly realized that, if they were to meet the challenging annual goals for improvement under NCLB and state accountability policies, they had to address the shortcomings of some teachers' performance, which they had been ignoring or tolerating. For the first time ever, teachers throughout the school had to perform effectively. Faced with the challenge of improving instruction schoolwide, some principals and teachers started to rethink their use of human resources. Many realized that a school can't effectively function as a collection of solo teachers in isolated classrooms if it is to truly serve all its students. Because those students move over time from class to class and grade to grade, their education ultimately is the sum of all those experiences. However, if a third-grade teacher neglects a required learning standard, such as teaching her students how to calculate volume in math class, they will stumble later when they try to solve a practical problem in science. For too many students enrolled in low-income urban schools, the education they experience is disjointed and their various learning experiences don't add up to much.

Therefore, teachers in some schools began to look beyond the students in their class and take into account what was happening across their grade level and in other classes where either their subject or their students were taught.[16] For example, they might agree to modify the list of texts they assigned so that all students in their grade would have comparable reading experiences. Or teachers in grades 3 through 5 might forego having a self-contained class so that students all could benefit from being taught by the best math or language arts teacher in the grade.

One indirect effect of these accountability policies has been to promote organized, rather than chance, collaboration among teachers as members of instructional teams or professional learning communities (PLCs).[17] If teachers meet regularly to do what Little calls "joint work" by planning curriculum, reviewing students' progress, and revising their lessons together, students stand to benefit schoolwide.[18]

Recognizing the many challenges that educators face when they take steps to organize collaboration, we sought to learn more about teachers' working relationships with their colleagues, especially in low-income and high-poverty schools. Did they collaborate? If so, when and how? What was their purpose in meeting—reviewing test data and monitoring students' ongoing progress, developing supports for struggling students, sharing resources, learning to teach better, and/or coordinating their use of the curriculum? There were many possibilities, but what did they hope to gain and what did they in fact get?

Given the difficulties that schools typically experience as they implement teams, it is important to understand not only what works, but also what doesn't work.[19] Principals and teachers can learn from the challenges and mistakes of others as well as from their successes. In the discussion that follows, we first consider what we learned from our Teaching in Context study of 2010–2011 about why and how teams in three WCSD schools worked well, while those in three others did not. We then move on to consider the central role that teams played in the Successful Schools study of 2014–2015. These teams dealt with issues of both content (curriculum, lessons, and assessments) and the student cohort (discipline, norms, and culture). Administrators carefully protected scheduled team time and remained engaged in the teams' work. In an especially promising practice, teacher leaders in three schools formally facilitated teams.

TEACHING IN CONTEXT: SUCCESSES AND FAILURES OF TEAMS IN DISTRICT SCHOOLS

We were very surprised to find that all the WCSD schools we studied in 2010 arranged for teachers to meet at least once a week with colleagues who shared their grade level, subject, cohort of students, or specialized assignment, such as special education or art.[20] When we asked those teachers about their interactions with colleagues inside and outside of school, they repeatedly pointed to team meetings as their most regular and valuable collaborative experience. Given past research, we expected them to judge their teams' value by whether it helped them teach their own students better. However, we found that teachers within these high-poverty schools had not one, but two, criteria in mind as they assessed their teams. As expected, the first focused on themselves as individual teachers: does my team help me teach better? However, the second criterion was organizational: does my team contribute to improving the school?[21]

Not all teachers judged their school's approach to teams favorably. In fact, while teachers in some schools were full of praise, those in others were bitterly critical. Although teachers' views varied from team to team within the same school, we found the school-to-school differences far more striking. Across all six schools, teachers believed that teams had great potential to both enhance their work with their own students and promote school improvement, but in only three of the six schools we studied that year did large proportions of teachers assess their team experience positively.

Three Schools Where Teams Worked Well

Teachers in three WCSD schools—Angelou Elementary, Morrison K–8, and Giovanni Elementary—generally found their teams worthwhile. As we saw in chapter 2, Angelou was in the first year of a state-mandated reorganization due to poor performance and faced the real possibility of state takeover. As a result of work completed by the school's design committee, much of teachers' team time focused on learning how to use the district's curriculum in ways that would provide a more coherent learning experience for all students. Some of Angelou's teachers believed that their colleagues were the best source of knowledge and advice about curriculum and content and, therefore, they turned to them during team meetings for expertise and advice. For example, one fourth-grade teacher described how the new curricular consistency across her grade made it possible to learn from others' experience as they taught the same content: "It's nice. Most of us are at similar points in the curriculum. So we might say, 'Oh, today I taught lesson 4.5, did you?' Or, 'How did that go for you when you taught that?'" Teachers set the agenda and facilitated their meetings, while administrators attended often and sometimes offered their views, which most teachers found supportive and helpful.

Teachers at Morrison K–8 did not experience the same threat of state takeover, but they were seriously concerned about their school's standing because students' test scores had slipped in recent years. Because their school was relatively small, teachers and administrators could easily identify students who struggled academically and then use team time to diagnose their needs and decide how best to intervene and support them. Teachers spent team meetings analyzing data from various assessments, which they found helpful as they planned what to do in their classes and how to allocate resources for tutoring.

At Giovanni Elementary School, where students were performing relatively well, the principal, Mr. Gilmore, created grade-level teams so that teachers could explore and develop new instructional approaches. Whereas teachers at Angelou spent team time discussing curriculum implementation and those at Morrison concentrated on individual students' test scores and learning needs, Giovanni's teachers used the time to improve their pedagogy. Under their principal's leadership, they examined student work, analyzed videos of their colleagues' teaching, experimented with new instructional strategies that had been introduced during professional development sessions, and explored ways to adapt their curriculum and lessons to meet the diverse needs of students within their classes. Teachers repeatedly said that their work together enhanced their own instruction and simultaneously helped the school progress toward its larger goal of providing consistent, high-quality instruction across the grades.

Three Schools Where Teams Fell Short

Teachers in the remaining three schools—Thoreau High School, Whitman Academy High School, and Stowe Middle School—criticized their teams, saying that they didn't help them teach better, were misaligned with their school's larger purposes and programs, or focused excessively on improving test scores. Their complaints suggested that they were expected to participate in the kind of "contrived collegiality" that Andy Hargreaves cautioned about nearly two decades earlier.[22] For example, since the mid-1990s, teachers and students at Thoreau had worked together in small learning communities (SLCs), where an interdisciplinary team of teachers convened regularly to share information about their students and curriculum and to plan SLC events. Ms. Thomas, who had been appointed principal four years earlier, was concerned that the SLCs had too much autonomy and perpetuated inequities among subgroups of students in the school. Therefore, she and other administrators created schoolwide subject-based teams, which they thought would moderate the influence of the SLCs and generate instructional consistency throughout the school. However, many teachers prized their SLC experience and distrusted the principal's motives. They also said that time spent with their subject-based colleagues was not well used and that the topics under discussion seldom aligned with what they were currently teaching. Although some less experienced teachers appreciated the chance to learn from senior colleagues, most teachers suggested that their subject-based team lacked purpose and offered little to help them improve their own instruction or students' schoolwide experience in studying their subject.

At Whitman Academy, a successful magnet high school that featured technology, administrators and teachers went to great lengths to know each student well and to customize the academic program to meet individuals' needs. Teachers were encouraged to follow their own interests and create unique elective courses, such as biotechnology and Latin American history. Although these specialized courses might have dampened teachers' interest in formally collaborating, the teachers did not work alone and the professional culture of the school was not fragmented. Each week all teachers and administrators joined in an extended meeting during which they reviewed individual students' progress, appraised the school's programs, and explored opportunities for integrating and improving them. Teachers were devoted to their school and revered their principal, Ms. Wheeler. Although they spoke favorably about the weekly whole-faculty meetings, they expressed little enthusiasm for meeting with their departmental team. One physics teacher said, "I think they make us have meetings just to have meetings."

The one exception to this general lack of enthusiasm came from Whitman's team of English teachers, who said they learned a great deal from one another. However, they suggested that their team succeeded primarily because of the individuals involved. One said, "We work incredibly well together. We share materials. We set a bar really high." These teachers appreciated their team because it benefited their own instruction, but they didn't see it as a means to improve the school. Overall, the content-based teams at Whitman were not well aligned with the school's commitment to individualized learning.

Whereas teachers at Thoreau and Whitman were disappointed with their team experiences, teachers at Stowe Middle School seethed as they described theirs. Many said that their principal, Ms. Sterling, narrowly defined and closely managed their team's work in order to raise test scores, especially those of students who appeared to be on the brink of falling into the "needs improvement" category. One said, "[Ms. Sterling has] an agenda based on test scores. So everything is about test scores." Another explained that the work assigned to his team by administrators "can seem disjointed or unrelated to what I'm going through during the day. [As a result], we never have enough time to meet, and [meaningful conversation] just gets lost in the shuffle." Teachers suggested that the time available during team meetings was consumed by mandated topics and activities, leaving little opportunity for them to work with colleagues, whose views and expertise they respected.

The Principal's Role in Effective Teams

Amy Edmondson explains that when teams are effective in other sectors, such as product design and health care, the manager sets an "aspirational" purpose for the team's work, encourages team members to learn together rather than simply "execute" a task, and provides a "psychologically safe" environment in which members can explore possibilities and take risks without fear of retribution or humiliation. She characterizes the manager as a team's "crucial partner."[23] By comparing the work of teams at Stowe Middle School and Giovanni Elementary School, we can see how a principal's actions can determine the effectiveness of school-based teams.

Setting an aspirational purpose

Arguably, Stowe's principal, Ms. Sterling, had good intentions and her school's interests in mind when she focused teachers' time and attention on students' performance on standardized tests. She was well aware that continued funding for the school's extended learning time might be cut and the state could sanction Stowe if students' test scores continued to drop. However, by defining student learning narrowly and essentially equating it with gains on standardized tests, Ms. Sterling ignored much of what teachers cared about and did on behalf of their students. Stowe's teachers wanted to awaken their students to new ideas, strengthen their skills, and encourage their creativity—all goals that the principal probably would have agreed were worthwhile. However, in Edmondson's terms, the teachers thought that Ms. Sterling had abandoned an "aspirational" purpose for their meetings and substituted a "defensive" one by which the school could avoid punitive sanctions.[24]

In contrast, Giovanni's principal, Mr. Gilmore, had been an instructional coach before becoming principal and he carried his zeal for instructional improvement into his new school. He believed that, by working together, teachers could improve both what they did as individuals in their own classroom and what they did collectively across the school. In committing his own time and becoming actively involved with the grade-level teams, Mr. Gilmore generated enthusiasm and confidence about what teachers' collaboration could yield within and across classrooms. Teachers were inspired by being committed to a goal they regarded as worthwhile—increasing and enriching opportunities for their students to learn as they progressed through the school.

Promoting shared learning, not lockstep execution

Virtually no teachers at Stowe said that the work they did on their team encouraged or supported better instruction or improved students' learning. Instead, they reported that administrators and external consultants set the agenda, ran their meetings, and required them to complete activities meant to tightly align instruction across their classes. One said his team time was consumed by completing required paperwork. Others reported that their teams spent much of their time discussing logistics, such as "getting the kids downstairs quickly and efficiently. It's about forms; it's about the assembly. . . . For the most part, it is not educationally focused." Another teacher elaborated: "It just doesn't work. It's like we're doing it just to show the state that we're doing something. And it's, in my point of view, a complete waste of time." Teachers said that the consultants' routines were disconnected from the issues of teaching and learning that mattered to them. One explained, "It's sort of like going to a group of people and telling them, 'Well, I want to see [you do] this, although I'm not a teacher, although I don't know what your needs are, but I want to see this.'"

By contrast, Giovanni's teachers enthusiastically described team meetings where they explored instructional challenges and opportunities. Teachers used protocols to examine student work, analyzed video recordings of their own teaching, shared and experimented with instructional approaches they had learned at professional development sessions, and investigated how to use and adapt the curriculum to meet students' individual needs. The fifth-grade team watched videos about reading comprehension strategies and then planned to conduct teaching and observation cycles where they would introduce and practice them. One teacher explained, "[We] plan lessons together and then . . . we've been teaching sample lessons, and the principal's there, and we all kind of give each other feedback. . . . We'll talk about what strategies we used, what we could do to improve it." While team time at Stowe focused on completing predetermined tasks, Giovanni's teachers were actively engaged in planning the course of their professional learning.

Providing a psychologically safe environment for teams

Stowe's teachers not only resented being micromanaged, but also feared reper-cussions if they failed to comply with their principal's expectations. One teacher said that any feedback she offered Ms. Sterling usually went "in one ear and out the other." Another explained that she and her colleagues refrained from object-ing to the administrators' tight agenda because the principal might "make some-one's life hard." As a result, most teachers kept their head down and complied with the requirements, even when they were convinced that they made no sense.

Giovanni's principal had high standards and held teachers accountable for their participation on teams, but did so in an environment where teachers could raise concerns, explore practices, and even fail without penalty or fear of humili-ation. Rather than telling teachers what to do, Mr. Gilmore encouraged them to use team time to puzzle over challenging problems and explore possible so-lutions. Within the school's professional culture, inquiry and exploration were valued and many teachers suggested their team meetings provided a vital arena where they could voice their opinions, solicit responses, and influence others. Offering an example of how teachers shifted his expectations, Mr. Gilmore said, "A first-grade group will say to me, 'I don't care what you say, Mr. G., . . . they're not ready for small moments [a strategy for teaching writing] in first grade. They don't know how to write a sentence. Could we please teach them the structure of the language?'"

Our study led us to conclude not only that teams are increasingly common in urban school districts today, but also that teachers are more likely to engage seriously with them than they were in the past. In the right context and with the right conditions, teachers welcome collaboration and thrive as they work to-gether. However, as we have seen repeatedly, schools differ as work environments and those differences matter—not only for teachers, but also for students. In the three schools where teachers widely reported that their teams were worthwhile, principals conveyed a meaningful purpose for their work together, encouraged teachers to focus on learning and school improvement, and ensured that teachers felt safe to experiment, raise concerns, and disagree. School leaders were key players, although not always—or even often—at center stage. They remained either actively involved or continuously informed about the teams' work. Teachers understood why they were working together and endorsed that purpose, convinced that they and their school would benefit if they collaborated effectively. In the three schools where teachers said that their team added little or diminished their effectiveness, key supports for effective teams were seriously compromised or missing altogether.

TEACHER TEAMS IN SUCCESSFUL SCHOOLS

Informed by these findings, we sought to learn whether and how teams functioned in schools that state officials judged to be successful. We found that all the schools we studied in 2014–2015 put a premium on collaboration among teachers, and that five of the six relied on teams as a key means for developing and maintaining an effective instructional program and monitoring students' experience and progress.

At the sixth school, Rodriguez Charter, collaboration was ongoing, but less formalized than at the other five schools. Pairs of regular education and special education teachers at Rodriguez cotaught an inclusion class at each grade. Otherwise, teachers had few, if any, colleagues who taught the same subject or the same students. Ms. Rega, principal of the K–4 school, encouraged teachers to work together when their preparation time coincided, but didn't schedule common planning time because, as she explained, such time was scarce: "The big problem, honestly, is [finding] meeting time. These teachers are so stretched that to put another hour in to meet someone else. . . . It's very hard to add another meeting."

Teachers Relied on Their Teams

However, in the other five schools, teachers repeatedly said that they relied extensively on their team members. For example, at Fitzgerald PreK–5, we asked a teacher where she went for support. She responded quickly: "My team members." We then asked what kinds of support she might look for and she answered, "Everything." We probed further about when this occurred and she said, "Every day, many times." Similarly, a teacher leader of instruction at Kincaid Charter—a restart school operating within WCSD—characterized the team as the teacher's "first line of defense," saying, "It's just a cohesive unit. . . . People are unified in their efforts here. You don't want to see anybody fail." Principals, too, cited the positive effects of teams. Fitzgerald's principal, Ms. Forte, attributed her school's rapid improvement after state officials placed it in turnaround to the formal process of collaboration among teachers: "I would say a lot of our success is because we really work at teams. The primary unit is the grade-level team. . . . It's really like you are married to your team."

Teams Focused on Instructional Content and the Student Cohort

Across these five schools, teams essentially had two areas of focus. *Content* teams included teachers who taught the same subject, such as those teaching self-contained multiple-subject classes in the primary grades or a single subject (or two) in upper elementary or middle school grades. Content teams also monitored student performance data (e.g., interim assessments, running records, exit tickets, and unit tests) to gauge whether students were learning what they were teaching.

Meanwhile, *cohort* teams focused on students' needs, behavior, and the school culture that they experienced. In some primary grades, the same group of teachers met to address both content and the cohort, although in grades 5 through 8, where teachers typically taught only one subject, separate teams focused on content and the cohort. A teacher at Kincaid Charter explained teachers' team assignments there: "You basically are always part of two teams. You're part of a cultural [cohort] team and you're part of a department [content] team. Your department team teachers will never teach together, but you will plan [instruction] together. On your cohort team, you never teach the same subjects, but you all teach the same kids."

Teachers in all five schools had daily blocks of fifty to sixty minutes scheduled as common planning time for teachers in the same grade level or content area. During at least one of those blocks each week, subgroups of teachers met in teams to address academic content, the student cohort, or both. Teachers then used their remaining blocks of preparation time to work independently or meet informally with colleagues.

Content teams addressed instruction and learning

As we saw in chapter 2, these schools relied much less on prepared curricula than many traditional schools. Both new and experienced teachers throughout these schools said that their grade-level and content teams helped them to meet the continuous demands of planning, teaching, assessing, and revising their curriculum throughout the year. In three schools—Kincaid Charter, Fitzgerald PreK–5, and Naylor Charter—teachers took this one step further and shared responsibility for lesson planning. Based on their team's curriculum design and unit planning, individuals wrote lesson plans to be used by all team members. In some cases, as we've seen, these were sometimes very detailed, including scripted introductions, explanations, and discussion questions that the teachers could pose to promote deeper thinking and analysis.

As a Kincaid Charter School history teacher reflected on the benefits of his content team, he said, "[It has] turned the job of curriculum design into a much more manageable beast." However, one Kincaid administrator acknowledged that the process of team-based lesson planning had advantages and disadvantages: "When it works it's great because the team's collective understanding of the standard and how to teach it is just rich and pushes each individual forward." However, "if it's not working well, it pulls everyone down. . . . It's really tough." For example, an eighth-grade teacher at Kincaid was assigned to teach math, but had no prior teaching experience. He recalled that, although he found the grade-level content team very helpful, the process was "touch and go for a little while." He explained, "The fact that I was only responsible for one-third of the lessons I taught and that the other two people in my department were more experienced meant that I saw and taught lessons that I didn't write. They were written by people who knew more than I did. Because of that model, I wasn't left to learn on my own what works and doesn't work. I was able to learn from and with them." However, his colleagues were not satisfied. He recalled that they "sat [him] down in December and said, 'Okay, we need to have a talk. . . . Some of your lessons are great, some are not so great, and we think there are some guiding principles you should know.'"

Teachers did not simply exchange and then use their colleagues' lesson plans, but first reviewed and revised them together during team meetings. A science teacher at Naylor Charter explained, "It's not that other people don't have any input. . . . We'll all give feedback on it." He said that teachers sent out their proposed lessons in advance of team meetings "so that then we can say, 'Hey, I really would like to see this in this lesson,' or 'I'm really confused about this part of the lab. How's that going to work?'" Another Naylor teacher described the interaction: "It's great because I'll have an idea and they'll make mine just so much better, so much stronger."

All five schools dedicated some content team time to analyzing data about students' learning, a process where they tried to discern whether their planned curriculum and current instruction were working as they intended. In doing so, teams reviewed a wide range of data from state tests, interim assessments, unit tests, and students' homework.

Cohort teams addressed students' needs, behavior, and organizational culture

Cohort teams were dedicated to ensuring that students could and would do their part as learners in the school. The teachers achieved this by systematically reviewing the needs and progress of individual students within their grade-level cohort, appraising the students' behavior as a group, and taking steps to strengthen aspects of the cohort's culture. At Dickinson and Fitzgerald, both preK–5 schools, this focus on the cohort largely occurred during grade-level meetings.

Each school had a dress code (including uniforms), rules for how students should behave as they walked in the corridors (silently at Naylor and Kincaid; calmly at Fitzgerald and Hurston), and expectations for how they should conduct themselves in classes (respectfully and attentively in all schools). Rules and norms were designed to promote an orderly environment that was conducive to learning, and teachers tried to make their expectations explicit and to respond consistently across classes. During cohort meetings, they took stock of students' behavior, with Kincaid and Naylor Charter Schools demanding strict compliance and expecting teachers to respond to individual violations quickly, consistently, and firmly. Teams in other schools also considered whether students were upholding the rules, but focused more on their social interactions, noting when disputes erupted or individuals were disorderly, withdrawn, or being bullied.

When they met in cohort teams, teachers also created new activities, incentives, and rewards to motivate students in their grade level or cluster. For example, Hurston's middle school teachers had adopted a set of behavioral norms called PRIDE (Perseverance, Respect, Integrity, Daring, and Excellence). When individual students acted in line with a PRIDE norm, teachers rewarded them with a small certificate; if a student received twenty certificates within a month, he could attend the cohort's ice cream party. At no-excuses Kincaid Charter, one teacher explained that she and her colleagues who taught the three cohorts that composed the grade "all run our classrooms the same way, [have] the same expectations for kids. We have the same consequences. We have the same incentives. We have the same cheers, the same chants." She said that, although all Kincaid students were expected to "call out answers or raise their hands in similar ways," the prizes awarded for "highest homework completion might be customized by cohort."

Factors Contributing to the Teams' Effectiveness

Across these successful schools, teachers and administrators identified four factors that contributed to their teams' effectiveness—sharing a clear, positive purpose for their teams' work; having sufficient, regular time for meetings; having administrators who remained engaged in or informed about their progress; and, in three schools, having teacher leaders serve as team facilitators.

Aspirational purpose

Each of these successful schools had an explicit mission of achieving equity, which then guided teachers' collaborative work as they developed curriculum and lessons, assessed the effectiveness of their instruction, and monitored students' behavior, needs, and progress. It was, in Edmondson's terms, an "aspirational" rather than a "defensive" purpose. Teamwork contributed to the school's progress as these educators sought to eliminate racial, ethnic, and economic achievement gaps by providing their students with the curriculum, instruction, and support they believed all students deserve.

Sufficient, predictable time

These schools also gave scheduled team time priority over other activities. Teachers could count on that time being protected, which made it worthwhile for them to prepare and actively participate in meetings. Other studies have found that, when team time is short, interrupted, or unpredictable, meetings often become occasions for check-ins with colleagues about routine matters, such as playground monitoring or field trip plans, or opportunities for individuals to socialize or prepare for their next class.[25] Team time in these successful schools was inviolable and, with few exceptions, teachers prized it. As one Hurston teacher said, "At no point was it ever 'Oh [let's] slack off and just hang out for a couple of hours.' . . . Why would you just sit around and not do anything?"

Because these schools were regulated by different policies, expectations for teams and what they might accomplish varied across the sample, largely based on how much time was available during the teacher's workday and whether a teacher's contract limited the principal's say in how that time could be used. Of the successful schools we studied, Dickinson PreK–5, which had no special autonomy or extra resources, had the least amount of dedicated time for team meetings, while Naylor Charter had the most.

Dickinson's teachers were required to be in school for 6.25 hours and were guaranteed five periods of common planning time each week, one of which the principal could direct. Dickinson's principal, Ms. Davila, made the most of this comparatively small block of time by convening and facilitating a series of three weekly meetings, each including teachers who spanned two grade levels (K–1, 2–3, and 4–5).

By contrast, Naylor Charter School teachers had a 9.25-hour workday. Teams met daily for a content meeting focusing on curriculum and instruction and convened again weekly to review data about students' achievement and progress. They also met as grade-level (cohort) teams weekly and had another one to two hours for professional development on Friday afternoons, when grade-level teams could continue their work. Ms. Nelson, codirector of the Naylor CMO, explained that the school had "big expectations for collaboration. . . . One of our four big organizational values is 'We grow best together.'" The school's generous allocation of team time reinforced and highlighted that priority.

Ongoing, engaged support from administrators

Like the teams that teachers judged favorably in the district schools of the Teaching in Context study discussed earlier (Angelou, Morrison, and Giovanni), the teams in these successful schools benefited from administrators' support and attention, either close up or from a distance.[26] Several principals attended meetings often, but only Dickinson's principal, Ms. Davila, regularly chaired them. Each Hurston administrator took responsibility for following teachers' work on four content teams. For example, Hurston's principal, Mr. Hinds, was responsible for ELA teams in three grades as well as the schoolwide arts team: "Those are my four teams. So I go to almost all of their meetings." Every team maintained a Google Doc that included meeting agendas, notes, and links to data. Teams could enter additional data during their meeting, which they then referred back to in subsequent meetings. Thus, the Google Docs structured, supported, and tracked the teams' progress, while also informing administrators schoolwide about all the teams' work. One explained, "All of us, the administrative team, are on Google Docs for all the teams . . . so that we can follow electronically what's happening, even if we're not there." He reported emphatically that Mr. Hinds "reads it all."

A middle school math teacher at Hurston said that Mr. Hinds "doesn't micromanage, but he plays a role in some of the small decision-making we have in our different teams. He'll pop up and attend different team meetings or he'll read the notes and give feedback. But it's not 'Okay, you guys, you have to do this. This team, you have to do this. This team, you have to do that.'" However, several Hurston teachers did object when Mr. Hinds stepped in after ELA test scores in grades 3 through 5 failed to improve and, as one teacher said, "laid down the law," requiring the team to focus on skills called for by the Common Core State Standards, such as close reading. Other teachers, however, thought the intervention was warranted.

Facilitation by trained teacher leaders

One of the most notable and successful practices in the three schools that had received extra funding after the state intervened (Hurston K–8, Fitzgerald Elementary, and Kincaid Charter Middle) was appointing teacher leaders to facilitate teams. In addition, Hurston committed the equivalent of another administrative position to supervise the facilitators' work. During the year we studied the school, Mr. Hanover, Hurston's Director of Professional Development and Data Inquiry, met weekly with each facilitator to review that team's prior meeting, offer feedback on facilitation, and help the facilitator plan the next meeting. Across these schools, teachers widely praised their facilitators, who themselves appreciated having the opportunity to exercise leadership. One facilitator said, "We work as a team, but I am the point person. . . . [T]he opportunity for constant discourse is super enriching and fulfilling for me as a teacher—knowing that I'm making an impact not only in my classroom, but I'm affecting the entire grade."

Supported by funds from federal School Improvement Grants, Hurston and Fitzgerald provided $6,000 stipends to each facilitator, but funding ended when the schools successfully exited turnaround. In order to keep this valuable practice going, Mr. Hinds secured a small grant from a local foundation, reduced the number of team facilitators, and reallocated administrative time so that a single administrator supervised two experienced teacher leaders, who in turn supervised other facilitators. Fitzgerald's facilitators lost their stipend, but acceded to the principal's request that they continue to facilitate teams voluntarily during the following year, when we studied the school. At Kincaid Charter, where team facilitators also were paid $6,000, participants said that they expected the stipend to drop to $2,500 the following year, leading several to suggest that interest in the position might decline, given the demands of the work.

All three schools where the state had intervened improved rapidly and, within several years, they achieved the state's highest rating. Not surprisingly, this is not the typical outcome of state intervention. Teachers and principals credited the teams with playing a major role in their improvement by supporting teachers as they collaborated to develop new curriculum, devise better strategies to support students' learning, continuously review their progress using data from many sources, and support teachers as they learned to manage and monitor their new practices.[27] Teachers told of working closely with peers to align their expectations for students, and individuals variously spoke of "increasing rigor," setting "high expectations," and establishing "consistency across classrooms." Strong, positive professional cultures within the schools, which many suggested emanated from their teams, encouraged and sustained teachers as they shared responsibility for this very challenging work. Meanwhile, teachers often mentioned that they chose to stay at their school because of its steady support for teams.

CONCLUSION

Based on our studies and others, evidence is growing that if teacher teams are well implemented, they minimize teachers' isolation, support their instruction, improve their school as an organization, and increase students' learning. In the five successful schools that relied on teams, teachers and administrators reported that teams led to greater instructional coherence both within and across grade levels as well as within subject areas throughout these schools. Teachers said they could be candid with members of their teams about their successes and failures. One Naylor teacher explained that having a shared stake in their students' success "creates a really open, honest environment." She said she could "walk into any of the other kindergarten teachers' classrooms and say, 'I just taught a lesson and it was bad. This really didn't go well at all. What did you guys do that I could do better?'" Such exchanges, long absent in schools where professional norms stifle candor, suggest that teachers may be ready to relinquish traditional assurances of privacy and expectations of self-reliance in return for productive work and interdependent relationships with colleagues.

Teams were not without their demands and drawbacks, however. As one Kincaid teacher explained, coordinating teaching inevitably reduces the independence that teachers are accustomed to: "When you work as a team, you don't have that autonomy." Asked what she would tell a prospective teacher interested in working at her school, she said, "Be ready to be on a team and be ready to be accountable to your team." Without that readiness to participate, she explained, "You're going to have some hard conversations with your team, perhaps with your [supervisor]. Just get on board." However, teachers in these schools continued to search for the right balance between holding true to their professional judgment about what and how best to teach, while also accommodating and adjusting to their teammates' views, which sometimes diverged from or conflicted with their own.

No one said that their school had created teams to support the induction of new teachers, but we repeatedly heard that teams served that purpose. In these schools, novices were not assigned individual mentors. Instead, from the first day they arrived, they were socialized to embrace the norms of interdependence that flourished in these schools. Novices quickly became engaged with their peers in making important decisions about what and how to teach, and they received advice from their more experienced, trusted colleagues about how to do this work better. Rather than waiting for periodic meetings or intermittent attention from an assigned mentor (whose interests and teaching style might not align with their own), they could observe colleagues' classes and be observed teaching as part of their team's routines.

Unquestionably, teams would never have flourished in these schools without the strong leadership of their principals—all serious, long-term educators. Importantly, administrators managed the school schedule to provide weekly opportunities for formal and informal collaboration. In these schools, there was virtually no mention of principals being intrusive or high-handed in supervising their work, as Ms. Sterling at Stowe reportedly was. Also fundamental to these teams' success was the teachers' confidence in their peers' knowledge, skills, and good intentions—confidence that many attributed to the thorough hiring process described in chapter 1 and the intensive supervision that all teachers received, which is the focus of chapter 5. First, however, chapter 4 examines the important role that students play in teachers' success by closely considering their needs and conduct as learners and how the school addresses them.

CHAPTER FOUR

Who Addresses Students' Needs and Conduct?

Teachers choose a career in the classroom because they want to work closely with young people and contribute to their learning and growth. Again and again, teachers offer similar explanations for why they teach. They want to "raise up" the next generation, "give back" to society in thanks for their own education, "unlock" their students' potential, and celebrate moments of insight when "the light goes on" as a student suddenly grasps a difficult concept or finally masters a challenging skill. With few exceptions, teachers are motivated by the prospect of experiencing intrinsic rewards from such experiences.[1] Like other researchers, my colleagues and I have found that teachers who achieve a "sense of success" with their students are more likely to remain in the profession than those who do not.[2]

Somewhat paradoxically, whether teachers attain the intrinsic rewards they seek hinges on the very students they hope to inspire, enlighten, and guide. Because those students are varied and unpredictable in their background, abilities, and interests, they inevitably bring uncertainty with them when they enter the classroom, possibly putting at risk the very success that a teacher hopes to achieve. As Dan Lortie explained over forty years ago, "Uncertainty is the lot of those who teach."[3] Therefore, in any classroom of any community, an effective teacher is constantly engaged in diagnosing, promoting, and managing the learning of twenty to thirty students, whose interests, behavior, and responses she can, at best, only partially predict.

Urban students who live in high-poverty communities often pose additional challenges for teachers. They may be academically far below grade level; stressed by poverty, homelessness, or the threat of violence in their neighborhood; or frightened that their friends or family might be deported. They also may feel unwelcome or mistreated by those in the school itself, and misbehave or act out in response to discrimination or injustice they encounter from teachers, administrators, or staff.

Education reformers regularly warn teachers not to take a "deficit perspective" toward their students by blaming them or their families for those challenges, rather than blaming the disjointed education system, failed public policies, racial and ethnic prejudice, and social injustice that afflict them and their communities.[4] Yet, whether or how teachers allocate blame, they still must face the array of challenges that many of their urban students experience. A teacher in a high-poverty charter school explained that her work was hard because her students' lives were shaken by violence: "And so you never know who's going to come in and say, 'Oh, my cousin was shot last night.' You look at the news and you know that there's a shooting, and you wonder who it's affected. . . . That tends to play a role, take a toll." Whatever their source, these problems—both dramatic and routine—exist, and teachers must deal with them, even as they marvel at their students' many talents and strengths.

To be clear, teachers in our two Walker City studies repeatedly said that many of their students were well behaved, inquisitive, even-tempered, kind, and studious, and that most parents were devoted to their children's well-being and passionate about the importance of education. Yet, as we interviewed teachers working in the city's high-poverty schools, they raised common questions and worries: Would their students be sufficiently prepared for the academic level of their class or grade? Would they have the basics of food, housing, health care, and warm clothing? Would they attend school regularly and on time? Would they take school seriously day to day? Would they be well behaved and show respect for adults and fellow students? Would they do their homework and study for tests? Would their parents support the school and the teachers?

Based on their experience, many teachers expressed doubts. One told of students in her school "who don't have enough to eat, who don't have medical facilities that they go to, kids who have toothaches, kids who need glasses." Another explained, "We have children who have parents who are incarcerated and who are living in shelters, and [those students] can't always be expected to just park it and be able to focus on a rigorous academic curriculum that we expect them to." An elementary teacher said that the threat of violence compromised her students' learning: "A lot of the children are traumatized. . . . And I'm not saying all of them, but, you know, a large chunk of these children [are]." She speculated that the school might be "the only safe haven" some students have. Given these possibilities, many teachers, like this one, described the excitement and pride they experience when students succeed: "One of the things I like most about them is also the most frustrating. . . . They have so much potential and you can see it in them, but then they also shut down so quickly. So I really like just getting through to at least one or two kids, and you can see a change and you're just like, 'Yes! Yes! Success!'"

Despite the challenges and uncertainty they encounter, teachers of urban students often say they choose to remain in their schools because of their students, not despite them. A teacher in the Fitzgerald Elementary School explained why she stays: "It's very rewarding work. . . . What makes it most challenging is also what makes it most rewarding. . . . We all know that this school is altering the course of these kids' lives . . . ensuring that all our kids can read well by third grade alters the course they are on." Time and again, when we have asked teachers why they stay in their high-poverty, urban schools, they have said it's because of "the kids." At Hurston K–8 School, one middle school counselor said, "The longer I stay, the harder it is to leave because I'm so incredibly happy with what's happened here. Mostly, I'm happy for the kids."

A SPECTRUM OF APPROACHES

However, not all urban schools make success likely for teachers and their students. In fact, researchers who track teachers' employment using large data sets report that teachers steadily leave schools that enroll black and brown students from low-income communities, transferring to schools that are, on average, whiter and wealthier than the school they left.[5] There's no dispute that this exodus occurs; rather, the dispute centers on why it happens and whether it is inevitable.

Some scholars infer from these broad transfer patterns that teachers who leave urban schools do so to flee their urban students. However, other researchers have concluded that these broad patterns of movement obscure crucial school-to-school differences.[6]

In our effort to understand how the school affects teachers' work with their students, we have found that schools fall along a spectrum.[7] At one end are schools that develop effective organizational strategies for improving students' attendance, minimizing disruptive behavior in corridors and classrooms, ensuring respect for adults and peers, supporting students' individual needs, and productively engaging parents. These schools reliably attract and retain teachers.

Toward the other end of the spectrum are schools that, at best, respond partially and sporadically when students' needs or behaviors reach a crisis level. Otherwise, administrators take a somewhat helpless, hands-off stance, leaving teachers to fend for themselves and devise their own solutions in the isolation of their classrooms. Given that teachers typically are responsible for 20–25 elementary or 100–150 secondary students at any one time, this expectation is unrealistic and far exceeds the time, energy, and skill that most teachers have. It's these schools that teachers continuously leave and that students would leave if they could.

What Challenges Do Urban Students Present?

Teachers in high-poverty, urban schools express concern about three broad areas of challenge. First, teachers say that effective education depends on their students being present, well behaved, and focused on learning. However, many of the schools where they teach are themselves disorderly, mismanaged environments, where truancy and tardiness are tolerated, rules are not enforced, and bullying is ignored.

Second, teachers struggle to meet the academic and socioemotional needs of their students. Many arrive to their class far below grade level, largely the result of inadequate schooling in prior years. They may lack stable housing and sufficient food and clothing. Personally, they may be troubled by the effects or threats of violence, abuse, and racism. Understandably, they may see no promising future for themselves and, therefore, may not be willing to engage in the work that their teachers encourage and expect.

Third, teachers express concern about the lack of parental engagement and apparent support for their students. Most recognize that urban parents often contend with their own personal challenges, such as being unemployed or having to juggle the demands of several part-time jobs with unpredictable schedules. Many recognize that parents may distrust the school because of mistreatment they experienced as students. However, teachers believe strongly that when parents convey to their children the importance of school and ensure that they attend and complete their homework, students are more likely to succeed. One Walker City teacher said:

> You really want to make a difference with the kids and with families. I've tried really hard to build a relationship with families because I feel like we all have to

work together to help their child. . . . I'm [only] with each child so long [during the day]. If I can build a relationship with families, do home visits, through parent-teacher conferences, just through not even formal [interactions], I think it makes a difference when there is a problem.

TEACHING IN CONTEXT: WHEN TEACHERS MUST FEND FOR THEMSELVES

In our Teaching in Context study, many teachers were left largely on their own to manage discipline. At Thoreau High School, for example, teachers criticized their administrators for adopting pointless rules that were seldom enforced. Signs posted throughout the school warned "No hats, No cell phones, No skipping classes," rules that were largely ignored by students, teachers, and most administrators. Metal detectors at the entrances discouraged students from bringing weapons to school, but did little to increase their sense of responsibility or of being cared for. One teacher described with frustration his students' initial encounter with the school: "[On the] first day, I walk in and there's kids coming in the door going through the metal detectors, and there's some guy saying, 'Come here, you.' And he goes over the three rules and says, 'Now you know I'm going to be watching you.' And it's like, that's a kid's first experience on the first day of school?"

Further, teachers said that Thoreau's students ignored rules about class attendance and congregated noisily in the halls. "Activity in the hallways stinks," one teacher said. "I hate it. I try to avoid the hallway. I can't stand what I see. I can't stand what I hear." In fact, when I arrived one day to interview teachers and stopped, as required, at the main office, the assistant urged me to wait until after students changed classes to avoid turmoil in the corridors. Banking on my own experience as a teacher, I went ahead anyway, but I did see why teachers complained. Some described frequent fights in the hallways and students' contempt when they or their colleagues tried to "sweep" the area clear of students and send them off to class. One teacher complained that the administrators' only response to students who broke the "no skipping" rule was to walk them back to their class. "There is no incentive for the kids to not do that every day. Like, why not come to your English class forty minutes late every day? I mean the only thing that happens is somebody brings you there late."

The school provided no meaningful forums where teachers and administrators could develop a shared understanding of appropriate behavior and agree about how to respond to these everyday problems. One teacher said that "most of the teachers deal with things independently," which means they had to spend "so much time handling discipline issues." Another said that dealing with disruptive students' behavior kept her from "focusing on preparing really great lessons and helping students." Another concurred: "I'm ready to teach. I'm ready to not worry about discipline." Many Thoreau teachers we talked with were frustrated, and several said they were likely to transfer to a different school. One spoke for herself and two colleagues: "I know personally that the three of us don't feel supported by [the principal]. I feel like we're not making a difference because the behavior is so bad [that] the teaching is not happening."

In other schools, teachers spoke about the need for more student support services, which they felt unable or unqualified to provide. Often they pointed to a few promising programs or initiatives, but said that those fell short of meeting their students' needs. Most schools had a part- or full-time social worker or psychologist who counseled students individually, but teachers said that one or two specialists could never meet the ongoing demand for services. Morrison K–8 School sponsored a student support team that met regularly to discuss students who were referred by individual teachers because they struggled academically or personally. In response to a referral, the student support team might recommend tutoring or counseling. However, because the team focused primarily on students whose standardized test scores were low, they sometimes missed others whose personal needs deserved attention.

All schools invited parents to attend annual open houses to meet the teachers, although only some made genuine efforts to encourage attendance and welcome the parents who showed up. Two schools that did, Giovanni and Angelou Elementary Schools, also hosted special evening events to help parents understand the subjects their children were learning and offer advice about how to help them with homework. One Giovanni teacher described her school's efforts: "A couple of times during the year [we] will have a bedtime story night, math night, all different nights, pasta night, and we have a huge [number of parents] showing up."

At Angelou a family coordinator, whose primary responsibility was to maintain productive relationships with parents, offered a class to help parents deal with their child's socioemotional needs. That year, the school also required teachers to make home visits for all of their students twice a year. The principal, Mr. Andrews, who lived in the community, offered to accompany any teacher on the first visit. A few teachers said they appreciated the offer, and some, but not nearly all, of Angelou's teachers visited their students' homes. Most teachers viewed each of these initiatives positively, though they also expressed concern that the students' needs far exceeded the supports they or the school could provide.

SUCCESSFUL SCHOOLS: CRAFTING A COHERENT APPROACH TO STUDENTS AND PARENTS

Although we identified promising practices in several district schools in our Teaching in Context study, they seldom were interdependent components of a coherent system designed to address the needs of students and families. It was not until our subsequent Successful Schools study that we found comprehensive organizational approaches to the three challenges of maintaining an orderly environment for learning, addressing students' academic and socioemotional needs, and establishing schoolwide approaches for working with parents. Teachers in these schools were not left on their own to create effective practices classroom by classroom, but instead were expected to actively participate in the established grade-level or schoolwide systems designed to address those problems.

Schools Operating as Open or Closed Systems

Beyond the striking fact that each of these successful schools had adopted a deliberate organizational approach to students and families, we found notable differences in how they viewed the scope of their responsibilities and the kinds of rules, supports, and relationships they adopted. All of these schools functioned within complex, dynamic environments that included families, neighborhoods, businesses, and an array of public and private agencies. Two schools took the position that their work could and should be done with few interruptions by elements of that environment and minimal concessions to those who were part of it. The other four schools assumed that their organization was inevitably permeable to environmental influence and, therefore, they broadly defined both their responsibilities and the resources they might draw on. Organizational analysts Richard Scott and Gerald Davis distinguish between these differing viewpoints, labeling the former a "closed systems" perspective and the latter an "open systems" perspective.[8]

Kincaid Charter and Naylor Charter proceeded largely as if they were closed systems that could establish clear and effective boundaries for their organization. They centered their attention on the students' experience and behavior within the school, relying primarily on rules and procedures to regulate their conduct, address their needs, and define parents' responsibilities and interactions with the school.

In contrast, educators at Dickinson, Fitzgerald, Hurston, and Rodriguez Charter conceived of their schools as open systems, believing that their students were inevitably and substantially influenced by their environment, which in turn affected their learning. In fact, from the perspective of these schools' educators, students themselves were part of that environment, moving back and forth daily from their homes and communities into the school's classrooms and corridors. Teachers, administrators, and other staff in these open-system schools sought not only to be responsible for students' experience within the school, but also to influence and often moderate the environmental factors that compromised their students' learning and development.

Two schools—Kincaid Charter and Dickinson PreK–5—illustrate how conceptions of the school as a closed or open system led to markedly different approaches for teachers and their students.

Kincaid Charter Middle School: A Closed System

Administrators at Kincaid Charter Middle School proudly referred to it as a "no excuses" school. They claimed virtually full responsibility for educating their students and firmly discouraged teachers and students from shirking their obligations or explaining away their failures. Teachers were not permitted to attribute their students' shortcomings to external causes, such as poverty or homelessness.

Unlike some charter schools that select their students or require them to enter a lottery, Kincaid's administrators worked hard to enroll all students who had attended the middle school Kincaid replaced after the state intervened and closed it. Approximately 25 percent of the students were English language learners and 25 percent had disabilities of various kinds. Mr. Kaplan, the school's founder and current head of the Kincaid CMO, said, "We're able to serve students who have been in the school district. We're able to serve the student population that we think is most in need of a really good school. This is very important to us." Another administrator emphasized that there was "no sifting of students who might or might not help us achieve our goals."

Kincaid's principal, Mr. Kain, explained why the school relied on a comprehensive system of rules and practices: "When students come to us in sixth grade from schools all over the district, with proficiency rates and gaps all over the map, they need more structure." In serving their students, Kincaid's educators concentrated almost entirely on what occurred within the school, which most viewed as being within their control. One teacher said that factors originating outside the school, such as poverty, generally were not discussed. "[The school] seems to operate almost ignoring that, almost ignoring students' backgrounds." Although 85 percent of Kincaid's students lived below the poverty line, another teacher said, "It's not something we address. We don't have professional development around it."

Detailed, firm expectations for achieving a "rigorous and joyful" school culture
Mr. Kain said that Kincaid was devoted to creating a "rigorous and joyful" school culture, although some teachers suggested that the goal of combining rigor and joy had not yet been realized. The school's attention to rigor was apparent in its detailed expectations for both students and faculty. A twenty-eight-page *Field Guide* for teachers included step-by-step explanations for Kincaid's many systems—"best practices for nearly every facet of the school." Separate sections dealt with topics such as grading, the "joy factor," the classroom learning environment, staff dress, and coaching sessions, including detailed requirements and suggestions for each. For example, it explained how teachers should conduct the morning homeroom. They were to "shake hands with all students as they enter[ed] the classroom. The best position for handshaking is to straddle the doorway and monitor the hall and classroom simultaneously." Meanwhile, students were required to "silently place their breakfast on their desks, take their backpacks and jackets to their lockers, and bring their homework folders to their desks along with two writing utensils."

The Field Guide also detailed the school's system of merits and demerits for students. Teachers, it said, should grant students merits in "sincere recognition for exceeding expectations," not to "bribe" them to meet expectations or award them for things the teacher asked them to do. The guide explained that "merits help students internalize our values so that, over time, they do the right thing because it's the right thing to do." The guide also specified ten unacceptable behaviors that warranted demerits. Among them were speaking out of turn, leaving one's seat without permission, being "unprepared for class (e.g., no writing utensil)," putting one's head on the desk or "slouching down or away from the desk (e.g., tipping chair)," and having a shirt untucked or a necklace out. The Field Guide explained that a "good ratio of merits to demerits is 3:1."

Further, the Field Guide said that teachers should impose "swift accountability for disrespect" by assigning students to detention for violations such as "reacting disrespectfully or negatively to a demerit or direction either verbally or nonverbally (e.g., lip smacking, teeth sucking, eye rolling, 'Why?' etc.)"; "low-level curse words or low-level disrespect towards other students"; "being in the wrong place at the wrong time"; "self-tattooing"; or "spending more than four minutes in the bathroom." Students were assigned to detention if they received more than four demerits in a day.

Teachers and administrators agreed that Kincaid's explicit, strict rules ensured a quiet, orderly environment for teaching and learning. Unlike those I experienced at Thoreau High School, corridors and classrooms at Kincaid were virtually silent and students appeared to know what they were required to do or not do. Mr. Kain said that the system of merits and demerits created "a set of basic, clear expectations for behaviors we want students to internalize and avoid." He explained that faithful implementation by administrators and teachers throughout the school meant that "a whole group of people are enforcing in the same way every day" and that across the school "on-task learning" had increased, likely contributing to the school's rapid improvement in test scores. Another administrator, who said Kincaid's "behavioral systems [were] really strong," elaborated: "I think one thing that we do really well as a school is hold an incredibly high bar for what students are expected to do and how they're expected to treat each other." Many teachers, especially those new to the school, were grateful not only to be well informed about Kincaid's rules and expectations, but also to be confident that their colleagues would enforce them.

However, not all teachers agreed with Kincaid's exacting system and some found it unnecessarily constraining. One described a situation in which she was obliged to assign detention: "One of my kids said, 'That's a force,' so I had to give him a [detention.]" She went on to explain that his comment suggested that she was demanding too much and that "the school takes that as a low-level [sign of] disrespect, which is an automatic detention." When asked why it was important to assign detention, she explained: "If you have teachers that are holding different ground rules, that's really difficult for students this age. . . . If you don't keep that consistency, they don't really—they get lost. They don't know what's going on. They don't know what rules to follow."

Although this teacher complied with Kincaid's behavior system, she said she planned to leave the school because of it. "I can't deal with the fact that [students] have no recess. They don't move. They're in their seats all day. . . . They're only allowed to walk silently in lines. They're only allowed to go to the bathroom about four times a day. During breaks, which are ten to fifteen minutes long, they're allowed to switch seats, but then they have to sit right back down."

She went on to explain that during detention students were required to complete "a huge packet explaining what they did that was wrong and how they were going to fix it . . . they write a bunch of sentences a million times [and] write an apology note." She worried that such practices caused students to "hate writing." Another teacher, who was surprised to find that Kincaid resembled a "military school," expressed concern that students who depended on the structure to regulate their behavior would fail when they left for high school. "They're going to bomb. It's going to be complete culture shock."

Limited supports for students' socioemotional needs

Two deans supervised Kincaid's behavior system and met with students who committed serious violations or repeatedly broke rules. The school also had a counselor and a psychologist who met individually with students, primarily those receiving special education services. Although teachers praised their skills, one said that the specialists were "totally overworked" and another explained that they were "fully booked." A seventh-grade teacher complained about the school's lack of "full follow-up" for other students who "just need a little bit more love, a little bit more support, who the systems [of demerits and detentions] are not particularly working for." When she sought help from administrators after a "few cultural issues" emerged in her students' cohort, she was told simply to "rely on the systems."

Controlled relationships with parents and families

Kincaid's Field Guide also delineated how teachers should communicate with families so that the school could "build a united front." Each teacher was assigned ten advisees and was expected to communicate with those students' parents every two weeks, as well as if they were absent or tardy twice in a week or received multiple demerits or detention. In addition, teachers were required to be available to meet with them, if asked. According to the Field Guide, teachers should regard parents as "experts on their students" and treat them respectfully. Also, teachers were encouraged to initiate other events for parents, invite them to volunteer, and visit their homes, although no teacher described doing any of those.

Teachers provided parents with the required information about their child's behavior and academic performance, but few went beyond that. One who did said that she had been able to "grow a very strong relationship with parents [of my advisees]. I am able to get to know particular students very well, know what works, know what doesn't." She said that, based on her "limited experience speaking with [her] advisees' parents," the only major concern they expressed was that the school's system of merits and demerits was "a little too strict." In practice, Kincaid expected parents to support the school by ensuring that their children attended regularly and punctually, did their homework, and abided by the rules. Otherwise, parents were not regularly present or engaged in activities at the school.

Dickinson Elementary: An Open System

Educators at Dickinson PreK–5 Elementary School, a traditional neighborhood school where 75 percent of students were English language learners, conceived of their responsibility far more broadly than their counterparts at Kincaid. Both schools had high expectations, but no one would have described Dickinson as a no-excuses school. The principal, Ms. Davila, was unequivocally devoted to students' academic success, saying that, although she and her teachers were committed to addressing personal needs, "we get paid to do a job, and our job is to make sure that these children are going to be successful when they leave us." However, Dickinson's educators also believed that academic success depended on their students being healthy, safe, and happy. Ms. Davila explained that they often relied on community agencies for "support in that." In contrast to Kincaid, Dickinson dedicated far more time and resources to systems that provided support for students and their parents.

Flexible rules and discipline

Whereas rules were prominent at Kincaid, Dickinson relied mainly on norms to ensure order. Most students understood that they were expected to attend school regularly, respect others, and move quietly through the corridors. The school didn't specify how students should behave in class, leaving those decisions to individuals and teams of teachers.

Reportedly, some teachers devised their own expectations and approaches to enforcing discipline, but most relied on decisions made with their grade-level colleagues. For example, most teachers in the lower grades used a visual "stoplight" system of green, yellow, or red to convey to the student and his parents whether his day-to-day behavior was appropriate, borderline, or unacceptable. Teachers in the middle grades were increasingly using a yardstick with colors arranged in a rainbow-like continuum. The teacher who introduced this approach had convinced his third-grade colleagues that the graduated colors gave students a better chance to reflect on their behavior, adjust it, and watch their ratings gradually move down the yardstick. Meanwhile, the teachers in fourth and fifth grades had adopted a "three strikes, you're out" approach. A student who "struck out" was assigned one hour of detention; serious offenses led to two detentions within a week.

Detention, which teachers endorsed and supervised, was a new practice at Dickinson. Ms. Davila described the type of notice the school might send home to the parent: "Your child was very disrespectful to the lunchroom attendant and cursed. We don't accept this behavior at the Dickinson School. You can choose the day they work [the detention]." Then, she explained, "the parents sign off. Child brings it back. We have a log of it. It goes in the book."

The principal and teachers acknowledged that, although the school was orderly, some students' behavior continued to present problems. Ms. Davila said, "I'll be honest with you. Like every other school, we struggle with it. We do struggle with behavior and children acting up." A veteran third-grade teacher said that students with behavior problems could "make our lives miserable." However, she went on to explain that the school had "channels" for dealing with these students, which included informing the principal, meeting with parents "if it's a very big, hard case," and searching for solutions. She emphasized that Ms. Davila kept close watch on disobedient students: "Those who don't behave, she knows them—each and every one of them completely. She knows them completely."

Another experienced teacher, who also was dissatisfied, said, "We've had many difficult years with behaviors and families that are dysfunctional." She thought that the school needed "to have more discipline . . . like stricter consequences. 'You're disrespectful and you're going to have to be sent home. Your parents need to be called. This cannot happen again.' Stuff like that. We talk about it, but it's happening, I think, in such great numbers, that you would be sending half the school home. We just need stricter discipline rules, but I don't think public schools can enforce those."

Nevertheless, the same teacher expressed surprise to see that many students succeeded under the current system: "With some students, their lives have been so chaotic, I feel like I can't believe how much growth they have made. To be honest with you, I'm astonished."

Many supports for students' socioemotional needs

Without exception, the principal, teachers, and staff at Dickinson pointed to their student support team as their primary schoolwide means for ensuring their students' success. This team, which included Ms. Davila, the nurse, the resource room teacher, an occupational therapist, and a family coordinator, met "religiously" every Wednesday at 8:00 a.m. They systematically monitored students' performance and identified a wide array of academic, medical, social, and psychological supports for those who needed them. Based on a schedule established in September, every teacher met at least twice a year with the team to review her students, one by one. Ms. Davila described the process: "They have to come down and tell us, student by student by student, how they are doing academically in all areas, how they are doing socially, and if there are any issues going on. Are they having a hard time with behavior? Homework? Do they need intervention? Do they need any services?"

The starting point of the review process was a student's academic performance, but the team often moved on to discuss the student's well-being and any underlying problems. Ms. Davila explained: "If it's a child that we think is sad, depressed, [has] family issues, if my parent coordinator says, 'You know what? The parents are going through a divorce.' [Maybe] the mother has reached out because the husband's being abusive to her and the children are seeing it."

Based on their review, the team developed a strategy for addressing any problems. For example, according to Ms. Davila: "If it's a case of [the teacher saying] 'I don't think he sees the [black]board. I think maybe he needs glasses,' then the nurse reaches out for that medical piece." A parent might, with the school's referral, be offered counseling at a partner agency. The student support team kept detailed notes for each student and designated a date to review individuals placed on their "watch list." In fact, the nurse had kept records over many years and the team referred to those when students' problems persisted or siblings began to experience difficulties.

By requiring teachers to report on each student's performance and progress, the student support team ensured that all students, not only those with obvious needs, received attention. On alternate weeks, the team considered referrals from teachers who sought immediate advice about a student. For example, Ms. Davila said it could be one who "just had a really bad week." They also focused on students on the watch list when concerns were raised prior to their scheduled review. Ms. Davila described three students in one class who had been placed on the watch list in January, but then took a "nosedive" by April. The teacher had "done outreach, but absences had gone up. We're coming to realize it's a family issue. We have the [WCSD] attendance office involved." The principal said that the established review procedure "makes us [who sit] at the table all accountable to our own roles. Then we're always meeting back and talking about where we're at—what this one did, what that one did, how we can keep tabs and not let these kids fall through the cracks."

During team meetings and throughout the school day, adults consulted one another as they identified and responded to students' problems. The nurse, who was widely viewed as the linchpin of the school's student support system, credited others with its success: "It's a cliché, but everyone really does work together here." While moving in and out of classrooms, she might mention to a teacher, "Jimmy's not feeling well. Has he said anything to you about what's going on at home? Or is he just struggling with math? Because he always seems to come down [to the nurse's room] about 10:00." She said that sometimes the answer was straightforward—"he really has a stomachache and needs to go home"—but "more often than not, there's a pattern going on, there's stuff going on at home."

An early-career classroom teacher explained that she played multiple roles in the school: "I'm not a psychologist or psychiatrist, even though I feel like I am that as well, many times. I feel I wear many, many different hats." These overlapping roles were part of an intentional strategy to engage all the adults in addressing students' needs and problems. Like many others, the nurse credited Ms. Davila with ensuring that "the vast majority" of students would succeed: "Her passion is that every kid does as well as they possibly can academically. Also, that they come here and are happy and safe. That just shows through in almost everything that we do."

In addition to referring individual students and families for help and intervention either at the school or at medical or counseling centers throughout the community, Dickinson maintained partnerships with organizations that sponsored programs for students before and after school. In several cases, teachers were compensated by the agencies for providing those additional services. For example, four days a week at 7:30 a.m., Dickinson's occupational therapist and a fourth-grade teacher ran a popular exercise and nutrition program for approximately forty students. An athletic company sponsored it, paying the teachers for their time. Another teacher facilitated student groups in a year-long program called "Saturdays for Success," which was designed for students struggling to deal with aggressive or inappropriate behaviors at school, including bullying.

Parents and families treated as partners

In addition to including parents in the student support process, Dickinson sought to engage them regularly throughout the school. Because virtually all students lived in the neighborhood, teachers could count on seeing parents frequently as they walked their children to and from school. Ms. Davila said that meeting them in person was important because most were immigrants, and many did not have a phone or speak English. Also, some parents were unfamiliar with cultural expectations about the US education system. The parent coordinator explained:

"In their countries, when you drop the kids at school, then it's the school's job to do whatever they have to do. The parents don't have to be involved with that." Therefore, teachers appreciated having frequent, informal interactions with parents and receiving help from someone on the school's staff to translate as needed.

Parental engagement at Dickinson went well beyond the periodic programs for parents that schools such as Angelou and Giovanni offered. Every week Dickinson held a well-attended breakfast for parents and other key family members. Ms. Davila explained, "Every teacher gets a week [to] present some aspect of their teaching to their group of parents." Teachers from a single grade level sometimes provided sessions several weeks in a row in an effort to help family members understand what their children were studying and learn how to help with their homework. During the entire month of March, partner organizations from the community visited the school's breakfasts to familiarize parents with their services. For example, the community health center described its program on nutrition for parents, and a mental health center provided an overview of its classes on parenting. WCSD sponsored an annual Parents University at a local university, and Ms. Davila used funds from her Title I budget to rent a bus so that parents could attend.

Public schools routinely hold an open house for parents each fall, where teachers explain the curriculum and their expectations for students and parents can ask questions or briefly share information about their child with the teacher. These events usually set the stage for the year ahead. However, open-house attendance is often sparse in low-income schools because, even if parents are encouraged and would like to attend, many work evenings or cannot arrange child care. Therefore, Dickinson's teachers held a parent conference for each student. Ms. Davila said, "They reach out to them individually until they get 100 percent. . . . They meet with every single parent and talk with every single parent." Also, when report cards were distributed each quarter, teachers held back those of students who were frequently absent so that they could speak with parents to explore whether the school could provide any supports to ensure regular attendance. As Ms. Davila said, "We need to have that conversation. . . . We do use the parent as a partner."

Therefore, educators at Dickinson saw their school as being deeply embedded in its environment, which they believed profoundly affected their students. Sometimes, that environment was the source of problems that interfered with their learning. However, the environment also served as a resource for solving problems when community agencies worked with families or provided additional supports to the students themselves. These educators never contemplated limiting their attention to in-school behavior. In fact, most considered the challenges that their students encountered inside and outside school to be their challenges as well, and they sought to address and resolve them through their ongoing interactions with parents and community organizations.

Other Successful Schools as Open and Closed Systems

Other successful schools fell along the continuum between open and closed systems. Educators at Naylor Charter, another no-excuses school, viewed their responsibilities much like Kincaid's educators did, deliberately concentrating on students' in-school behavior. One teacher said that, after a student in her class had a "family tragedy," she and her colleagues discussed whether they should consult with the school psychologist about their concern, but ultimately decided that they should mention it to the principal, who then assured them she would "route it" properly. Thus, in this case as in routine activities, Naylor's educators relied on formal rules and procedures to ensure that learning time was well used and that students were responsive to assignments and respectful of adults and peers.

One distinctive feature of Naylor's approach was its effort to develop a positive organizational culture throughout the school by creating events and routines designed to reinforce their norms and values. For example, students in grades 3 through 5 participated in a weekly community meeting planned by teachers. One described a meeting where she and her colleagues presented skits illustrating what it meant to be "a good Naylor scholar," exhibiting integrity and being a team player. Teachers and students joined in repeating the school's "chant," which expressed its core values. The teacher said that she and her colleagues made a "pump-up" video prior to the state tests by rewriting the lyrics of "popular songs that the kids like," making them "MCAS-related." She said students responded enthusiastically and several asked whether they could see the performance again on YouTube. In their homerooms, teachers taught "character education," focusing on "what it means to be a good person." A kindergarten teacher said, "We're constantly working on character education, starting from the very first day of school and what it means to be a nice friend and what kindness looks like, and what to do when you're feeling angry, and what kinds of choices are acceptable choices when you're feeling upset and what is not acceptable, and why it's not." Teachers spoke favorably about these initiatives. One said, "You walk down the hallways and always see kids with smiles on their faces. I think that culture transcends all aspects of the school, which is awesome."

As at Dickinson, teachers and administrators at three other schools—two turnaround district schools (Fitzgerald Elementary and Hurston K–8) and one charter school (Rodriguez K–8)—viewed their organization as an open system, which was substantially influenced by its environment. They, too, developed systematic approaches that administrators and teachers could rely on to enhance their effectiveness with students.

For example, Rodriguez Charter viewed its responsibilities to students and families very broadly, leading one administrator to describe Rodriguez as a "full-service school." The middle school had both explicit rules and an organized discipline system for students across all classes. However, it also had a student support team that considered concerns about individual students raised by teachers. The team then arranged follow-up supports with specialists from the school and community organizations. In addition, the school sponsored a year-long program of professional development designed to help teachers understand and respond effectively to students' social and emotional concerns. A nonprofit agency provided professional development for teachers and administered student surveys that teachers then used to identify students' problems, assess their severity, and devise possible responses. Teachers who taught the same children completed and compared their assessments of those students. They then developed "action plans" for individuals, which might include counseling, group participation, or incentives designed to change behavior. As one teacher explained, "We all sort of play the role of school psychologist at certain times. . . . Helping the kids cope and deal with their emotions and feel free to talk to us about things is a major goal of ours."

Rodriguez also had recently focused on issues of race and poverty by sponsoring discussions among both students and teachers. A male, African American teacher led a program called "Men in the Making," developed by a local family agency to address the concerns and needs of black boys. He said, "It's like a forum, a space for the boys to talk about issues that are directly affecting them, enhancing [them] through their reflective and expressive skills. They, in turn, are able to understand and see their behaviors, responses, and reactions to things a lot better." Another teacher said that many in the school had joined conversations about race that the program generated: "We've been doing a lot of talking as a staff about our attitudes toward black boys, what we do, and what we don't do, which has been really great, thinking about that and the culture piece of that."

Initially, Fitzgerald Elementary had only an academic student support team, which met weekly with representative teachers from every grade, the psychologist, nurse, speech and occupational therapists, and resource room teacher. That team's main responsibility was to screen referrals for students to receive special education services. However, in response to teachers' concerns about individual students' needs and conduct, they added a student support team for behavioral issues. Both teams relied extensively on in-school specialists because, as the principal, Ms. Forte, said, "we really felt like you could not reward or punish your way to good behavior." She explained that the school had adopted a program called "Peaceful School Climate . . . an approach that's pretty different than a lot of high-poverty schools. [It's not] 'These are the rules, these are the consequences.'" Instead, she explained, the philosophy is, "If a child's not behaving, there's some unmet need."

Ms. Forte described Fitzgerald's students as "very fragile" due to poverty and family problems and observed that, "the parent piece is quite hard here." A kindergarten teacher said that five of her current students lived in homeless shelters, the fathers of two were deceased, and six students had a parent who was incarcerated. Because many parents were not inclined to reach out to the school for help, Fitzgerald sought ways to encourage them to visit the school. One of the most effective was to host a local agency's food bank within the school, which attracted many of the school's parents. Knowing who was likely to show up, teachers would stop by so that they could informally speak with parents about their children.

Hurston K–8 also was deliberately organized as an open system and, as at Fitzgerald, a monthly food bank attracted parents to the school. However, a counselor said that parents had become a constant presence since the school entered turnaround. "There are parents in this building all day long. Whether it be dropping off, picking up, or stopping by as they walk from the bus home. It's just 'Oh, I'm going to stop by and see how Jamile is doing.'" She said that many parents worked in the school "as lunch moms, as secretaries, as paraprofessionals. It wasn't always this way. This school was a place parents didn't feel welcome at for many, many years." She credited Hurston's family coordinators with having successfully "market[ed] involvement in the school to families," helping them to "advocate for themselves and their kids in a way that's productive."

CONCLUSION

The six successful schools adopted different and distinctive systems and practices to engage and deal with students and parents, depending on whether their educators viewed their school primarily as a closed system, a protected space that could exclude or keep at bay problems and environmental influences (e.g., poverty, violence, prejudice, and homelessness), or as an open system, a permeable space that is inevitably affected by such factors. Kincaid and Naylor, both no-excuses schools, took a closed-system stance, concentrating resources and attention on students' in-school conduct and participation. All teachers were expected to enforce the rules uniformly and hold students to high standards, without regard for their experiences outside school. Educators also sought to strengthen students' allegiance to the school and commitment to its values by promoting a consistent, positive organizational culture using symbols, such as banners, chants, and stories. Adults' roles and responsibilities were defined explicitly. These two schools had a small number of specialists, including psychologists and social workers, who counseled some students, usually those designated for special education services. Teachers were not encouraged to take on counseling roles. Parents were expected to support the school's established values and practices by seeing that their children attended school regularly and punctually, completed their homework, and gave their best effort to learn and improve throughout the day.

The four other successful schools—Dickinson, Fitzgerald, Hurston, and Rodriguez—took an open-system stance and sought to create an orderly learning environment schoolwide by establishing a set of basic expectations for students. Relying more on organizational norms and less on rules—especially detailed, prescriptive ones—they generally called on teachers, usually as grade-level teams, to establish classroom practices. Educators in these schools engaged medical and psychological specialists within the school to counsel students, and they arranged for additional services with community agencies outside the school day. Teachers assumed that their urban students' life experiences with poverty, racism, and violence created challenges for their learning and therefore sought ways to moderate these effects. Teachers, administrators, staff, and specialists often had blended roles and shared responsibility for noticing and addressing students' academic, physical, behavioral, and socioemotional problems. Each school had a family coordinator who cultivated relationships between parents and teachers. These schools viewed parents as essential partners in their work and encouraged them or other key family members to visit the school informally and to become involved with ongoing programs designed for them. Although the main goal was to ensure students' success and well-being, these schools actively addressed the needs of parents so they could support their children.

Choices and the Tensions They Create

Given these contrasting perspectives and practices, the choices of individual schools had implications for teachers and their efforts to succeed with their students. Overall, most of the teachers we interviewed thought that their school's particular approach to students and families was sound and that it supported their teaching and students' learning.

However, some teachers expressed concern or doubt about their school's stance and day-to-day practices. Systematic efforts by closed-system schools to establish uniform expectations for students led some teachers to question whether students' physical, social, and expressive needs were being unwisely ignored or suppressed. These teachers raised concerns about whether, in their effort to closely control students' behavior with rewards and punishments, they were making them too dependent on the school's tight behavioral system. Other educators, especially teachers of color who had experienced discrimination in their own lives, questioned whether it was fair or realistic to discount the consequences of race or poverty in their students' lives.

Meanwhile, some teachers in the open-system schools said they would prefer stricter rules and more accountability for students and families, arguing that valuable learning time was wasted when teachers had to repeatedly address students' misbehavior. A few suggested that they were overwhelmed by their school's expectation that they should be open, responsive, and accommodating to the full array of challenges that students and families presented, although others were reassured by the help they received from colleagues, administrators, and staff.

Despite some teachers' reservations, all of these schools had an explicit and deliberate approach for addressing students' conduct and needs as well as the relationships they fostered and maintained with parents. By relying on these established systems, teachers could reduce uncertainty in their classes and potentially be more successful with their students. The fact that all the schools had achieved Level 1 ratings from state officials suggested that having such a system may have contributed to students' improved performance. However, which of the two approaches—closed-system or open-system—is superior remains a matter of professional judgment. It is a question that will remain unanswered until researchers assess whether the students who experienced one or the other achieve the long-term academic and personal success that all these educators hope for.

How schools respond to students and the uncertainty they introduce into the workplace of urban school teachers gets far less systematic attention than matters of curriculum and instruction. And yet, as we saw with the Thoreau teachers who were leaving the school because of poor discipline, these are crucial issues that can drive able and committed teachers out of a school. If a school fails to implement a coherent, consistent plan for establishing order and discipline across classes and grades, and to provide the resources and training for teachers consistent with that plan, then those teachers are unlikely to achieve the academic success with their students that they otherwise might. However, if teachers are well aware of their school's expectations and resources from the time they are hired, they can confidently rely on the support of colleagues and team members and use their own energy, attention, and instructional time more efficiently and effectively.

Therefore, in schools that organize for success, teachers can count on guidance and support from colleagues and administrators, both as they decide what to teach and as they address the behavior and needs of their students. As we will see in chapter 5, teachers also are not left on their own to improve their instruction, but can count on their supervisor's ongoing classroom observations, judgments, and suggestions for improvement.

CHAPTER FIVE

Using Evaluation to Improve Instruction

Beginning in the early twentieth century, when the efficiency movement claimed the attention of school superintendents across the nation, teacher evaluation took its place as a bureaucratic staple of public schooling.[1] Administrators began conducting annual or biannual reviews of individual teachers' instruction and completed written assessments, typically a checklist of items, such as "maintains an orderly classroom," "presents material clearly," and "supports students in their learning." That assessment, ending with a summative rating, usually "satisfactory" or "unsatisfactory," then became part of the teacher's personnel file. Some administrators discussed the evaluation with the teacher, but often they didn't. On rare occasions, an evaluation was presented as evidence in a dismissal hearing, though usually it had no consequence for either the teacher, her students, or the school.

The process of evaluation began to change in the 1980s. Formal appraisals of public education in the US, such as *A Nation at Risk*, led some districts and states to adopt more detailed criteria and ratings for evaluators to choose from.[2] Meanwhile, as they bargained new contracts, teachers unions and school boards formalized the assessment procedures, often requiring an evaluator to justify a negative rating with documented evidence. Despite these changes, few administrators or teachers who participated in the evaluation process would have said it was worthwhile, especially if was supposed to improve teachers' instruction.

Experts, too, found much to criticize about the process: primitive checklists, infrequent or "drive-by" observations, incomplete follow-up, uninformed summative judgments, and reluctance to dismiss ineffective teachers, even when all observation forms had been completed and the case for termination was strong.[3]

From the perspective of many teachers, evaluation continues to be an uninformative, bureaucratic process. In teaching graduate students about evaluation, I typically start class by asking those who have been teachers to raise their hands. Most hands go up. Then I say, "If you were regularly evaluated, keep your hand up." Some hands go down. Next, I ask, "Were you regularly observed as part of the evaluation?" Suddenly many hands go down amidst puzzled looks and nervous laughter. How could they have been evaluated if they weren't observed? Then I move to the more difficult questions: "Did you receive feedback about how to improve?" "Did you learn something important from the process?" "Did you think this was a worthwhile experience?" By the end, only a few hands remain in the air.

What follows then is a lively, often humorous, and sometimes painful discussion as students describe their professional experiences with evaluation. Inevitably, someone calls it a "dog-and-pony show." Another explains that she was never observed after her first year. Yet another adds that, whether or not he was observed, he always received a completed form in his mailbox in the main office, which he was expected to sign and return as evidence that he had read it. Some forms included a space where the teacher could comment on the assessment, although there was no assurance that her administrator would respond. A very few students might say that their principal offered good advice about general approaches, such as how to maintain discipline or ask higher-order questions. One or two might describe their principal as someone who could model the practices she recommended. By the end of our discussion, it had become clear that these former teachers generally saw evaluation as a bureaucratic process designed to document teachers' weaknesses, not one dedicated to making them better teachers.

Yet, unquestionably, even the best teachers must continue to improve if they're to meet current needs and expectations.[4] This is true even for those who have completed a strong teacher preparation program, including a lengthy stint as student teacher, although many teachers today entered the classroom following a short, alternative preparation program that lacked a clinical component in a regular school setting.[5] Over time, a school's curriculum, courses, testing, and students inevitably change and the teacher must keep up with those changes. However, because most classrooms remain private, protected spaces, teachers typically have little or no access to informed and regular feedback about how well they teach or sound advice about what they might do differently. As they participate in workshops, professional development sessions, and discussions with their colleagues, teachers may acquire a sense of what they *should* do, but it's quite another matter for them to discover whether they actually do what they intend, whether they succeed at what they try, and why things turn out the way they do.[6]

Many elementary schools now provide instructional coaches in the tested subjects, math and language arts, although it's not common for those coaches to systematically observe even this group of teachers, and rarely do teachers of untested subjects receive coaching about their instruction. As we saw in chapter 2, when schools provide instructional coaches in tested subjects, their assignments often focus on providing resources for teachers' lessons or strategies to improve students' test scores, not on individuals' pedagogy. As teachers try to assess and improve their own instruction, they may reflect on their students' in-class responses and scrutinize their performance on quizzes, tests, and papers, but beyond that, they're largely on their own. The reality is that, within the work environment of most schools, teachers still have very few opportunities for personalized feedback and coaching about their instruction.

POLICIES MEANT TO IMPROVE TEACHER EVALUATION

In their effort to improve public education, policy makers in most states recently instituted changes intended to produce a more robust teacher evaluation system. In doing so, some reformers focused on improving assessment procedures so that schools could better identify and dismiss ineffective teachers, while others sought to promote teachers' development. The first purpose relies on a strategy for improvement that gradually transforms the composition of a school's staff, while the second calls for an organizational change strategy meant to benefit all teachers.

Better Assessment Procedures: Using Value-Added Methods to Judge Performance

In the early 2000s, when economists began to use quantitative *value-added methods* (VAMs) to identify individual teachers' contribution to students' learning, they concluded that performance evaluations were rarely used to make employment decisions, such as reappointment, tenure, and dismissal.[7] In response, Eric Hanushek concluded that school officials could dramatically improve their students' performance by using student achievement data to identify and "deselect" (dismiss) 5 to 10 percent of the schools' least effective teachers and replace them with average or excellent teachers.[8] He and other scholars contend that dismissing teachers in the lower tail of the performance distribution will gradually improve the effectiveness of an entire school as less effective teachers leave and more effective teachers replace them. This assumes that more effective teachers are available to fill the positions and that the costs of such changes are modest, neither of which may be true in many high-poverty, urban schools.

Many policy analysts and journalists embraced this recommendation as a call to action. In a widely circulated 2009 report, TNTP (formerly known as The New Teacher Project) assailed what it called "the widget effect" in public education, by which all teachers are treated as if they are equally effective, even though test scores and peers' reports suggest otherwise. Only 1 percent of teachers in the twelve districts TNTP studied were evaluated as unsatisfactory, even though 81 percent of administrators and 57 percent of teachers reported that at least one ineffective tenured teacher worked in their school.[9] In 2010 the headline on a *Newsweek* cover boldly asserted: "The Key to Saving American Education: We Must Fire Bad Teachers." In that issue's lead article, the authors denounced the decline of public education as a "national embarrassment" and urged that it be reversed through the dismissal of ineffective teachers.[10]

Other reformers doubted that swapping out the weakest teachers for stronger ones would appreciably improve students' experiences and learning. John Papay argues persuasively that, however well intentioned, a strategy that concentrates on dismissing weak teachers is misguided: "With nearly three million teachers in the United States, rapid improvements in instructional effectiveness will not be possible by simply replacing low-performing teachers. . . . Instead, for evaluation to realize its potential as a widespread instructional reform, it must work to raise the performance of all teachers." Further, he recommends that in order for evaluation to support "transformational change," policy makers, researchers, and reformers should refocus their attention and resources on teachers' ongoing development.[11]

Competing Purposes in Evaluation Policies?

Therefore, researchers and reformers identified two distinct purposes for an improved process of teacher evaluation—promoting teachers' development schoolwide and informing job decisions, especially dismissals. This raised the question of whether these purposes are complementary and compatible or competing and mutually exclusive. Following the 2008 recession, the prospects for improving teacher evaluation received a big boost when federal policy makers used large financial incentives in the federal Race to the Top (RTTT) competition and waivers from NCLB to compel states to reform teacher evaluation and improve teacher quality. They urged school districts to link evaluation to high-stakes personnel decisions, including teachers' dismissal, tenure, and compensation. Further, they called for incorporating measures of student achievement into evaluation. Although these were guidelines, not requirements, states desperately needed the additional funds that RTTT might provide; thus, the recommended components essentially functioned as mandates. By 2015, forty-six states and Washington, DC, had received waivers and sizeable grants in exchange for making significant changes in their evaluation processes.[12]

In deliberating about how best to improve evaluation, these states often included a wide range of interested parties—teachers, administrators, state and local officials, advocates from nonprofit organizations, teachers union leaders, and citizens. Given the breadth of these participants' views and goals, it's not surprising that the states eventually enacted policies designed to meet both purposes—better assessing and better developing teachers. For policy makers, the former purpose took precedence and received considerable attention by the media. Gradually, however, it become clear that many administrators did not see this as an either-or choice, but rather as an opportunity first to focus on improving teachers' instruction and subsequently to pursue dismissal if efforts to help a teacher improve failed.[13]

IMPROVING EVALUATION WITH OBSERVATION-BASED INSTRUMENTS

Several developments in the field of teacher evaluation reinforced this "both-and" approach to reform. As these deliberations about new policies were under way, many school districts already were replacing their traditional evaluation checklists with more comprehensive and complex instruments for observing and assessing teachers' instruction. The most influential and widely adopted model was created by Charlotte Danielson.

Danielson's comprehensive framework includes four domains of teaching responsibility: planning and preparation, classroom environment, instruction, and professional responsibility. Each domain includes five or six components, and each component includes three or four elements. For example, the instruction domain has five components, one of which, engaging students in instruction, includes four elements: activities and assignments, student groups, instructional materials and resources, and structures and pacing. Beyond being comprehensive and detailed, the feature that most distinguishes Danielson's framework from earlier instruments is its rubrics, which describe what teaching practice looks like at four levels of effectiveness for each of the model's seventy-six elements.[14] The framework is complex and demanding to master and use well.

Importantly, the system was designed to apply to all grade levels and disciplines and to support formative (developmental) and summative (accountability) purposes. Administrators could summarize a teacher's scores from the domains to decide and subsequently justify whether he should be rehired, granted tenure, or dismissed. Evaluators and coaches could also use the rubrics to support teachers' learning and development by recommending specific changes they might make in their practice as well as supplementary learning opportunities they might pursue, such as peer observations, instructional coaching, or outside workshops.

Danielson believed that her framework could support efforts to identify ineffective teachers based on their instructional practice, but she also cautioned that more must be done: "We must create educative systems that actually result in learning, that are worth doing from the standpoint of teachers."[15] A two-year study conducted in the Chicago Public Schools found that Danielson's model was an improvement on the district's prior instrument and effectively introduced evidence-based assessments into the evaluation process.[16]

DEBUNKING THE PERFORMANCE PLATEAU

In a second important development, researchers found that teachers could improve their performance over the course of their career. Although this finding didn't surprise teachers themselves, it did run counter to a widely held belief that, on average, teachers rapidly improve early in their career, then level off after a few years. This empirical "fact," based on average growth trajectories for large numbers of teachers, quickly became the foundation for ill-informed advice. For example, TNTP reported in a 2012 fact sheet that "teachers gradually reach a plateau after 3–5 years on the job."[17] Even Bill Gates asserted in 2009 that "once somebody has taught for three years, their teaching quality does not change thereafter," a position he later revised.[18]

I'll never forget participating in an advisory meeting with the influential superintendent of a large urban district in 2008. He said that he was not concerned about retaining experienced teachers because they were not likely to improve once they hit the plateau. Believing that students should benefit from the best years of teachers' practice, he said, "Give me those four years." Unconcerned about turnover, he said that a school could always hire a fresh replacement. Like others who held this view, he assumed that the performance of a novice would be at least equal to that of a teacher with four years of experience and that this process of swapping out teachers would not be costly. However, research supports neither assumption. New teachers are, on average, far less effective than teachers with four or five years of experience, even if they improve no further. This, of course, means that a replacement strategy carries not only financial costs for the district, but more importantly, learning costs for its students as well.

Recently economists have documented that teachers can continue to improve, especially when their schools are supportive work environments.[19] Analyzing data from one very large urban district, Matthew Kraft and John Papay tracked individual teachers' improvement throughout their career and found that they continued to improve "at least in their ability to raise student test scores," well beyond their early years. In fact, they estimate that "35 percent of a teacher's career improvement happens after year 10." Kraft and Papay also coupled their analysis of student performance data with assessments of the school as a work environment. Importantly, this analysis revealed that the rate and extent of teachers' improvement are influenced by the school context in which they work: "Some teachers do plateau, whereas others continue to improve. And teachers in some schools improve at greater rates than others."[20]

This research demonstrates clearly that a teacher's improvement depends not only on what she brings to her work, but also on what the organization provides; a school may enhance or compromise a teacher's efforts to improve. Therefore, as principals and other administrators set forth to evaluate teachers under new state policies adopted in response to RTTT, they could do so with more complex assessment tools and increasing confidence that investing over time in teachers' improvement would pay off.

FOCUSING ON BOTH DEVELOPMENT AND ACCOUNTABILITY

Researchers who tracked new evaluation laws highlighted different features of these policies. For example, Matthew Steinberg and Morgaen Donaldson reviewed forty-six new state evaluation policies and concluded that most took "a developmental stance towards evaluation by requiring a summative rating to be linked to professional development for teachers, including those judged to be under-performing."[21] In contrast, the federal Institute of Education Sciences (IES) reported strong evidence of a move toward accountability in the new laws.[22] However, as any veteran of past education reforms knows, the true impact of education policies must be assessed not only in what the laws say, but also in how they are implemented.[23] In this case, the question is whether and how laws that call for new approaches to evaluation change teachers' day-to-day practice and the employment decisions of school officials. Do they give priority to development or accountability for teachers? Do they incorporate both goals? Or do they simply reinforce bureaucratic procedures that are likely to have no impact on teachers' instruction or students' learning?

Our research in schools serving students from high-poverty communities in Walker City addressed these questions. First, in our 2010–2011 Teaching in Context study, after WCSD adopted a new standards-based evaluation instrument based on Danielson's model, we studied evaluation practices in six district schools that performed at various levels. Then, in our 2014–2015 Successful Schools study, three years after a new state policy was enacted, we studied evaluation practices at six high performing district and charter schools. Our findings from the Teaching in Context study illuminate the challenges that principals and teachers faced as they began to use the new, more complex instrument, while our findings from the Successful Schools study show how high performing schools set their priorities and organized their resources to implement the new state policy. Both studies have lessons that can help policy makers and administrators anticipate the difficulties schools are likely to encounter in implementing evaluation policies as well as the practices that effective schools from both studies adopted.

TEACHING IN CONTEXT: EVALUATION IN WCSD, 2010–2011

In 2006, WCSD adopted a new standards-based instrument and evaluation policy, which all principals were required to use. Given prior studies of implementation, we expected to find that school-based practices would vary, even though principals were supposed to implement the same policy. And, in fact, they did vary—widely.[24]

The district's policy, which had been negotiated with the local union, was designed to increase opportunities for teachers to improve while also ensuring that they would be regularly assessed. It states: "True performance evaluation involves analysis of an employee's strengths and weaknesses, resulting in diagnosis and prescriptions which lead to desired professional growth."[25] Administrators were required to conduct classroom observations and assessments each year for probationary teachers and biannually for tenured teachers. Evaluators could rate teachers either as "meeting" or "failing to meet" expectations for each of eight dimensions, ranging from "instructional planning and implementation" to "partnership with family and community." Evaluators then assigned each teacher a summative rating of "meeting" or "failing to meet" expectations. Further, the policy seemed to suggest that the evaluation process was meant to be a tool for holding teachers accountable in meeting basic professional expectations. For example, the guidelines describe only the support that administrators were required to provide teachers who failed to meet expectations, not what they should make available to teachers who already met them. Further, in a memo to WCSD principals, the superintendent briefly mentioned using evaluation to support professional growth, but went on to provide detailed directions about how to properly execute the assessment process, especially in response to ineffective teachers, who might be dismissed only if procedures were followed to the letter.

During our 2010–2011 interviews, teachers in four of the six WCSD schools described experiencing perfunctory, bureaucratic evaluation practices, which had little impact on their work. In those schools, evaluation was used neither to inform high-stakes decisions about teachers' careers (rehiring, awarding tenure, or dismissing teachers), nor to support their development. However, as we'll see shortly, in two other schools, Thoreau High School and Giovanni Elementary School, evaluation was a prominent and consequential process that was intended to improve the school. Notably, however, the two principals' strategies differed markedly, as did their teachers' responses.

Endorsing Accountability for Their Colleagues

Teachers across all six schools expressed concern about their colleagues' performance, saying that everyone had to be effective, given the state's authority to sanction or close the school if students' poor performance continued. For example, a mid-career teacher at Angelou Elementary School said, "[T]here needs to be a little bit more push . . . about people who are doing their jobs and people that aren't. . . . [W]e're in such a crisis of [possibly] losing the school . . . we need to be a little bit harsher." A Thoreau High School teacher offered a similar perspective: "There are some incredible teachers and there are some people who have absolutely no business in the classroom." Therefore, many teachers endorsed using evaluations to dismiss weak teachers, although they did not think that accountability should be the sole, or even the primary, purpose of evaluation.

Resenting Insufficient or Unhelpful Feedback About Their Teaching

Both novice and experienced teachers said that they hoped their supervisor would observe their classes and provide feedback to help them improve. A mid-career, middle school teacher at Stowe explained, "I want to be evaluated. Come into my room. You know, here's a teacher that wants to be evaluated. And I feel like I do a good job, but I know I could do better." Her colleague, an early-career teacher, said that she was disappointed when she was not evaluated during her third year and felt ignored rather than reassured: "[A] lot of people . . . said, 'Oh, that should make you feel good.'. . . It doesn't, though." A high school teacher at Whitman Academy also wanted more feedback: "The more, the merrier. Give me some ideas. Ideally if you're evaluating me . . . jot down a note and tell me what you thought, so I can learn from it." Teachers were annoyed when they weren't observed yet received a written evaluation nonetheless. Other teachers objected when they received only vague, general feedback, what one called "fluff." Teachers suggested that hurried, brief visits by their evaluator seriously compromised the validity of the process. For example, another Stowe middle school teacher said: "It's a little weird, I mean, I've only been observed once, maybe twice . . . [S]he looked at the board, watched the instruction, watched the 'do-now,' and she was really only there for fifteen minutes and then she was gone. And that was really all it was, to be honest. But the next thing you know, [I received] the [written] evaluation."

At four schools (Angelou Elementary, Morrison K–8, Stowe Middle School, and Whitman Academy High School) teachers offered similar accounts of a per-functory and uneven evaluation process in their schools. For example, a new teacher at Stowe recalled, "[The evaluation said that] I met or exceeded [expecta-tions] on everything and then I had to sign it. He gets a copy. I get a copy. And I guess they do that every year." An experienced teacher at Whitman Academy also focused on the steps in the process: "You have a pre-observation meeting, then she observes, and then you have the post-observation meeting where you go over the evaluation. And if you agree, you sign. If you don't agree, you don't sign, and you write a response."

When asked if they thought the evaluation process was helpful, most re-sponded much like this Stowe teacher: "Not helpful, no. Honestly, not at all." Even teachers who were neutral in their judgments described a process that had minimal, if any, impact on their practice. A Whitman Academy teacher said, "It's not threatening, but to me, it is not useful also." A second-year teacher at Mor-rison responded with indifference: "They'll just walk through and they'll look around and they'll be like, 'okay,' and they'll leave and then I'll get some sort of feedback later, or not."

Taking Evaluation Seriously at Thoreau and Giovanni

Teachers and administrators at Thoreau High School and Giovanni Elementary School took evaluation much more seriously. Thoreau's principal, Ms. Thomas, and her team of six administrators were committed to implementing the district's evaluation policy by observing and assessing all seventy teachers at least every other year: "We've done a massive amount of evaluating. . . . We're evaluating about 70 percent of the building because that's what you need to be doing in a two-year cycle." Her administrative team convened biweekly to improve their practice by discussing a guide for administrators about how to conduct evaluation, calibrating their use of the ratings and rubrics, and standardizing how they debriefed observations with teachers.

In describing evaluation at their school, most Thoreau teachers said that administrators concentrated on documenting the shortcomings of the least effective teachers so that they could be dismissed. And throughout their lengthy explanations of the process, these administrators confirmed that evaluation at Thoreau was intended primarily to increase teachers' accountability rather than their development. Ms. Thomas described their current efforts: "So those are the two teachers that . . . we needed to get out and I think what we're going to do with the other four or five that are really [weak is that] . . . they'll probably all get [an overall rating of] 'meets [expectations]' with 'does not meet' in two or three areas. But we're reserving the option to [give] them a 'does not meet' [overall rating] by the end of the year."

She said that this preliminary assessment was intended as a "wake-up call" to warn these teachers that they would be evaluated again in January "and that's how much time you have to get better."

Without intending to, administrators sowed fear and distrust among other teachers who were not the focus of dismissal efforts. In fact, very few teachers at Thoreau had reason to think that they might be fired, and most saw evaluation as an empty, symbolic process. However, many expressed concern about the anxiety and distrust generated among others when observations were assumed to be geared toward dismissal. As one said, "Some people feel targeted." Another described "a real sense that they were out to get you. They had like a preconceived notion of who the not-so-good teachers were, and they kind of insensitively went after them, which kind of made other people say, 'Whoa!'" Several teachers said they were worried about who would be next on "the list."[26] Despite the school's enormous investment of administrators' time, none of the twenty teachers we interviewed at Thoreau described receiving feedback that helped them improve.

In contrast, professional growth was the primary goal for evaluation at Giovanni Elementary. In administering WCSD's evaluation policy, the principal and sole evaluator, Mr. Gilmore, integrated assessment with Giovanni's ongoing improvement work. He held his forty-five teachers responsible for high levels of professional practice, while also supporting their development. He explained, "[W]hen I do evaluations . . . I'm not after anybody; I'm really after . . . how do we improve?"

Mr. Gilmore conducted a comprehensive evaluation process with each teacher at least every other year, adding components to the district's basic requirements.[27] Teachers submitted lesson plans for the classes he observed and completed a self-assessment, including professional goals and a record of professional development experiences. Mr. Gilmore also asked for evidence of their communication with families, use of student data, and involvement in schoolwide teacher leadership opportunities. He then met with every teacher before and after each of two formal observations. He said that the process was very demanding for him, but worthwhile because it ensured that he spent time in classes and promoted teachers' improvement. Teachers described the process as time-consuming and stressful, but also very helpful.

In emphasizing development, Mr. Gilmore did not ignore accountability. In fact, teachers said that if their principal had serious questions about their performance, he would address them long before their formal evaluation began. One teacher said that the pressure of being assessed made her nervous, but not excessively so, because she knew that Mr. Gilmore was there "to help you grow." She explained: "He does have strict expectations . . . you do have fear. I do respect him . . . but I don't fear him in the way that it's going to make my teaching go down. It's to help me support my teaching, so that's great." She and others said that Mr. Gilmore often modeled the practices that he expected them to learn, especially in literacy, his area of expertise. The fact that he might coteach on an impromptu basis, even during a formal observation, convinced teachers that he was a skilled instructor, committed to their improvement.

Therefore, we found wide variation in how these six schools implemented the district's evaluation policy: perfunctory compliance in four schools; aggressive use of evaluation to dismiss unsatisfactory teachers in the fifth; and, in the sixth, integration of formal assessments with the school's ongoing program to develop teachers' instruction. The case of Giovanni serves as both a counterpoint to the other cases and as proof that evaluation can simultaneously serve the purposes of development and accountability.

Confronting the Challenges of Insufficient Time and Inadequate Expertise

In all six schools, it was the principal who decided whether evaluation would be a serious endeavor and what purpose it would serve for the school. We don't know from our study why the administrators who barely complied with the requirements did so, but there are many possibilities. They may have decided to invest in different strategies for improving teachers' instruction. Or they may have learned from past experience that it would be difficult to dismiss a teacher, even if they presented a strong case. They may have known that it can be difficult to replace an underperforming teacher with a better one. They may have wanted to avoid undermining staff morale by using evaluation to pursue dismissals. Or, as other research suggests, these principals may have lacked the time and expertise to do evaluations well. In fact, both time and expertise presented problems for most principals.

Finding time

It takes a great deal of time to effectively conduct a robust and useful schoolwide evaluation program. School administrators often must evaluate twenty teachers or more each year. Done well, every evaluation requires one or more observations, each with a pre-observation and post-observation meeting. These meetings often call for reviewing related lesson plans and student work. And, finally, the evaluator must complete a complex evaluation form. Evaluating novices and experienced teachers who do not meet standards typically requires additional observations and meetings. Some principals can share this work with other administrators, although many elementary principals, like Mr. Gilmore, have no assistant administrators to call on. As the principals we interviewed explained, simply completing the tasks that evaluation requires is a daunting challenge; doing them well can seem impossible.

Others who have studied administrators' responses to new evaluation instruments and policies also report that principals view time as a major challenge. Connecticut principals interviewed by Morgaen Donaldson and Casey Cobb said they found it hard to complete the six observations for every teacher (three formal and three informal) that the new state policy required.[28] Similarly, William Firestone and his colleagues reported that New Jersey's principals found the state's evaluation requirements exceeded what they could do in the time they had available.[29] Timothy Drake and colleagues, who interviewed central office personnel in five large, urban school systems in five states, also reported that the time required to implement new evaluation policies was a barrier to completing them.[30]

Running short on expertise

Finding sufficient time is not the only problem that principals face, although it may be the easiest one to identify and report. Effectively supporting teachers' development calls for expertise in instruction, especially in the subject being taught. It's relatively easy for an evaluator to tell whether a teacher's lesson is well organized, whether his explanations are clear, and whether he responds to all students, not just those who eagerly raise their hands. Most evaluators can assess such skills across a wide array of subjects and grades by listening to the teacher's presentations and observing students' attention and responses. However, as Lee Shulman explained many years ago, understanding how to teach ratios in a math class or narrative stance in an English class calls for both subject-based knowledge and pedagogical content knowledge—that is, knowing a subject and knowing how best to teach it.[31]

A principal who is responsible for evaluating teachers across a wide range of subjects may not have the expertise needed to assess a teacher's subject-based practice, although that may be exactly where the teacher most needs help. The Danielson model (and others it inspired) does not address subject-based pedagogy, and therefore has the advantage of being broadly useful, though that's also its limitation. For example, if an evaluator relies only on a generic instrument, the teacher may never learn where his history lesson falls short, much less how to improve it. Notably, although Mr. Gilmore could draw on his own knowledge and prior work as a literacy coach, when he wanted to help teachers improve their math instruction, he called on an experienced, skilled math teacher to provide additional feedback and model effective practices.

Finally, principals need to understand how adults learn and improve. In preparing administrators to evaluate teachers, school districts often hold meetings where principals view videos of teachers' classes and then practice calibrating their responses so that they can reliably score what they see. However, those meetings generally don't deal with how evaluators might talk with those teachers so that they can improve their work. Although Ms. Thomas's administrative team practiced rating teachers' instruction based on videos and role-played how they would give feedback to ineffective teachers, they reportedly did not use this process to learn how they could help adequate or proficient teachers improve their practice.

In 2013, Matthew Kraft and Allison Gilmour interviewed twenty-four principals in one large urban district in order to learn how they conducted observations and feedback. Participants said that, during post-observation conferences, they focused on evidence that supported their ratings. However, they had little to suggest about what the teachers could do to improve.[32] This is not surprising, given that many principals teach for only a few years before moving into administration, and their understanding of pedagogy may be limited. Further, most professional development for principals focuses on issues of management rather than either pedagogy or coaching, and rarely do they have the chance to learn how to help teachers improve. Many principals who would like to use evaluation to develop their teachers simply do not know how to do so. Given such findings, Mr. Gilmore's rich feedback and modeling of exemplary literacy practices stand out as exceptional and exemplary.

EVALUATION IN SUCCESSFUL SCHOOLS, 2014–2015

We conducted our subsequent study of six successful schools in Walker City after Massachusetts had adopted its new 2012 evaluation policy, which gave us the opportunity to learn about the schools' evaluation practices as they were implementing the new law.[33] It would be tempting to simply compare the practices of the schools from the first and second studies and attribute any differences we found to the new policies, but that would be unwarranted for at least two reasons.

First, during the four years between our studies, evaluation received considerable attention nationwide. It was widely held that a principal could not be an instructional leader unless he administered an effective evaluation system. Inevitably, this increased principals' attention to the task and possibly led them to improve their skills. Second, while the schools in both studies served similar students from low-income communities, they differed in important ways. Those in the first sample all were responsible to WCSD, but they varied on three key dimensions: their level (three elementary, three secondary), their students' performance, and their teachers' views about their work environment. In planning our second study, we hoped to identify and describe best practices. Therefore, our first criterion in choosing schools was that they be successful in educating low-income students. We limited our sample to elementary and middle schools so that we could better compare them. We also wanted to explore practices in charter schools, where some researchers had found more ambitious and innovative evaluation practices.[34]

All schools in our study were required to implement the new state policy. However, they also were subject to additional regulations that differed from school to school. Three district schools (Dickinson Elementary, Hurston K–8, and Fitzgerald Elementary) were subject to WCSD policies, including provisions of the local teachers' contract that covered evaluation. However, after turnaround, Hurston's principal retained considerable autonomy to hire, fire, and transfer teachers, and therefore didn't rely exclusively on evaluation to dismiss ineffective teachers. As a restart school within WCSD, Kincaid Charter Middle School was exempt from contract provisions that specified evaluation practices, and its administrators could dismiss teachers at will. The remaining two schools in the sample, Rodriguez and Naylor Charter Schools, were responsible only to their charter board and could dismiss teachers at any time.

There is much to be learned from how administrators in these successful schools conceived of and conducted evaluation. Because each had a unique history and was subject to different policies, it is impossible to attribute the practices we found to a single policy or school leader. Yet, when we compared the practices of these schools with those in our prior study, we found remarkable differences. Before exploring those differences, however, it's helpful to understand some basics about the state policy.

Developing a New State Policy on Teacher Evaluation, 2011

The Massachusetts teacher evaluation policy was developed by a forty-one-member task force composed of administrators and teachers from public education as well as representatives from universities, foundations, business, unions, and nonprofit agencies. In its report, which proposed an evaluation policy for the state, the task force explained that it sought to "transform educator evaluation from an inconsistently applied compliance mechanism into a statewide catalyst for educator development and continuous professional growth."[35] The policy's five-step cycle for continuous improvement required teachers to set "specific, actionable, and measurable" goals for improving their practice and students' learning. It was explicit in identifying teachers' development as the primary purpose for evaluation. However, in recommending the report to the state board of education, the commissioner urged that their regulations balance the proposed policy's focus on teachers' development with the schools' obligation to ensure accountability—to "dismiss educators who, despite the opportunity [to improve], continue weak performance."[36] The board subsequently endorsed both purposes.

The state also created a comprehensive model system that incorporated the statewide standards for a teacher's effectiveness in four areas (curriculum, planning, and assessment; teaching all students; family and community engagement; and contribution to professional culture). Like the Danielson framework, this system included sample rubrics for each standard, describing practice at four levels of proficiency (proficient, exemplary, needs improvement, and unsatisfactory). Districts were required to incorporate multiple measures of effectiveness in their assessments. Initially the policy called for using standardized test scores, although that was never enforced. Districts and schools could "adopt or adapt" the state's comprehensive model system or "revise" their existing evaluation system to meet the new regulations.[37]

In partnership with a statewide teachers union, Massachusetts officials also developed model contract language for evaluation that districts could adopt. In addition, state-level education staff posted on their website templates, planning and implementation guides, and other resources that districts and schools could use as they implemented the law.

Enacting Similar Evaluation Practices in the Successful Schools

Although these six schools were distinct in many ways, we found their approach to evaluation remarkably consistent, much as their approach to hiring had been. All schools used the supervision and evaluation process primarily to develop teachers, rather than to hold them formally accountable.[38] Most not only complied with the new law's regulations, but went beyond them, providing teachers with far more frequent observations, feedback, and support than the policy required. Teachers widely corroborated their principal's report that evaluation in their school was meant to improve their performance, and they strongly endorsed that priority. In fact, a number of teachers said they wanted more frequent feedback than they currently received, especially more subject-specific feedback. However, we also learned that, because the schools operated in distinct policy contexts, they encountered different opportunities and constraints as they implemented the policy.

WCSD and therefore its three district schools (Dickinson, Fitzgerald, and Hurston), along with Rodriguez Charter, adopted the state's model system, while Kincaid Charter and Naylor Charter revised their existing approaches to meet the state's new requirements. All schools used detailed, standards-based frameworks for observations and assessments. Teachers participated actively in setting individual goals for student performance and professional practice and completed self-assessments prior to formal evaluation meetings.

Development was the primary goal

Administrators in all six schools said their main responsibility as principal was to develop their teachers, many of whom they had hired. For example, Naylor's CMO, Ms. Nelson, explained that her school's commitment to improvement called for frequent observations: "We do believe that our whole mission is to be a human capital organization. We are here to develop our kids. We are here to develop our teachers. We are here to develop our administrators. This is what we do and what we're all about."

As a result, Naylor's administrators focused much of their time on conducting observations and providing feedback. Ms. Nelson explained, "[W]e think that the most transformational thing is just being in people's classrooms, talking with them afterwards."

When we asked the administrators about teacher evaluation, all of them began by describing their approach to formative, not summative, evaluation. An administrator at Kincaid Charter explained, "We believe that teachers, or just people in general, grow with immediate feedback and real-time instruction on how they are performing and [having] an opportunity to fix that in the moment." Kincaid's principal, Mr. Kain, realized that some teachers would encounter more challenges than others, but he expressed confidence that his school had the expertise needed to support them: "If we have teachers who are struggling, it's oftentimes . . . rooted in a lack of skill. Our job as coaches is to help them with that." Administrators in this sample provided detailed explanations about how, as one Fitzgerald evaluator said, she and others "coach [teachers] or find them the help they need."

Ninety-two of the ninety-seven teachers we interviewed in these six schools confirmed their administrators' accounts that evaluation focused primarily on helping them become better teachers. For example, a Naylor Charter teacher said she appreciated her administrator's "continuing to develop [her] as a professional." Her colleague explained that teachers at Naylor truly wanted to improve: "[I]n order to be an employee here, regardless of if you're an academic teacher, co-curricular teacher, even a staff member, you need to want feedback . . . to get better . . . [to] help [our] kids."

Further, teachers across all six schools said that their evaluation process was embedded in a professional culture that promoted continuous improvement. Many described their school much as this Rodriguez instructional coach did: "[T]here is a culture here that is about continually getting better. . . . [T]hat means that every teacher, whether they're getting feedback from an administrator or not, is trying to get better in their own practice."

Frequent observations with feedback

Under the state's model system, the number of required observations during the school year depended on a teacher's summative rating in prior years. Every new teacher and any experienced teacher who had been rated "unsatisfactory" had to be observed once during an announced visit and four times during unannounced visits. A returning teacher with a history of "proficient" or "exemplary" ratings had to be observed only once, unannounced. A teacher who had received a "needs improvement" rating had to be observed at least twice, unannounced.

In this sample of schools, most teachers, regardless of their summative rating from the prior year, described participating in an intense, yearlong cycle of observations, followed soon after by written or oral critique and recommendations. Approximately 40 percent of the ninety-seven teachers we interviewed said they were observed and received feedback at least twice a month. Approximately 20 percent estimated that they were observed and given feedback between five and ten times a year. The final 40 percent estimated that they had been observed one to four times per year, consistent with state and district policies. Although all schools met or exceeded the state's recommendations, the frequency of observations varied within schools, with novice teachers and new hires being observed more often than others.

Administrators at Kincaid and Naylor Charter Schools expected that every teacher would be observed and provided face-to-face feedback at least twice a month, and all teachers interviewed said that evaluators met, and often exceeded, that standard. At Hurston K–8 and Rodriguez Charter, administrators hoped to observe every teacher and provide feedback at least once a month, although participants from both said their school lacked the resources to maintain that level of supervision for all teachers. All administrators routinely conducted "walkthroughs" for quick observations, often providing feedback soon after. Dickinson and Fitzgerald teachers said their principals spent a great deal of time in classrooms throughout the school, but most described receiving formal feedback no more than a few times per year, consistent with the model system.

It's notable that the principals from these schools (and Mr. Gilmore from the Teaching in Context study) expressed similar beliefs about the benefits of frequent observation and feedback, which was not the case in earlier studies—our own and others'—where principals' views varied widely.[39] Perhaps even more important, these principals were recognized, themselves, as being strong teachers, who brought to the process of evaluation not only beliefs about the benefits of developing teachers but also knowledge and skills about what teachers should do and how to help them. A teacher from Naylor Charter expressed a view that was common among the teachers we interviewed: "[I]n my old school . . . you'd find out they were coming in [to observe]. It was like you were ready for a performance. You had to do it perfectly and then they never came in again until three or four months later. [Here], they're just always in and out of the room, so it's nice. It's a good way to just always keep getting better."

A colleague offered a similar perspective: "When I know something isn't going well, I will ask to be observed so that I can get help on that. That's totally the mentality here. I don't like someone seeing me doing something wrong. [But] I would prefer that . . . [to] not getting any guidance on it."

Making the Most of Principals' Time for Observations and Feedback

Three schools (Naylor Charter, Kincaid Charter, and Hurston K–8) had reorganized their administrators' responsibilities so that the principal could spend much of his or her time observing teachers and providing feedback, while other administrators handled responsibilities such as student discipline, contacts with parents, and operations (e.g., building maintenance, bus schedules, data analysis, and budgeting). All principals had considerable discretion in allocating their funds and could decide to hire an additional administrator to make that possible, although doing so would likely require making cuts in other areas. The director of operations at Hurston K–8 described how his role supported increased observations by Mr. Hinds and other evaluators: "My role has been to block and tackle so that [the evaluators] can spend their time in the classroom coaching teachers and [attending] team meetings."

Notably, however, Hurston's administrative team was the same size as Kincaid's, yet Hurston enrolled 800 students, while Kincaid enrolled 475, and Hurston had 65 teachers to observe, while Kincaid had only 40. Therefore, regardless of Mr. Hinds's intentions, he and other evaluators could not provide the same level of intense supervision for all Hurston's teachers as their counterparts at Kincaid and Naylor could. At Dickinson, Ms. Davila, the sole administrator, could not reassign management responsibilities to others in order to free up more time for observations. Although all principals in this study thought that observing teachers and providing them with feedback fostered improvement, those who had less administrative support coped with more demands and greater constraints on their time, affecting how they implemented the policy and how teachers responded to it.

Nevertheless, virtually all teachers we interviewed spoke positively about their experience with evaluation—a remarkable finding. A third-year teacher at Rodriguez Charter said, "Just the fact that my administrators are in my classroom on a weekly or biweekly basis, I think shows a lot. It means that they care, and they're here to help us." Another Rodriguez teacher, with twelve years of experience, said of her principal: "He knows my flaws. He knows what I need to work on. He knows me better than I know myself as a teacher."

Many praised their school's current approach to evaluation with phrases such as "hugely helpful" or "super supported." A Fitzgerald teacher said that evaluation kept her "on [her] toes" and "helped [her] to do better as a teacher." A Dickinson teacher echoed this sentiment, saying, "It's helpful always. A second person can notice things that you yourself in the job miss." One Naylor teacher, in her seventh year of teaching and her fifth at the school, said that "the constant feedback" she received was a highlight of her job: "I constantly feel like I'm getting better."

Most teachers said that their evaluator provided detailed feedback about a range of topics, including classroom management and pedagogy. For example, one Naylor teacher said that her supervisor had helped her improve the questions she asked during read-alouds so that they promoted higher-order thinking among her primary students. Naylor administrators provided written feedback on a Google Doc, which one said helped both the administrator and teacher keep track of progress made over time.

Hurston evaluators emailed their feedback within twenty-four hours and also recorded observations in a Google Doc, which was available to the entire administrative team. Teachers there repeatedly described their post-observation feedback as timely, specific, and relevant. Several showed us comments they received. Mr. Hinds wrote to one about how she paced a lesson and to another about how responding to every student's contribution before the next student spoke discouraged open exchange. In both cases, he suggested changes that the teachers found helpful.

Across schools, teachers often said that the process of observation and feedback led them to change their pedagogy, which they thought was improving. A Kincaid Charter teacher with six years of experience said that she had become "a drastically better teacher" in the three years that she had worked at the school, "because it's been this really close cycle of being observed and then feedback on what to work on, and then observed again and then feedback again." An experienced elementary teacher at Rodriguez Charter described how over time his principal's feedback had supported him in gradually but dramatically shifting his instructional approach:

> She kind of said, "Why don't you think about doing this, that, and the other thing?" I said, "Okay" and that first two, three, four weeks of changing my entire teaching style was a disaster. . . . I started tweaking it and figuring it out and she would come in and observe and critique and give good, positive comments and negative ones. . . . Looking back I can't even imagine how much of a disservice I was doing to kids back then in the way that I was teaching.

Linking Evaluation to Other Professional Supports

Evaluation did not stand alone in these schools' efforts to develop their teachers. Instead, it was coordinated with other professional learning opportunities, such as instructional coaching, teacher teams, whole-school professional development, and peer observation, each part of an integrated strategy for improving teachers' practice across the school. The evaluator's approach to instruction, therefore, was situated in and responsive to other related practice, which seemed to augment its benefits.

Although the teachers experienced observations and evaluations primarily as individuals, they often looked to colleagues on their instructional teams for additional feedback about their teaching and how to improve it. School administrators remained well informed about their teachers' instruction by routinely reviewing unit and lesson plans and participating in team meetings that focused on data analysis and curriculum planning. In responding to our questions about the instructional support they received, teachers often didn't distinguish between evaluation practices and other opportunities that the school provided. From their perspective, the ongoing process of being observed and receiving feedback was, in itself, valuable professional learning. However, many—including experienced teachers—identified the continuous cycle of classroom observations and feedback as the most valuable part of their school's developmental process. Julie Marsh and her colleagues, who studied evaluation practices in eight New Orleans schools, also found connections between evaluations and other practices. When teachers participated in organized collaboration and when administrators and teacher leaders shared responsibility for leadership, evaluation practices "appeared to foster a sense of accountability for continuous improvement" among teachers.[40]

Keeping Accountability a Priority

Policy makers and analysts may debate whether the goal of evaluation should be to improve teachers' performance or hold them accountable. However, neither teachers nor administrators suggested that this was a choice they had to make. They did not think that their school's focus on development made it difficult to dismiss weak teachers. Most appreciated having the chance to meet with their evaluator to discuss their ratings and to review their progress toward selected goals. Although these teachers realized that formal evaluation could be used to inform employment decisions, including dismissal, they viewed its use for accountability as a secondary purpose. Clearly, that perspective was reaffirmed by the time and effort that administrators invested in observing their classes and the quality of feedback they provided throughout the year.

Teachers widely endorsed the formal evaluation process, which included mid- and end-of-year meetings when they discussed their assigned ratings on the evaluation rubric and reviewed their progress toward selected goals. Evaluators rated teachers' performance on all four standards, each including multiple indicators defined by specific elements and descriptors. Accompanying rubrics depicted typical performance at different levels of accomplishment. With only two exceptions across six schools, teachers said that their evaluations accurately assessed their professional practice. Unlike ongoing formative supervision, which usually focused on no more than one to three issues at a time, summative evaluation was comprehensive.

Summative ratings—no surprises

Teachers frequently suggested that formal evaluation, as it was implemented in their school, was a natural outgrowth of day-to-day supervisory practice. One teacher described formal evaluation as "just a tiny piece of what we already do on a daily basis." Another teacher echoed many others in explaining that the summative evaluation process "shouldn't be a big deal. It really hasn't [been]." A third expanded: "I know exactly what my goals are and what I'm doing, so it wasn't surprising how she graded me. I graded myself really hard, but I knew what I was working on, so it made sense to me." Teachers believed that, when warranted, evaluators gave low ratings in summative assessments that could lead to dismissal. In fact, at all but one school, administrators reported that teachers in their school were currently, or had been, on improvement plans, with goals they had to meet in order to keep their job. Administrators at all schools also mentioned having teachers who were not offered a position the following year or, in unusual cases, were dismissed midyear for ineffective instruction.

Several teachers expressed respect for the fact that even the summative rating process encouraged improvement. This was especially true when teachers believed that their evaluators had a deep understanding of learning and teaching. A Naylor teacher explained that he was graded on "a rubric from 1 to 4, just like the students are." He noted that, despite receiving "mostly 1.5s, some 2s, and a 3," he was not discouraged, although "in another context, I would have felt like they were starting a paper trail to fire me." He explained that his current administrators had different expectations for beginning teachers. "They expect their first-year, maybe even second-year, teachers to be working hard, but not really mastering all the things they want you to master." His thoughtful, open-minded view reveals the high level of trust that existed among the teachers and administrators within his school.

Mr. Hinds explained his intentions for summative evaluations, which were consistent with these teachers' views: "I think evaluation without ongoing supervision is meaningless. It becomes only the way that you terminate employment. And so my belief is that I and every member of my administrative team needs to be in classrooms all the time, giving feedback, asking questions, pushing people. And then all of that just gets rolled into an evaluation. No surprises."

This contributed to a sense of accountability that made the evaluation process a serious one, but there was no evidence that it generated fear or undermined the teachers' trust in their evaluator or the system, as it had at Thoreau in the earlier study. The administrators' frequent presence in classes and their investment in teachers' improvement convinced them that they and their colleagues were being treated fairly.

Facing Ongoing Challenges with Time and Expertise

As they described evaluation practices within their school, both teachers and administrators raised the persistent challenges of finding enough time to do thorough observations and feedback and summoning sufficient expertise to meet teachers' needs.

Not enough time

Even in these successful schools, which dedicated a large share of their resources to supervision and evaluation, some participants said that administrators lacked the time they needed to provide comprehensive observation and feedback for all teachers, which confirms findings in studies discussed earlier. Virtually all teachers we interviewed expressed appreciation for whatever attention they received, but six of them—five having seven or more years of experience—explicitly said that they wanted more attention than their supervisors could provide. As one Fitzgerald teacher said, "I think it would be a lot more powerful if administrators were able to be in the classrooms a lot more." Principals at Dickinson, Fitzgerald, Hurston, and Rodriguez Charter talked about the daunting demands of conducting frequent observations and providing detailed feedback for all teachers. Most were responsible for supervising fifteen to twenty teachers, but some had more. With thirty-nine teachers to evaluate, Mr. Hinds at Hurston had the most. Ms.

Forte at Fitzgerald said, "We just can't keep up. We're lucky to have two of us, [the principal and assistant principal]." Similarly, Mr. Ryan, the middle school principal at Rodriguez Charter, said, "I have twenty people I evaluate and supervise, and it feels like too many to me. I'm always thinking, 'Oh, I haven't been [in that teacher's class] for so long!'"

At these schools, as at those studied by Richard Halverson and colleagues, teachers mentioned that administrators spent more time supervising new and struggling teachers than proficient, experienced teachers.[41] Several veteran teachers we interviewed said they understood why the needs of novices took precedence, but they still wanted more feedback and support for themselves, because they knew they could improve. For example, a Hurston teacher with ten years of experience said: "I would like more feedback [from] someone who knows my classroom, has seen student A in October and now can tell me how student A [has] progressed in March." Her colleague with nine years of experience said that she wanted to be observed more often so that she could have in-depth discussions about her "delivery of instruction," such as, "Did it make sense to do that activity in groups?" Nevertheless, these teachers still approved of their school's focus on development and valued the feedback they received.

Mismatched subject-based expertise

Although teachers expressed confidence in their evaluators' knowledge of classroom management and general pedagogy, some were disappointed about their lack of subject-specific knowledge, which limited what they could recommend about teaching the content. A middle school math teacher at Hurston K–8 said that, although she found her administrator's comments "affirming," her math colleague's feedback was more helpful. "He just knows more about the content. He can tell if students are understanding or not a little bit more than [administrators] can because not everybody's an expert in everything." A history teacher at Kincaid Charter who was supervised by a former English teacher said that his feedback often focused on how to teach writing through history, but neglected the "nitty-gritty of history." Teachers of students with special needs at Kincaid expressed concern that their supervisors lacked experience and knowledge about students with disabilities. One called the feedback "very standard . . . cookie-cutter." Another said, "I think there's still huge amounts of growth I could make, but it's hard accessing that growth when the [evaluators] don't know what you're doing [in your content area]." These were spontaneous comments, and other teachers may have held similar views but not mentioned them.

Several administrators acknowledged that they could not realistically provide pedagogical advice in every subject, at every grade level. At Fitzgerald and Rodriguez Charter, instructional coaches supported teachers in planning and teaching mathematics and literacy, which they appreciated, although those content experts did not conduct formal evaluations.

TAPPING EXPERTISE AMONG TEACHER LEADERS AND PEERS

Inevitably, there are limits—in both time and skill—to what a single administrator, or even a small team of administrators, can provide within a school. However, any serious effort to help teachers improve their instruction through the evaluation process brings with it increasing demands for expertise. One option, often overlooked, is to rely on teacher leaders with deep knowledge and successful experience teaching in specific grade levels and subject areas. Two schools relied on instructional coaches to conduct observations during the formative part of evaluation, a practice that could be expanded. As the previous teachers' comments suggest, when such teacher leaders know the subject being taught, their advice is likely to be more credible and useful than when an evaluator observes classes generically.

Peer Assistance and Review

For many years, I have been impressed by the effectiveness of Peer Assistance and Review (PAR) programs, which provide teachers with frequent, informative, subject-based support and assessment. In districts that have adopted PAR, a cadre of carefully selected consulting teachers leave their classroom for three to five years and assume responsibility for providing both formative and summative evaluation for novices and underperforming veteran teachers. After several months of giving detailed feedback and modeling exemplary practice, consulting teachers conduct a formal evaluation and file a report with the PAR panel, a joint labor-management committee overseeing the program. In 2007–2008 we closely studied PAR in seven districts and documented their practices in detail.[42]

If the consulting teacher's combined advice and assistance do not lead to improved practice by the teacher, the PAR program provides a clear path for the teacher's dismissal. The consulting teacher's report is either the sole or primary document that the panel considers in deciding whether to recommend that a teacher be reappointed or dismissed. Because PAR provides due process at all stages of the program, districts rarely encounter legal challenges to their decisions, even when they dismiss tenured teachers. Although some states or local teachers' contracts prohibit teachers from evaluating peers, the Massachusetts evaluation law explicitly permits districts to adopt PAR, and WCSD was conducting a small pilot program.

In our cost-benefit analysis of PAR, we found that the program affords a range of financial savings and organizational benefits that offset its costs.[43] The practices of PAR's consulting teachers illustrate the program's potential to reduce the demands of evaluation on administrators' scarce time and to compensate for subject matter expertise that a principal may lack. However, we concluded that, in order to ensure that consulting teachers in a PAR program have the professional authority and organizational skills they need to be effective, they should be selected in an open and competitive process, have clearly defined roles, and be well trained and supervised.

School-Based Peer Observations

Less formalized and consequential observations by peers also can supplement administrators' knowledge of different subjects and experience in different grade levels. Although peer observation was identified decades ago as a promising practice to support teachers' learning, it remains uncommon and virtually unstudied in schools today.[44] All six successful schools had introduced peer observation in some form at some time.[45] When the practice was sustained, it was embedded in other systems and structures that promoted collaboration and learning, such as team meetings or professional development sessions.

The charter schools—Naylor, Kincaid, and the middle school at Rodriguez—had the most developed and established practices. In the fall, Naylor's principal, Ms. North, required all teachers to observe one another in pairs every three weeks, focusing on a particular topic that was the focus of professional development; by the spring, peer observations were optional and more open-ended. At Rodriguez, teachers were required each year to observe at least four colleagues, who were randomly selected during a professional development session. Teachers asked their observer to focus on a particular aspect of their practice and the pairs then debriefed those sessions during weekly professional development meetings. Both schools provided a structured protocol for observations and a feedback sheet for taking notes. Certain features of how work was organized in these schools—shared space, coteaching, and shared lesson planning—made observing colleagues and providing feedback relatively easy to arrange, which seemed to moderate traditional norms of privacy and autonomy. The schools' schedules accommodated visits, and teachers-in-training at Naylor and Kincaid could cover teachers' classes when they were observing their colleagues.

The logistical challenges of finding time and paying substitutes to permit peer observations were greater at Hurston, Fitzgerald, Dickinson, and Rodriguez Elementary. Also, teachers at those schools were less accustomed to having peers watch them teach and expressed more apprehension about the process. These schools paired teachers to conduct peer observations, but the purpose of the visits differed. Dickinson and Rodriguez Elementary used the process explicitly and exclusively to benefit the observer, who might discover new instructional practices or learn from students' interaction and responses. As one Dickinson teacher explained, "You're not really there to critique. . . . You're going in with a . . . purpose for you, that you want to learn about."

In contrast, Hurston's practice was geared to assist the observed teacher, who could benefit from a colleague's insights and advice. A teacher leader organized Hurston's process, pairing teachers within and across departments and grade levels. Teachers received a printed protocol, calling for a pre-observation conference, in-person observation, and a post-observation debrief, all focused on an instructional challenge identified by the observed teacher. The pre-conferences, observations, and debrief meetings were scheduled by teachers on their own time.

Often those we interviewed said that the logistical challenges of scheduling and debriefing visits meant that they conducted fewer observations than expected. Other initiatives competed for their time. For example, Ms. Davila said that Dickinson's focus on conducting data inquiry cycles had "distracted" the school from allocating the time and support that peer observations required. In reflecting on peer observations at Hurston, Mr. Hinds candidly said, "People really liked it and then it fell apart." He added, "It was great for two years, but . . . we failed to do our part" to keep it going.

Sometimes it seemed that accounts of logistical challenges masked teachers' concerns about privacy. To moderate both the demands on time and teachers' underlying reluctance to be observed teaching by their peers, efforts were under way in several schools, including Dickinson, to use video recordings of teachers' instruction as the basis for discussion during professional development sessions. Still, at four schools (Dickinson, Fitzgerald, Hurston K–8, and Rodriguez Charter Elementary), despite widespread praise and optimism about the potential value of peer observation, the practice occurred intermittently rather than routinely.

CONCLUSION

Through these studies, we learned first and foremost that it is indeed possible to effectively incorporate both development and accountability in an evaluation system. Moreover, we found that combining both components in a single, on-going process can enhance the value of each. Some experts suggest that a "fire wall" should separate the support provided by a supervisor and the final judgment rendered by an evaluator.[46] However, no teacher or administrator we interviewed recommended that approach. In fact, teachers valued ongoing observations with feedback in part because they knew those observations contributed to their final rating, and they had confidence in that rating because it was informed by frequent observations, rather than a single classroom visit.

However, the benefits of a comprehensive evaluation process cannot be achieved unless the observations and feedback that teachers receive during the formative stage of evaluation are thorough and genuinely intended to help them improve. As we saw at Thoreau High School, perfunctory classroom visits that fail to provide feedback and support will likely backfire, fueling suspicion, undermining morale, and reassuring no one about the benefits of evaluation.

Second, we learned that, although conducting summative evaluations takes time, attending meaningfully to teachers' development takes more time—time that must be provided, protected, and adequately funded. There is no shortcut here. These cases suggest that reorganizing administrators' responsibilities can free up key evaluators so that they can observe classes often. Fortunately, all of these principals could reallocate the funds in their school's budget, within broad parameters. However, the administrative resources available in traditional district schools fell short of those available in charter, turnaround, and restart schools. This suggests that, if policy makers and administrators are serious about improving all teachers' instruction, then they must fully fund a robust, ongoing process of supervision and evaluation by increasing administrative support.

Third, we concluded that the benefits of an evaluation system will be augmented if it is embedded in a professional culture with strong professional norms that inspire improvement. This can be achieved when all educators bring a "growth mind-set" to evaluation and when the evaluation process is well integrated with other human capital practices, including hiring, grade-level and subject-based teams, and schoolwide professional development. Such a professional culture and related practices take time to build and considerable effort to sustain, but there is great payoff in doing so.[47]

Finally, we learned that when teachers experience frequent observations and useful feedback from skilled evaluators, they become more confident and report that their practice is improving. These teachers appreciated receiving detailed recommendations that were grounded in thorough observations, and they welcomed watching evaluators model the practices they were expected to enact. Therefore, to be effective, evaluators must have a deep understanding of instruction and, ideally, be able to demonstrate the skills they recommend. Principals can engage teacher leaders who are experts in various subjects to supervise and evaluate teachers as instructional coaches or peer evaluators, thus ensuring that all teachers receive the pedagogical support they deserve. For this and many other reasons, it is essential that those who appoint principals choose individuals who are experienced teachers, steeped in the expertise and judgment they need to be true instructional leaders.

In chapter 6, we move from the classroom out to the school, focusing on how teachers exercise professional leadership among their colleagues and administrators.

CHAPTER SIX

When Teachers Lead

THOSE WHO WORRY ABOUT PUBLIC EDUCATION but are unfamiliar with schools and how they work might expect principals to manage and lead with relative ease. Compared with complex, multilevel corporations, hospitals, and governmental agencies, schools are simple, flat organizations. At the top of the organization chart sit the principal and one or two administrators who supervise the work of the classroom teachers, positioned just below them in the school's hierarchy.

Given this spare structure, policy makers and administrators who are intent on quickly improving schools tend to think about change as an uncomplicated transactional process: the principal diagnoses the problem, lays out a strategy for solving it, and then expects teachers to promptly "buy in" to the plan and implement it. However, principals who approach reform in this top-down way repeatedly discover that they have less authority to change practice than either they thought or the organization chart suggests. If teachers disagree with their principal's plans for improvement, they can rather easily ignore or minimally comply with them. It turns out that the classroom walls and doors that isolate teachers from one another also protect them from close administrative scrutiny.

So far in this book, we've considered some of the challenges that urban schools face along with the shortcomings, outright failures, and best practices that educators within these schools used to address them. However, these accounts only hint at how those within a school decide—or decide to decide—what problem to address and how to approach it. This chapter deals with that process by exploring the role that teachers play in leading change.

Over the past thirty years, researchers have convincingly documented that both principals and teachers have essential, complementary roles to play in school improvement. These studies provide rich pictures of what schools look like when teachers actively collaborate in the process of school improvement.[1] However, we still have much to learn about what principals and teachers do to develop the kind of interdependence that is needed. Who takes the lead? Who follows? Or can everyone both lead and follow?

In exploring these questions, this chapter draws on the experiences of teachers and principals in all twelve Walker City schools we studied. First, we'll consider the nature of the most difficult challenges that are prominent in urban schools today—those for which there is no established solution for educators to adopt. Next, we look at teachers' experiences as members of their school, considering whether and how they participate in deliberations about its priorities and then influence the implementation and refinement of new practices. Finally, we turn to the potential contributions that teachers who hold formal leadership roles can make to improve their school, investigating what teacher leaders do, what their roles require, and what sustains them in their work.

RESPONDING TO CHALLENGES IN URBAN SCHOOLS

Let's begin by looking at the serious challenges that Ms. Thomas confronted when she became principal of Thoreau High School in 2008. Nearly 50 percent of the entering ninth-grade students had failed every core course the year before, and another 20 percent had passed only one. Although Thoreau's tenth-grade students performed reasonably well on the state's MCAS test, many continued to fail their courses, causing both teachers and administrators to fear that those who eventually graduated would not be prepared for college.

Despite sustained efforts over many years to create an effective learning environment for all Thoreau's students, the school was failing to serve many of them. Ms. Thomas and her teachers faced crucial, complex challenges and she saw no clear path to improvement. Like many urban principals, she recognized an urgent need for change and knew that her strategy would require teachers' endorsement, but she found that harder to gain than she expected.

The troubles at Thoreau seemed so pervasive that it was difficult to say for sure what caused them. Was it, as Ms. Thomas believed, the presence of ineffective teachers, the lack of a schoolwide curriculum, isolation of the small learning communities (SLCs), and a disjointed six-period schedule? Or was it, as many teachers believed, a problem with Ms. Thomas's leadership and management: lax discipline, lagging administrative support for the SLCs, and scant supervision for teachers who wanted to improve their instruction? Or was it something entirely different? As in many urban high schools, Thoreau's teachers and administrators could point to evidence of the problems they faced—chaos in the corridors, disregard for school rules, students' failing grades—but they never genuinely explored together what caused those problems. Where could they and should they begin?

Technical or Adaptive Challenges?

Ron Heifitz provides a useful way to think about the kinds of problems that Ms. Thomas and her teachers faced. He distinguishes between two types of organizational challenges. *Technical* challenges, such as how to efficiently schedule students for classes, are straightforward and responsive to established, routine solutions. However, *adaptive* challenges, such as how to ensure that instruction is inclusive and coherent for all students in all classes, have no obvious, established answers.[2] They call for everyone to better understand how their organization currently works before moving ahead to decide how to improve it. From Heifitz's perspective, until Thoreau's educators reached a shared understanding of what was not working in their school and why, they could not begin to develop a promising strategy to address it.

As Heifitz and Donald Laurie explain, the process of organizational learning requires everyone's earnest participation and calls for "the collective intelligence of employees at all levels, who need to use one another as resources, often across boundaries, and learn their way into solutions."[3] At Thoreau, that would mean engaging administrators, teachers, and specialists to work together in an organized effort to define and understand their problems, explore options for addressing them, and systematically implement and refine the solutions they decide to try.

HOW DO PRINCIPALS AND TEACHERS JOINTLY ADDRESS CHALLENGES?

How, then, do principals and teachers interact when they face adaptive challenges? What role, if any, can and do teachers play in diagnosing problems and generating solutions? In our 2010–2011 Teaching in Context study, almost all of our WCSD schools, including Thoreau, faced what they viewed as major challenges. Performance varied across this set of schools, but only Whitman Academy—a magnet, nonselective high school—was unequivocally successful, with its high test scores, large numbers of student applicants entering the school's enrollment lottery, and an excellent public reputation. The least academically successful school was Angelou Elementary, which was then under the state's watch as an underperforming school and would eventually be closed and restarted by a CMO. Other schools among the six we studied that year performed somewhat above the average for schools in the district, although many WCSD schools had low scores, so being above average wasn't a notable accomplishment. Educators in all these schools voiced concern for their students' current learning and future life chances. One elementary teacher at Angelou expressed the urgency that many others felt: "We've got to do better and we've got to educate our students better. We have to help and make sure that they achieve. . . . I think teachers feel a pressure to help in the standardized scores, but I think there's a lot of caring teachers here that also understand that we need to develop a group of students that is able to succeed, that they learn those skills that they can use for the rest of their lives."

The principal of each school had ideas about what to do so that students would meet higher learning standards. Most teachers said that they were ready to collaborate and actively invest in their school's improvement, even though they might not agree with their principal's current definition of the problem. Yet genuine "buy-in"—a commitment to invest in a plan and do whatever it takes to make it work—did not come easily. As Susan Rosenholtz explained in 1989, truly engaging teachers requires principals to do a great deal of groundwork: "Where teachers help principals define school goals and interact about how best to pursue them, where they help determine school policies that facilitate goal attainment, such as how students ought to behave or help to socialize new recruits, teachers engage actively in constructing their school reality."[4]

The teachers we interviewed in these schools realized that little would improve for their students unless their principal was committed to change and willing to create the conditions to support it. Therefore, they agreed that the principal should take the lead and set the direction for change. Because they felt intense pressure to improve their school—whether that pressure came from state officials threatening takeover or from their own concern about their students' future, or both—teachers generally gave their principal wide berth in deciding where to begin and what path to take. But they then expected to participate actively in an open process of exploring and explaining the school's problem before moving on to possible solutions. It would not be enough for the principal to get teachers' buy-in, which is often no more than a symbolic gesture that means little or nothing; they wanted a seat at the table where plans would be made.

Contrasting Approaches to Leadership: Instrumental or Inclusive?

Many people think of leadership as being rooted in the formal authority of administrators, such as the principal or superintendent. In fact, educators routinely use the term *leadership* to refer to those administrators, rather than to the process of leading. So what is leadership? Is it a position, a resource, or an interaction? Rodney Ogawa and Steven Bossert suggest that leadership is an "organizational quality."[5] As they see it, opportunities for leadership are not confined to those holding positions of formal authority. Instead, they say that leadership "flows through networks of roles that comprise organizations," creating opportunities for influence throughout. Leadership then emerges from the ongoing interactions among individuals as they seek to influence one another.[6] From their various positions, individuals may propose changes, disagree with suggestions, form alliances, withhold endorsement, or comply with enthusiasm—all in the exercise of leadership. According to this view, everyone in an organization has the potential to lead.

Principals of our six WCSD schools largely determined what opportunities teachers would have as participants and potential leaders in schoolwide change. We found that their approaches fell along a continuum ranging from *instrumental* to *inclusive* leadership.[7] Principals who relied on instrumental leadership preempted teachers from defining problems and devising responses; instead, they expected teachers to adopt practices that they or outside experts deemed effective. These principals tended to view the school's challenges as technical ones that could be successfully solved, if only teachers would consent to adopt their plan. In contrast, those who demonstrated inclusive leadership engaged teachers in identifying problems, devising solutions, and implementing changes. These principals viewed their school's problems as adaptive challenges that were situation-specific, not fully understood and having no established solution. Two schools, Stowe Middle School and Giovanni Elementary, illustrate salient contrasts between leadership practices that fell toward each end of this continuum.

Instrumental leadership at Stowe Middle School

Stowe Middle School, where Ms. Sterling had been principal for over a decade, enrolled approximately seven hundred students from throughout the district. Ninety percent were from low-income families and 95 percent were students of color. During the 1980s and 1990s, the school had enjoyed success and recognition, but lately was experiencing a steady decline in test scores. Since the early

1990s, Stowe had relied on outside funding to provide extended learning time for students, which included an array of enrichment courses. However, under Ms. Sterling's management, the additional time was increasingly used for extra instruction in core academic subjects. Because Stowe stood to lose its funding for the extended learning program if students' performance didn't stabilize and improve rapidly, Ms. Sterling intently focused her school's resources on improving test scores.

She hired consultants from a nonprofit organization to provide an improvement program that engaged teachers in systematically analyzing achievement data from interim assessments, which then could guide teachers' instructional decisions. However, teachers complained that they had little or no say in identifying the problems that the school faced or determining how to address them. Reportedly, Stowe's administrators and consultants decided which teachers would meet together, when they would meet, and what aspects of instruction they would focus on. In criticizing this top-down approach, one teacher raised concerns voiced by many others: "It just doesn't make sense. . . . A lot of people are really upset and angry about that. . . . And it just doesn't work. It's like we're doing it just to show the state that we're doing something. And it's, in my point of view, a complete waste of time."

Another teacher expressed frustration that teachers had no opportunity to diagnose their school's problems and propose responses: "Sometimes we feel like 'Why are we doing this?'. . . [W]e should have a say in what we want to do and what we need." She went on to explain what can be gained when administrators truly hear what teachers have to say: "When you have that conversation, you own it. You buy into it and you want to be a part of it, [as] opposed to someone saying, "'Well, I told sixth grade to do this. You do this and you do this.'" She speculated about the effect of such orders: "Do you really feel like a professional? And do you act like it?" One of her likeminded colleagues urged, "Give teachers back some control."

Ms. Sterling intended that the teachers' work with the consultants would give them the support they needed to improve and coordinate instruction. Yet, as she explained, she and other administrators decided who needed what support: "You know, we walk the building as much as we can to get information. You know, what's going on? And whenever you go into a classroom, you're always looking around. It's [as a result of] all of those little administrative observation things that we really try to tally information and say, 'Okay, where do people really need the support?' And that's where we provide support."

Teachers, however, thought that these activities were designed to direct, not support, their work. Although several credited Ms. Sterling for her tireless efforts on behalf of students, far more agreed with this experienced teacher: "You have to know how to do it and you have to build capacity. You cannot just have one person, or two people, telling everybody else what it should be." She further criticized the fact that the plan for change originated outside the school: "[The consultants] have their agenda. And so, yes, they're here to support us. But it's *their* thing."

Most Stowe teachers complied with the consultants' requirements, but did so reluctantly and superficially. Many suggested that the principal did not look to them for ideas, but instead used her authority to extract their compliance. Several said they feared retaliation if they resisted. Not one of the teachers we interviewed at Stowe described being involved in a process of exploring causes, generating ideas, deliberating about alternative approaches, or making more than routine decisions about the school.

By resisting or minimally complying with Ms. Sterling's plans for their improvement, Stowe's teachers also exercised leadership, but it was covert. They undermined the principal's agenda and pursued their own plans by turning their attention away from schoolwide initiatives and back to their classroom. One explained: "I try not to think about all the hard stuff and try to focus on the kids that are in front of me. You know, as people like to say, 'Close the door and just teach and try not to think about all the outside distractions and influences.'"

Teachers suggested that, if Ms. Sterling had truly sought their views, they would have gladly explored why their students were not doing well and what they might do to improve their experience by changing their curriculum, course offerings, schedule, and/or pedagogy. But no one asked and, in response, teachers' leadership went underground as Ogawa and Bossert suggested it might. Because teachers complied minimally, neither Ms. Sterling nor the consultants seemed to realize it was happening, but the fact that it was not visible made it no less consequential. Teachers tried to continue in their work together, despite Ms. Sterling's planned support, which many found intrusive. Some said they might leave Stowe for another school where teachers had more freedom and influence.

Inclusive leadership at Giovanni Elementary School

Teachers at Giovanni Elementary School had similar backgrounds and voiced similar interests as teachers at Stowe. However, they gave their principal, Mr. Gilmore, wholehearted approval, not the disdain that Stowe's teachers expressed about Ms. Sterling, and they told a very different story about their role in school improvement. Teachers described Mr. Gilmore as having a highly inclusive approach to leadership, engaging them regularly in identifying problems and opportunities, exploring options, and committing to new approaches.

Though younger, Giovanni's 450 students were demographically similar to those at Stowe: 95 percent lived in low-income households and 90 percent were students of color. Yet, on the state's measures of student growth, Giovanni's students performed substantially better than Stowe's in both ELA and math. As a literacy expert and former instructional coach, Mr. Gilmore had been Giovanni's principal for close to a decade. He expressed confidence that he and his teachers shared similar goals: "I think the teachers in this building have a clear understanding that I want the same things that they want, and that is for all our kids to achieve." In remarkable unanimity, the teachers we interviewed described Mr. Gilmore as taking an active lead in setting the school's improvement agenda, while also being responsive to teachers' concerns and soliciting their ideas for modifying that agenda.

Mr. Gilmore explained that, over time, he had found that the potential for positive change throughout the school rests with certain skilled teachers, who might or might not be formally recognized as teacher leaders: "I've found these really excellent and strategic thinkers that are embedded in schools, who really draw no attention to themselves. When you connect with those folks—if you're lucky enough to connect with these folks—you can advance the program over time."

In moving Giovanni's improvement agenda forward, Mr. Gilmore met regularly with several groups of teachers, including those on the school's instructional leadership teams (ILTs) for literacy and math. ILT meetings were open, so teachers who didn't have formal positions on these committees could also join the deliberations, as some did. All but two teachers we interviewed endorsed the contributions of their ILT colleagues; those two supported Mr. Gilmore, but complained that a few teachers, referred to as "power players" or "keepers of the data," had undue influence in the school.

When the ILTs met, Mr. Gilmore and the teachers generated proposals for improving the school's curriculum and instructional approach and then took those back to their colleagues to ask what they thought. One teacher described the process: "When we are talking about a new idea, [Mr. Gilmore] will say, 'Run it by your grade-level [team of teachers] and next time bring it back. . . . Test the waters. . . . And then we will figure it out. Was that a good idea or a bad idea?

What parts did people not like? What should we change?' So, before we bring it into the law, at least we kind of talk to every teacher. It's not just 'Here it is.'"

Another teacher elaborated: "We get to put in our ideas and show different things we've been trying [in our classes]. . . . And we definitely talked about 'Can you do that in the period [of time] that you're given? Are you using all of the resources that come with it?' Those kinds of decisions, like what's the best use of time?"

A third teacher said that Mr. Gilmore was "very open to hearing arguments and suggestions. . . . If we bring up an idea, we can all discuss it. If it's a good idea that we can support, it can be something we can change [throughout the school]." She, like others, said that the principal solicited their ideas: "So it [isn't] just like him telling us, 'This is what we are going to change.' [It's] all of us going through this together. 'Here is what is working right now. This is what we need to change.'"

Mr. Gilmore said his school "runs on consensus," not "democratic vote." He and others made sure that everyone had a say and that all views were considered. However, once they made a decision, everyone was expected to comply. Still, teachers could decide how to implement that decision in their classes. As one teacher said, "I think he gives us a lot of freedom and he trusts us. He's definitely not a micromanager."

Mr. Gilmore recognized the enormous potential for leadership among teachers. He not only believed that the potential for leadership rests with individuals throughout the school, but also understood that leadership is relational in nature, stimulating and implementing change through personal interactions. As Mr. Gilmore and Giovanni's teachers described their work together, their accounts seemed to echo James Coleman's explanations of how social capital can be used to augment human capital in the school.[8] Further, Mr. Gilmore realized that teachers throughout the school had the power to advance or stall the progress of their reforms, so he tried to surface objections early, drop ill-advised proposals, and solicit promising refinements before decisions were made.

No laissez-faire administrator, Mr. Gilmore did not shirk from using his experience and expertise or exercising formal authority. However, rather than using that authority to impose a solution, he drew on it to promote schoolwide participation in defining the challenges that Giovanni faced. He collaborated with teachers to develop sound solutions that could gain broad support and thus would be implemented widely and well. One teacher characterized Mr. Gilmore's interdependent leadership style: "He's the driving force, but the teachers are sort of pushing behind him. He's not like pulling us through."

Contrasting Responses by Teachers to These Different Leadership Approaches

When a principal's approach to adaptive challenges is inclusive, as Mr. Gilmore's was, many teachers become engaged in diagnosing problems, debating options, suggesting new approaches, choosing a path forward, and then implementing and refining their initiatives. Teachers' leadership at Giovanni was interactive and generative. When, as at Stowe, teachers are excluded from identifying and deliberating about the school's problems, yet are expected to comply with administrators' solutions, they report feeling disempowered and resentful. If they fear that the principal can use formal authority to reprimand or punish them, they may seem to comply while actually withholding their commitment and effort, thus undermining the possible benefits of the principal's strategy.

Defining and addressing leadership challenges at Thoreau

With those approaches to leadership in mind, let's return to Ms. Thomas at Thoreau High school. Her long-time predecessor at Thoreau had believed that hiring good teachers was the key to school improvement. He met with each candidate and selected those he thought were outstanding—often by virtue of their being graduates of elite colleges—and then counted on them to know what to do. His hands-off, laissez-faire approach to leading the school was neither instrumental nor inclusive. An experienced teacher recalled him saying, "I hire stallions to come in here and run." However, Ms. Thomas was not inclined to step back while teachers exercised leadership, nor was she adept at including teachers in diagnosing and addressing adaptive challenges. Instead, she liked to take charge and solve problems. As we saw in chapter 5, she was convinced that some of those veteran teachers whom her predecessor had viewed favorably were no long effective, and she set out with her administrative team to document their weaknesses and dismiss them.

Ms. Thomas said that teachers at Thoreau were inclined to "look the other way" when problems erupted outside their SLC, and she believed that the students would not succeed unless teachers accepted responsibility for implementing systemic schoolwide changes that she and her administrative team defined. She explained, "Like warfare, . . . you have to be strategic. You don't get this job done by having good teachers in every classroom and then no strategic plan." She reflected on the paradox of empowering teachers to implement a change, which necessarily curbed their freedom: "[T]he school can't get better if teachers don't buy into what's happening . . . so the teams of people have to take responsibility and run this. And I know that [in order to make this happen] I have to take away some of the independence people enjoyed because . . . people can't just come in and do what they want."

Ms. Thomas sought to find the right balance between using her authority to introduce new structures and sharing that authority with teachers who would implement and develop them. After three years, she had not eliminated the SLCs, as some teachers feared she might, but she had sought to create greater curricular coherence by instituting weekly meetings of schoolwide subject-based teams, so that teachers would begin to map their curriculum and create model lessons. As we saw in chapter 3, some teachers, especially novices, appreciated these opportunities, but many others saw little purpose in the subject-based meetings and thought that they consumed their time without benefiting their students or improving the school.

In another, more controversial schoolwide reform effort, Ms. Thomas recommended substituting a block schedule for the current six-period day. When teachers voted on the principal's proposed change—a right guaranteed by their union contract—they rejected it. A veteran teacher recalled: "We felt like something was up their sleeve. In general, the staff felt, 'This is not good for us. There is something funky going on here.' So people voted against it basically. The school was very divided. And maybe the schedule that would have been better for the school did not happen."

Ms. Thomas's approach to leadership at Thoreau High School fell between the instrumental leadership of Ms. Sterling at Stowe and the inclusive leadership of Mr. Gilmore at Giovanni. She neither actively solicited teachers' views and suggestions nor engaged them in reviewing or improving the changes she initiated, but she acknowledged that, because of the union contract, she could not impose a block schedule without their approval.

However, something interesting was happening when we visited Thoreau a year after teachers rejected that schedule change. A small group of administrators and teachers, calling themselves the "Revisioning Committee," began to hold open meetings with their colleagues before and after school to discuss how instructional time was organized and explore ways to use it better. They exercised leadership by initiating a process to review their current scheduling practices and explore alternatives. At the time of our study, support was growing for a newly proposed block schedule. Several teachers explained that they had rejected the initial proposal because they resented being excluded by Ms. Thomas from the process of developing it, but they were willing to consider a similar proposal that grew out of broader discussion that included teachers and was responsive to their influence.

One teacher involved said that Ms. Thomas's agenda was "still very young," and that "things are moving along, but pushing and pulling." Such "pushing and pulling" revealed both the limits of the principal's formal authority and the potential for teachers' leadership throughout the school. Some teachers (especially those early in their career who had been hired by Ms. Thomas and had less allegiance to their SLC) seemed inclined to support the changes, while others (especially more experienced teachers hired by the prior principal and committed to their SLC) opposed anything that might be interpreted as a concession to Ms. Thomas.

Some might conclude that Ms. Thomas encountered difficulty because the teachers contract limited her freedom to hire and fire teachers or decide to change the schedule without the teachers' approval. Assuming that the principal knows best, some reformers have called for increasing the principal's formal authority and reducing teachers' rights. However, our research, as well as that of others, suggests that having formal authority isn't enough—it all depends on how it's used.

SUCCESSFUL SCHOOLS: USING AUTHORITY EFFECTIVELY IN TURNAROUND SCHOOLS

As state officials have intervened recently in chronically low performing schools, they have granted principals far-reaching authority over most decisions and practices in their school, such as hiring and firing teachers, allocating funds, defining the daily schedule, requiring a longer workday for teachers, and regulating how teachers use that time. In most cases, this authority supplants the rights and privileges that teachers may have gained earlier through collective bargaining. These principals could exercise even more formal authority than Ms. Thomas, Ms. Sterling, or Mr. Gilmore could.

These changes in policy made it possible for us to consider whether expanded authority for principals affects how teachers might respond. Although our research in two successful turnaround schools can provide only suggestive, not conclusive, findings, the accounts of teachers and administrators suggest that, even when principals have extensive authority, they would do better to use it to lead inclusively with teachers rather than to direct them instrumentally.[9]

Different Responses to Principals' Use of Authority at Hurston and Fitzgerald

When state officials placed Hurston K–8 and Fitzgerald Elementary in turn-around status in 2010, the WCSD superintendent, with the state commissioner's approval, appointed Mr. Hinds and Ms. Forte, respectively, as principals of the two schools. At the time, both schools had failed to improve, despite receiving the state's formal warning as well as substantial grants to fund improvement efforts. The newly appointed turnaround principals had the authority to hire an entirely new staff, but they had to replace at least 50 percent of the current teachers. Both Mr. Hinds and Ms. Forte required any current teachers who wanted to continue at their school to reapply for their position.

Both principals were under intense pressure to quickly assess their current teachers' practice while simultaneously recruiting teachers from other schools both within and beyond WCSD. Administrators and teachers recalled a period of fear and resentment as these principals rapidly met with every teacher, informing them one-by-one whether they would be rehired or forced to transfer to another WCSD school. Fitzgerald's assistant principal, Ms. Forsythe, called the experience at Fitzgerald "dreadful, to tell you the truth. Some of the teachers . . . had been here for over twenty years or more. . . . Even though it was quite a dysfunctional staff and a not-so-good culture . . . people were close to one another." Ultimately, Mr. Hinds replaced 85 percent of Hurston's current teachers and Ms. Forte replaced 65 percent of Fitzgerald's.

Unlike this unilateral, top-down approach to initial staffing decisions, however, these principals' efforts to rebuild practices in their schools were notably collaborative and inclusive. Both principals faced "adaptive" academic challenges that had no easy answers, and they solicited teachers' advice about what to do. However, the principals also had their own views about what should happen, and therefore teachers at Hurston responded more favorably than some of their counterparts at Fitzgerald.

Leading at Hurston

When Hurston K–8 first opened in an attractive, well-equipped facility in 2003, the school was participating in a WCSD labor management reform that granted the school and its principal autonomy from the district office for making key decisions about curriculum and assessment, staffing, scheduling, and budgeting. Teachers were expected to participate in decision-making, but ultimately the principal had the final say. Despite the school's autonomy, however, Hurston never prospered. Students performed poorly on the MCAS and waves of teachers repeatedly left the school. Mr. Hinds, the seventh principal in seven years, characterized the rate of teacher turnover as "colossal," noting that Hurston had lost at least 50 percent of its teachers every year since it opened: "It just churned through people unbelievably." He said that the school had the reputation of being "the worst school in this state, in a horrible neighborhood that no one would ever want to work at."

Students, too, he said, "knew that there was no success at the school." Mr. Hinds recalled the first day of turnaround, when an assistant principal had opened an assembly by saying, "'I'm really excited to be here,' [and] kids actually replied, 'No, you're not. No one's excited to be here.' 'This is a SPED school.' 'You're lying.'" Mr. Hinds explained, "It captured their beliefs about themselves. It captured the beliefs they had built about being in special education. . . . The school was full of negative self-image and negative everything."

Hurston's position as "one of the five lowest performing schools in the state" led Mr. Hinds to ask: "Where do you start with seventh graders that have had abysmal failure for five years? You can't start with the seventh-grade curriculum. You can't start with 'what's the difference between a fraction and a ratio?' when the student can't actually explain what a fraction is, or a student can't multiply successfully." Viewing this instructional challenge as an adaptive one, he thought that teachers and administrators "needed to think at every grade, 'How do we tackle this problem of incredible failure? How do we set a goal that's attainable?' and not just say, 'Well, we'll be proficient,' because we're not going to be proficient in a year, or two years, or three." In his view, the school faced "deep systemic challenges that we had to tackle."

During the spring and summer before the school reopened under turnaround, Mr. Hinds convened a small planning group of administrators and teachers to review the challenges that they faced and decide what to do. Eventually, the group settled on establishing instructional teams at every grade, where teachers would collaborate in making decisions about curriculum and instruction. One teacher recalled, "It was the plan of what we were going to do, how [Mr. Hinds] was going to help us turn around this building, how we were all going to work together to make it happen." Mr. Hinds recalled difficult early days when they had no curriculum to rely on. Before the school reopened in September, the faculty met for professional development and teams began to form and plan the work ahead.

With very few exceptions, Hurston's teachers strongly endorsed Mr. Hinds's shared approach to leadership. He explained, "If you're a principal that micromanages the day-to-day work, the school fails. . . . I wanted people who could say, 'Here's the data. Here's what we need to do. This is what we're doing.'" Once teams had a plan and wanted to "give it a shot," he felt confident authorizing them to move ahead. As they did, Mr. Hinds said that he and other administrators helped the teams "problem-solve and think through some of the potential unseen consequences of that plan . . . [but] I couldn't be the person that had to be the 'yes man' for everything." One teacher described the principal's leadership as "a really good balance of really high expectations that we place on each other and that the administration places on us as educators. But then also giving us the freedom to take the risks to do things the way that we see best, not the way that somebody is dictating. High expectations, high demand, but freedom to feel like I have ownership of my own work. I have ownership of my own decisions, so I think that's very positive."

Another teacher told of a recent professional development session where the presenter asked small groups to discuss, "What's holding this thing together?" He recalled his team's response: "It wasn't really coming from a cocky place, but some of us said, 'You know what? *We* hold this place together. We're the total package. We put in a lot of work and a lot of time and a lot of effort and energy. We want the kids to do well . . . and that's why this place is successful.'"

Leading at Fitzgerald

Fitzgerald entered turnaround the same year as Hurston and faced similarly daunting challenges. Ms. Forte explained that the school had been "in a very steady decline," with test scores continuing to decrease "year after year." Sixty-five percent of Fitzgerald's students had failed the MCAS, a situation that assistant principal Ms. Forsythe called "devastating. How could this possibly happen? How could this be?" Not only was student performance unacceptably low—in the bottom 5 percent of schools statewide—but conditions for teaching and learning were dreadful as well. Ms. Forsythe said that parents "didn't feel that their kids were safe, . . . respected by their teachers, or cared about." Still, "the children [not the adults] ran the school." Ms. Forte concurred: "[T]he building was absolutely wild. It was filthy. It hadn't been painted. . . . It was like a prison—fire alarms pulled every week, fights." She recalled that initially all she and Ms. Forsythe did in this preK–5 school was "patrol the building with walkie talkies, just trying to focus on learning."

In addressing Fitzgerald's academic failure, Ms. Forte initially took more responsibility than Mr. Hinds did for defining an improvement strategy, although she gradually engaged teams in that process. She was determined not to have teachers focus on discrete skills, "as a lot of high-poverty schools do," but rather to "foster higher-order thinking."

Teacher teams at Fitzgerald were still revising their curriculum when we visited after the school had been released from turnaround. Ms. Forte said that a year earlier, the entire school had "completely changed how we taught math." She described how "the fourth-grade team went off campus for a day. The first day, they just took the state standards and no outside curriculum. They just mapped out the state standards, trying to figure out what's most critical for somebody in this grade level to know. Then they tried to peel back to the objectives."

During their next off-campus meeting, the team examined alternative curricula "to see how each approached instruction for those objectives." In the end they drew primarily from two programs that helped students understand the foundations of math, rather than simply learn to apply algorithms.

Teachers' views of their principal varied at Fitzgerald much more than at Hurston. Some were satisfied, like one teacher who described the school as "self-governed, with the leadership actually guiding us along. So far, so good." She said that Ms. Forte "presents ideas and we are allowed to run with it. Then she'll either agree or disagree with it. If she disagrees, she will say why and what we can do to improve it or change it around. You can pretty much try to bring her to your way of thinking. It may not always work, but she's open to listen. She'll say, 'Bring it on. Let's hear what you have to say, and we'll decide.'"

However, other teachers viewed the process of making decisions as neither open nor inclusive. One, who called the administrators "very difficult," explained: "It's very hard to know what is okay and what is not okay. . . . The expectations are very high, but there's not the kind of support that there should be. . . . I don't think they realize that when they say things, people really take them to heart." Another teacher, who called the school "a monarchy," said that Ms. Forte didn't accept teachers' views: "If [her approach is] not working, she has a hard time listening to teachers and taking their advice." A third, who said leadership was "a buzz word" at Fitzgerald, explained that she "[led] silently" among her peers, but didn't get invested in team meetings. "I help underground, in underground ways."

Different Ways of Defining and Authorizing Leadership at Fitzgerald and Hurston

What explains why teachers responded differently in these two schools? Both Hurston and Fitzgerald relied on teams to make important decisions about a wide range of matters, including curriculum and instruction. In those meetings, teachers were active and influential as they identified and responded to the adaptive challenges their school faced. One explanation for teachers' different responses lies in how these two principals defined and used their formal authority.

Although Ms. Forte scheduled time for regular team meetings and delegated day-to-day instructional planning, she firmly held on to her right to accept or reject the teams' decisions. In contrast, at Hurston, Mr. Hanover, who directed professional development, said the school had a "distributive vision" of leadership. Teacher teams had a very clear mission and set explicit, annual goals. Within those, he said, "they could make decisions that are in the best interest of the school to help meet those goals." In the process, there was "a lot of [our] asking 'why?' and 'is that aligned with our vision?' and then saying 'yes,' or tweaking it." When a team seemed to veer away from the school's mission, a Hurston administrator might say, "No, you don't get what we're trying to do here. Let's go back to the big picture." Whereas Ms. Forte rejected the teams' proposals and decisions that did not conform to her strategy for improving Fitzgerald, Mr. Hinds and his administrators turned the deliberations back to the teams, asking them to consider the school's goals and urging them to rework their proposals. Mr. Hanover recalled, "More often than not, it was saying yes to [teachers'] good ideas to solve challenges that we didn't have an answer to or we didn't even anticipate." Through this process, Hurston identified and addressed the kind of adaptive challenges that Heifitz describes.

At Fitzgerald, authority was treated like a fixed commodity, which Ms. Forte could delegate to teams, but then reclaim when she disagreed with their decisions. At Hurston, however, authority was far more fluid and shared throughout the school. Organizational psychologists Kenwyn Smith and David Berg provide a perspective on authority that echoes Ogawa and Bossert's conception of leadership as an organizational quality.[10] They argue that real authority doesn't reside in roles, but instead "flows through many places to many people" who can then enact it. Rather than focusing on formal authority—who has it and who doesn't—they urge participants to focus on an interactive process that they call the "dynamics of authorizing."[11] For example, teachers can authorize principals to propose a plan for school change, while principals can authorize teachers to test, modify, and develop that plan. Paradoxically, Smith and Berg explain, one gains rather than loses authority by authorizing others. It was this kind of give and take that characterized the generative approaches to leadership we found at

Hurston. Although Ms. Forte delegated considerable authority to Fitzgerald's teachers, they remained confined by their formal roles and the conventions of the school's hierarchy. As a result, the potential for leadership sometimes fell short of what Fitzgerald needed.

FORMAL ROLES FOR TEACHER LEADERS

So far, in discussing teachers' opportunities for leadership experience, we've considered only those that all teachers can regularly exercise in the course of their work, both schoolwide and as members of instructional teams. However, many reformers argue that, even if the principal's approach to leadership is inclusive, teachers' influence is inevitably limited or short-lived if they lack well-defined, durable roles as leaders. This usually means being compensated with additional pay or released time, and knowing that their position has ongoing authorization and funding. In the context of a school's hierarchy and well-established professional norms, such visible recognition, compensation, and assurances of continuation can give teacher leaders the standing they need with both administrators and peers to successfully lead schoolwide practices. However, as we learned, it also matters how these teacher leaders are expected to relate to their peers.

Teacher Leaders for Support or Supervision?

For the final four years of my high school teaching career, I was one of four teachers who held a new role called "house teacher." Despite its unassuming title, the role carried substantial administrative authority. We were each responsible for overseeing the attendance, behavior, and academic performance of two hundred students. We could call conferences with their teachers, their parents, or both. We could arrange counseling, suspend students, and readmit them. We also were members of the principal's cabinet and, alongside other administrators, generated proposals for improving the school. For this role, I was released from teaching two classes, but received no extra pay. Years later, when I began to study teacher leaders and the difficulties they often encounter from their peers, I wondered why we had met so little resistance from other teachers. In retrospect, I think it was because the role of house teacher not only sounded unassuming, but also was designed to support fellow teachers rather than supervise them.

In 2004 my colleagues and I at the Project on the Next Generation of Teachers wanted to learn about new roles for teacher leaders, which were becoming increasingly common in schools. Therefore, we interviewed twenty-five teacher leaders in a wide range of schools; they all held positions that were compensated with released time or extra pay. However, only some of these teacher leaders were expected to coach or assess their peers, while others were supposed to support them, as the house teachers at my high school did. We learned that, when teacher leaders tried to coach or assess their peers they often were rebuffed, their advice was ignored, or their expertise was directly challenged.[12] For example, a fifth-year teacher appointed to be a math coach was expected to organize professional development meetings, demonstrate sample lessons for other teachers, and provide feedback on their teaching. She said, "I cannot even enter one teacher's room because he is not open to me coming to his room while he teaches. . . . There are other teachers, especially teachers who have been teaching a long time, who aren't comfortable with being observed, period."[13] One explained that when a teacher leader was appointed without a competitive selection process, she risked being seen as "the principal's pet." However, in two schools where the principals explained to teachers how and why the teacher leaders were selected and in what ways their work would contribute to the school's improvement, they had more credibility among their peers and were better positioned to do their work.

Consulting Teachers in PAR

Several years later, we studied the role of consulting teachers (CTs) in the Peer Assistance and Review (PAR) programs described in chapter 5. Central to the success of PAR in each district was a cohort of well-respected CTs who were responsible for working with a caseload of novice and struggling veteran teachers. They offered advice and help, observed classes, provided feedback, and eventually conducted formal evaluations. In carrying out their responsibilities, CTs necessarily exceeded the traditional boundaries that separate teachers who consider themselves peers.

Several factors contributed to the authority CTs exercised and the respect they earned. First, their role and responsibilities were clearly defined in the teachers contract and in district documents. Second, they were selected in an open, competitive process by a panel of teachers and administrators who managed the program. Third, CTs had sufficient time for their work; most were not teaching or taught only part-time. In addition, most earned an additional stipend for the extra time their work required. Fourth, CTs gained respect for providing intensive support and valuable advice to both novice and experienced teachers. Fifth, teachers trusted CTs because they were truly peers who would return to the classroom after they completed their three- to five-year appointment. And finally, CTs were respected because they had the authority to make recommendations—usually decisive ones—about whether teachers in their caseload should be renewed or dismissed.

Combined, findings from these two studies suggest that when teacher leaders have well-designed roles, are carefully selected in an open process, and receive systematic support and compensation, they can make valuable contributions to both their peers and the school, even when they exercise responsibilities that teachers rarely hold and might be viewed as violating traditional norms.[14]

T3 Teacher Leaders in Turnaround Schools

Teacher leaders served as facilitators on instructional and student support teams during turnaround at both Hurston and Fitzgerald. In selecting and developing these teacher leaders, the schools relied on a national nonprofit organization, Teach Plus, which sponsored a privately funded program called T3. Teach Plus recruited nationwide for T3 positions, although many of those appointed at Hurston and Fitzgerald already were local WCSD teachers. Teach Plus then conducted an intensive selection process where candidates participated in group simulations, designing action plans, analyzing data, and demonstrating that they could collaborate effectively. Principals of the turnaround schools then interviewed finalists with their own school's needs in mind. One T3 leader at Fitzgerald recalled, "You needed to be able to work with other people and you needed to do it for the common goal of getting students really accelerated."[15]

Based on their anticipated needs during turnaround, Ms. Forte selected eight T3 leaders and Mr. Hinds chose eighteen. For the next three years, Teach Plus provided monthly training for the cohort of teacher leaders from three turnaround schools, including Fitzgerald and Hurston. Much of their training focused on skills for effectively leading teams, such as creating an agenda, facilitating discussions, and collaborating schoolwide with other teacher leaders. Each T3 leader continued as a full-time teacher, while also receiving an annual $6,000 stipend for the additional work, funded by federal School Improvement Grants. Administrators and teachers throughout the schools praised T3 leaders for contributing to their teams' success.

Although the T3 teacher leader's role was well defined, supported, and compensated in the turnaround schools, the work was still difficult, in part because it encroached on the traditional professional norm of egalitarianism. As Mr. Hinds observed, "It's harder to lead your peers than it is to be a supervisor." Ms. Forte had that concern in mind when she decided to appoint only T3 leaders who already had been rehired to teach at Fitzgerald. She said that she did not want "new people coming in" with the message, "We're going to fix the school." In our interviews, teachers at both schools strongly endorsed the efforts and accomplishments of T3 leaders, who, as one explained, were careful not to say, "'I'm the leader'. . . . You don't say, 'I'm the boss.' I need my whole team on this. . . . It's all of us."

Not only did the T3 leaders benefit personally from their new skills and expanded influence, but their work enhanced the leadership of other teachers within their school as well. However, several T3 leaders at Fitzgerald suggested that they were constrained by Ms. Forte's narrow definition of their authority. One recalled a meeting that he and other teacher leaders requested with her, where they explained the problem: "We're the little leaders. We're the ones in the school that are creating change and leading the change, but [we] have no real authority." He said that they were asking her, "How do we work together [with you]?" In retrospect, he thought that the meeting "worked very well." As evidence, he noted that four years later, seven of the eight original T3 leaders were still at the school exercising leadership. This suggests that an ambitious plan of school improvement can be enhanced by a cohort of teacher leaders if their qualifications are vetted, their roles are well defined, and supervisory support is ongoing.

Hurston further invested in T3 facilitators by supplementing Teach Plus's funding for a half-time "embedded" supervisor with an additional administrative position. Mr. Hanover, who had deep experience as a teacher leader, instructional coach, and high school principal, explained, "Teach Plus and our T3 teacher turnaround teams were an integral part of the turnaround [strategy] right from the start." By the final year of turnaround, he was meeting weekly with each T3 leader to review the prior week's meeting and plan for the next. He also advised the school's full cohort of T3 leaders, who created Hurston's agenda for professional development. Without exception, the T3 leaders praised Mr. Hanover for his skilled guidance. One said, "He's a natural leader. He gives really great advice. He's just always really level-headed and he's always thinking. . . . He's just my go-to-person."

When the funding ends

The initial investment in T3 leaders occurred prior to our research and well before Hurston and Fitzgerald achieved Level 1 status. However, one important development in this story played out the following year while we were conducting our study. Once the schools were released from turnaround, funding for T3 roles, ongoing training, and school-based supervision ended. As with many supports for school improvement, reformers apparently assumed that additional funds were needed only until the school stabilized and had been successfully "turned around." Then the scaffolds of support were removed, presumably with the new roles for teacher leaders standing strong.

At that point, unless Mr. Hinds and Ms. Forte were willing to abandon the T3 roles—which they weren't—each had to devise a plan for continuing them. They chose very different approaches. Mr. Hinds raised $25,000 from a local foundation to pay facilitators a reduced stipend and to fund two head teacher leaders, who in turn supervised a cohort of facilitators. Mr. Hanover said, "I wouldn't say that we have it all figured out, but the idea is that people are getting collegial support for that work and not from me all the time." His vision for his own role was that:

> ultimately it ceases to be needed [and] the things I do become part of the way teacher leaders support one another and . . . the kinds of strategic things, [such as] the way we use our meeting times and the way we use data and other student work, are embedded in the culture. . . . I want that culture and that knowledge base to not be tied to individuals but be part of the school's culture. I don't know if it's possible, but that's my vision, that's my goal.

One of Hurston's new T3 cohort leaders described the new process as "gradual release" and said it was working well. The second concurred, explaining, "We're constantly adjusting it. I think it's the right path."

Ms. Forte had always thought that the $6,000 stipend for T3 teacher leaders was too high. Therefore, after Fitzgerald emerged from turnaround, she decided, with the teachers' endorsement, to end all funding for the positions and require every teacher in the school to serve in one or more leadership roles—as team facilitators or members of schoolwide committees. Also under her initiative, Fitzgerald applied to become an Innovation School within the state, which would continue some of the school's autonomy over its schedule and assessments that it had exercised during turnaround. Central to this proposal was the principle that all teachers would be leaders. Except for a few—such as the head of the student support team, whose responsibilities demanded extra time—no teacher leader received extra pay.

When we visited during the first year of this new arrangement, teachers said that the former T3 facilitators continued in their roles, although some thought that their influence might diminish over time. Several wondered whether these facilitators would gradually reduce their effort once that funding ended. Would the recognition that reinforced the efficacy of the T3 leaders' role dissipate if they were no longer recognized as having special expertise? One former T3 leader at Fitzgerald voiced her doubts about eliminating the paid positions and expecting all teachers in the school to be leaders:

> I don't know if that's necessarily a realistic vision or goal. . . . When there's so much piled upon you at a school like ours and you're so worried about all the things you need to do for your own classroom, sometimes people don't just automatically step up. . . . I think we have really cohesive, hard-working teams. . . . There's still always somebody who's getting the ball rolling. But that's usually the people who did it for the last three years. Maybe that's a little bit of a downfall. It's hard to transfer that.

CONCLUSION

As they work to improve their schools, urban educators like those at the schools described here inevitably face complex adaptive challenges that are poorly understood and therefore don't have obvious solutions. If schools are to effectively address those challenges, then teachers must be key agents of change, rather than the objects of change they are frequently expected to be. The knowledge they have acquired about their students, coupled with their insiders' grasp of how their school currently works, is a valuable resource to mine, not one to ignore. Because the possibility of leading—whether by initiating, joining, or resisting change—runs throughout the school, teachers can find many ways to influence their school's direction and the pace of change, even when formal leadership opportunities are unavailable to them. However, if schools are to make steady progress in improving students' learning opportunities and accomplishments, then teachers' potential to exercise leadership by diagnosing and addressing problems should be encouraged and cultivated.

Handing off this work to outside consultants, as Ms. Sterling did at Stowe, or trying to impose top-down reforms, as Ms. Thomas did at Thoreau, not only excludes teachers from understanding the problems they face, but also deprives the school of their insights about what might work better and how. A principal who takes an instrumental approach to leadership may extract teachers' reluctant acquiescence, but will also likely fuel quiet resistance as teachers' leadership goes underground. By contrast, at Giovanni, Mr. Gilmore's inclusive approach to leadership kept teachers in the game by stoking their interest and fostering their commitment to identify and solve problems together.

However, inclusive leadership is not the norm in most urban schools. Recently, Richard Ingersoll and his colleagues analyzed teachers' responses to the TELL survey conducted in sixteen states between 2011 and 2015. They found that in schools where teachers reported having a substantial say in schoolwide decisions such as those discussed here, students performed significantly better on state tests, suggesting that engaging teachers in leadership pays off for students as well as teachers. However, only 8.5 percent of the respondents who taught in high-poverty schools said they had such influence.[16] Our cases illustrate both what happens when a principal forecloses opportunities for teachers' leadership and what results when she opens and cultivates them.

Our research also highlights the important role that school-based autonomy played in the progress made by Hurston and Fitzgerald as they moved from failure to success. The principals had freedoms that their counterparts in district schools did not. However, what mattered in these successful schools was far less the autonomy of the principal to run the school, as some might think, than the autonomy—and therefore the responsibility—of *all* the school's educators to address their problems together. In fact, Mr. Hinds observed that immediately after Hurston opened in 2002, the seven principals who preceded him had access to much the same autonomy he gained under turnaround. However, he explained, those principals had failed to effectively "leverage" the school's freedom to define and implement an improvement plan.

Formal teacher leaders, selected and trained by Teach Plus, were key to implementing reforms in both schools, and the ongoing support provided both by Teach Plus and school-based administrators increased the value of teachers' contributions to those reforms. However, here, too, the principal's stance toward teachers as leaders made a difference. At Fitzgerald, Ms. Forte retained tighter control of formal authority than Mr. Hinds did at Hurston. Some Fitzgerald teachers reported feeling limited and dissatisfied by her constraints, while Hurston's teachers said they were energized and encouraged to take risks and experiment with new practices. As a result, Hurston's teachers and administrators benefited from a continuous process of authorizing one another to pursue further change.

To the extent that teacher retention data reflect a school's success in promoting leadership among teachers, both Hurston and Fitzgerald were successful. Each school was losing no more than a few teachers annually, who were said to leave for personal reasons rather than because of dissatisfaction with the school. Each school's reputation as a good place to work also generated interest among prospective teachers. Mr. Hinds reported that 102 candidates applied for a recent opening, whereas "four years ago, I'd have four." However, whether this stability and growth continued would likely depend on how current and subsequent principals viewed teachers' potential for leadership, as well as whether there would be sufficient financial and organizational support for teacher leaders' roles.

Whether and how teachers can influence change in their schools often turns on whether they have sufficient time to do so. With that in mind, we turn in chapter 7 to teachers' time—how much they have, and how it is allocated within schools.

CHAPTER SEVEN

Making the Most of Teachers' Time

AN EXPERIENCED WCSD TEACHER was livid when he read in the newspaper that teachers are "paid high salaries" for "part-time work." Complaining that critics never account for all the time teachers must spend that is "not in front of kids," he challenged: "How did those papers get graded? How did those tests get graded? How did those lessons get planned? How did those phone calls get made to parents? How did those resources get into that classroom? Who shopped for them? Who paid for them?"

Though seldom studied, teachers' time is arguably the most important resource available to their school, and many critics believe that teachers don't spend enough of it there. However, international comparisons suggest otherwise. The average US teacher is required to work 7.6 hours in school each day, considerably longer than his counterparts in other developed countries, whose workday averages 6.4 hours. US teachers also spend more time per day instructing students—an average of 5.5 hours—than teachers in other developed countries, who teach an average of 4 hours daily. In fact, teachers in two of the highest performing nations—Finland and Singapore—spend far less time than US teachers instructing students each day, 4.2 hours and 3.4 hours, respectively.[1]

Nevertheless, many critics of US education call for increases in the teachers' workday with more time instructing students. This is not surprising, given convincing evidence that the individual teacher makes the greatest in-school contribution to students' learning.[2] These reformers apparently reason that requiring teachers to spend more time in school and on instruction will help students learn more, even though international research casts doubt on that expectation.[3] However, little attention is given to the time required to complete the many activities that support instruction, such as planning classes, grading papers, meeting with parents, and collaborating with colleagues, which must occur either during the noninstructional hours of the teacher's in-school workday or on her own time.

The demands of successful teaching virtually always exceed the time that teachers have available during their workday, especially in US urban schools. In 2015, the American Federation of Teachers, the union representing teachers in many large, urban school districts, found that "time pressure" was the "everyday stressor in the workplace" most frequently cited by teachers in its 2015 Quality of Worklife Survey.[4]

Although teachers might disagree about how best to use their time in addressing the complex demands of their students and schools, most would agree that there is never enough of it. But time to do what? To teach students? To meet and plan curriculum and lessons with colleagues? To gather materials and prepare for class? To grade students' work and review their progress? To confer with students or their parents? To learn new skills? Realistically, if their students are to succeed, teachers must do all of the above, despite having scarce time.

This chapter explores the complicated challenges that time presents for urban teachers as they work to educate their students and improve their schools. Drawing on case studies of twelve district and charter schools serving low-income students in Walker City, it first examines key issues about teachers' time—how much is required, how it is used, and who decides. Then we consider two recent changes in policy and practice that center on time—common planning time for teachers and extended learning time for students—both of which have introduced new opportunities and expectations for teachers about how they manage and spend their time.

THE TEACHER'S WORKDAY

Of the twelve schools located in Walker City that we studied between 2010 and 2015, the required workday for teachers ranged widely, from a minimum of 6.5 hours to a maximum of 9.25 hours.

However, four of the eight district schools in our samples (Whitman Academy High School, Stowe Middle School, Hurston K–8 School, and Fitzgerald Elementary School) were free to set their schedule as a result of state and local policies, and in all of them, teachers worked a longer school day than WCSD required. In addition, teachers in these schools often spent more hours of that workday instructing their students than their counterparts in the charter schools we studied. Therefore, even across the WCSD schools, wide variation existed in the length of the required workday and the hours teachers spent instructing students.

How Schools Allocated Teachers' Time

In addition to their instructional time, teachers in all schools had time set aside for planning and preparation. All but one, Rodriguez Charter, designated time for formal collaboration among teachers. In addition, most teachers in district schools were required to spend one to two hours each week supervising bus arrivals and departures or monitoring the school's cafeteria, corridors, and restrooms. In the charter schools, these responsibilities often were assumed by teachers-in-training, aides, or administrators. All schools also required teachers to attend periodic staff meetings and professional development sessions, which occurred once or twice a week in the charter schools and biweekly or monthly in most district schools.

In charter schools, administrators decided how teachers used their time during the workday, while in district schools, these decisions emerged from a combination of union contract provisions, the principal's priorities, and teachers' preferences, usually in that order.

How Teachers Allocated Their Time Beyond the Formal Workday

We learned from both teachers and administrators that virtually all teachers in these schools complied with the formal requirements for their in-school workday. Even so, most said that they could not complete many essential tasks during that time—grading, reading, planning lessons, calling parents—no matter how efficient they were. With very few exceptions, these teachers worked additional hours to get their job done, and they were on their own to decide how much additional time to spend as well as when and where to do so. As they did, various factors influenced their decisions, including how much teaching experience they had, the prevailing professional norms and expectations of their school, their personal commitments and responsibilities, and how well their school was organized and managed.

Teaching experience

Beginning teachers need extra time as they learn to teach. As a first-year English teacher, I quickly discovered that reading and commenting on students' essays is a surprisingly difficult and time-consuming task, one that I had never practiced in my preparation program. To a novice teacher, everything is new, and being unprepared not only shortchanges students but also risks humiliation. Therefore, the new teachers we interviewed tended to work long hours at their school, whether or not they were required to do so. Often they arrived at school before sunup and left after sundown, working "dark to dark," as one teacher quipped.

More experienced teachers had decided how much time they needed to spend in order to do a good job and established their own routines. Many reported that, although the decision was theirs, they still worked long hours. For example, one teacher from Morrison K–8 School described her workweek: "I get to work at about 7:10 in the morning and then I stay until 5:30 or 6:00 most nights. And then I'll go home and sometimes I'll even finish up with more lesson planning. . . . It takes me a lot of time. I sit down over the weekend and all of Sunday I look at my books and I make my lessons."

In contrast, another experienced teacher from the WCSD magnet school, Whitman Academy, said, "Some of us more than others live and breathe our jobs. I don't think I'm one of those people. I definitely have a very strict cutoff about what I'm willing to do and not do as it intrudes into my personal life." However, like most of his colleagues, he still worked more hours than his school required.

School expectations and norms

As these teachers' comments suggest, many teachers work well beyond the required workday. In some cases, the principal might urge teachers to be available to meet with parents after school or, as at Angelou Elementary, visit parents in their students' homes. Often teachers gauged their real obligations by watching their colleagues. A Thoreau High School teacher said: "It's a very common part of the school culture to be here early and to stay late." In other schools with different professional practices, a teacher might conclude that it's acceptable to arrive and leave at the same time as his students, yet that was not the case in any school we studied.

Personal commitments and responsibilities

Some teachers cannot arrive early or stay late because they have young children. Although we know from decades of research that teachers choose to teach primarily because of the intrinsic rewards their work offers, a teaching career also provides an important secondary incentive—having a schedule that is compatible with family responsibilities. Teaching has long offered what one teacher called "mom's hours." Teachers could leave for the day in time to be home with their children after school and get back to their work after their children's bedtime. However, as Fitzgerald principal Ms. Forte explained, many urban schools such as those we studied are "on a mission," and that mission obliges teachers to remain longer at school. For parents of young children, this creates an ongoing and stressful tug-of-war between the needs of their job and the needs of their family.

Over the past twenty years, I have interviewed many young teachers who work a frenetic pace of 24/7 in high-need, urban schools. They often describe how exciting, important, and fulfilling their work is, only to quickly add that they could never sustain its demands if they had children. One fourth-year teacher at Stowe Middle School said, "From the minute I come in at 6:45 until the minute I leave at maybe 4:30, my brain has no time to stop." She predicted that her exhilarating but exhausting schedule would end before long because she was planning "to have children in the next couple of years." She explained: "I don't think I would be able to sustain the level at which I am going right now. . . . It is consuming my life. I have to make a concerted effort to have [both] school time and life time. . . . Sometimes it blurs and it gets really difficult and I try to balance the two, but it is difficult."

Such accounts of early-career teachers are common and raise pressing questions. How much on-the-job time can schools realistically expect of their teachers? And what is the tradeoff between requiring more in-school time and avoiding unnecessary turnover among them?

The organization and management of the school

Arguably, schools should be organized so that teachers can use their in-school time well, although in many urban schools, that's not the case. For example, when schools provide teachers with the curriculum, books, and teaching materials that they need, they can use their preparation time efficiently to plan for their classes. However, when they're obliged to scour the internet, libraries, and used-book stores to find relevant sources, texts, and materials, little time is left to plan. For example, a Thoreau High School teacher complained about having to "spend a ton of time on curriculum development" because the only math book available for her class included concepts and methods no longer in use.

In a related problem, several teachers said that they could not copy the materials they needed for class because the school failed to maintain its photocopier. One told of arriving at school early so that she could make copies for her first class. But after "run[ning] around and [finding] every single photocopier broken or out of toner," she realized "45 minutes have gone by and I don't have these 20 copies. This is a complete waste of my time. What am I doing?"

Often overlooked is the price that teachers and their students pay when their school is poorly managed. If teachers think that their time during the workday is misused, they may be less willing to arrive early, stay late, try harder, or do more. The teachers we interviewed in Walker City said that they needed a reasonably quiet, orderly, and purposeful environment if they were to use their teaching and prep time well. For example, if a school lacks an effective system to ensure that students attend their classes on time, then those students may show up late, congregate in the halls, distract other students, and disturb their teachers. A Thoreau High School teacher was busy preparing for class when she was interrupted by a group of students who had congregated noisily outside her door. She stopped her work to intervene, making sure that each student returned to class. Then she realized how angry she was about the disturbance and the precious time it claimed: "You feel like, what was that little half-hour blip? You know, that wasn't part of my job. That wasn't part of my plan. That wasn't positive. It's horrible and it took all that time."

Teachers also were troubled by having their instructional time and plans upended by administrators. A teacher at Stowe Middle School described being dismayed by sudden changes in the daily schedule: "I just found out yesterday that there is going to be a field trip tomorrow, [for] a select group of children [in my class] . . . not everyone." She had planned to give a test, then realized that "half of the kids will get the test and the other half won't. And then I found out I'm going [on the field trip]. I just found that out today. So now nobody is going to get the test and there is going to be a sub." She added in exasperation: "You have to be really flexible to work here . . . because every day there's something interrupting the schedule." One of her colleagues complained about a similar disruption when staff from a local hospital spent several days at Stowe working with students from various science classes, which caused some of her students to miss class. Although she recognized the benefits this experience had for students, she criticized the administration for "overscheduling" them and "not following through with the management of those things." She said she felt "lost in the shuffle" when the principal, Ms. Sterling, failed to inform teachers about "exactly what's happening."

Several teachers complained about being required to fill out forms or respond to "bureaucratic" requests for information that seemed only remotely connected to their work. One teacher said, "The less time you spend asking for the attendance list, the more time you get to teach. And the less time you're frustrated about not [having it], the more time you have to think proactively about 'How I can make my [class] that much better?'" In joking with her "nonteacher friends," she explained that it was not the students who made her job difficult: "I'll take crap from twelve-year-olds and I'll come back the next day and, to the best of my ability, give them a blank slate. But adults should know better."

Annoying tasks, broken equipment, and sudden interruptions or changes in the schedule intensify the stress that teachers already experience as they try to make the most of scarce time. Ultimately, that stress is likely to affect not only how much time they spend outside of school, but also the quality of the work they can do. Many teachers do their best in frenzied school contexts despite such interruptions and annoyances, but some teachers eventually decide to leave either their school or their career after what one teacher called "a thousand small cuts." A Stowe Middle School teacher who described her colleagues as "awesome," went on to ask rhetorically, "Why would you leave?" She quickly answered, "Because it is crazy. It is so crazy."

Therefore, the length of the teachers' required workday is, at best, a starting point for understanding the important role that time plays in teachers' lives. Not only do their personal needs and experience as teachers influence whether and how they can manage the demands of their schedule, but also schools differ in how they allocate teachers' time and how much discretion teachers have in deciding how to use it. Further, the quality of administrators' leadership and management is crucial in creating and maintaining a school environment where teachers can use their time well. These factors are important to keep in mind when considering reforms that substantially change the schedule and the allocation of teachers' time.

REFORM IN THE TEACHER'S WORKDAY: THE EMERGENCE OF COMMON PLANNING TIME

International comparisons reveal that US teachers have far less time available for planning and preparation than teachers in other countries.[5] In response, many reformers and administrators over the past twenty years have not only increased teachers' noninstructional prep time, but also arranged the school schedule so that the teachers' planning periods align with those of colleagues who teach the same students or subject, an arrangement widely referred to as common planning time (CPT).

Starting in the mid-1970s, public school teachers gradually gained more time during their workday for planning and preparation. Often these increases were won for teachers by their local union, rather than being introduced by administrators in an effort to improve instruction. Secondary school teachers have long had a daily "free" period, which could readily be arranged because students changed classes throughout the day. However, because elementary teachers traditionally had full-time responsibility for an entire class of students, providing planning time introduced the extra expense of hiring specialists in music, art, and physical education to teach students when their classroom teacher had prep time. Therefore, increases in elementary teachers' preparation time lagged behind those of secondary teachers.

The pace of change in providing preparation time for WCSD's elementary teachers offers a typical example. In 1987 they won the right to have two preparation periods each week, which increased to four in 1991 and then five in 1995—one per day. After the negotiators deliberated about whether teachers or principals should decide how that time would be used, they specified in the 1991 contract that preparation time should be "teacher directed," but also that teachers should use it "primarily for educational planning, team meetings, and parental contact." Apparently, this did not satisfy administrators' concerns, because in 1995 principals gained the contractual right to direct how teachers used one preparation period every other week, which increased to one period weekly in 2010. Therefore, when we studied WCSD schools, both elementary and secondary teachers had approximately fifty minutes daily for preparation and planning; the principal could decide how teachers used one period each week, while teachers could decide what to do with the remaining four.

Notably, as districts granted teachers more preparation time, the purpose was not to create opportunities for more collaboration among colleagues. In fact, preparation time was largely conceived with the individual teacher in mind—time when she could complete some of the many tasks good teaching required. Therefore, very few administrators scheduled the same free period for colleagues teaching the same subject or students. If the preparation periods of two fourth-grade teachers or two first-year algebra teachers coincided, it probably was unintentional. Nonetheless, teachers might take advantage of this fortunate coincidence to share materials, exchange advice, or even coplan classes during their prep periods. By contrast, in many of the charter schools that opened after 2000, designers deliberately incorporated substantial blocks of CPT for teachers during their workday.[6]

How Schools Included in the Teaching in Context Study Organized CPT

At the time of our 2010–2011 Teaching in Context study, most WCSD schools had scheduled teachers' preparation periods as CPT, and in the schools we studied teachers reported considerable variation in how that time was used. For example, at Morrison K–8 School a fourth-grade teacher whose colleague was "just a door push away" said, "We talk almost every day about what's happening in the classroom. . . . We're doing similar things. . . . We try to stay on the same pace, to follow the same subjects, the same content. Like if I make a work sheet, I'll share it with her and if she makes one, she shares it with me. So there's a lot of stuff that you'll see both classes doing."

She acknowledged that, although she found such collaboration "incredibly useful, it really depends on the pair. It's people and personalities. I feel like I got lucky because the teacher I work with, she's great and we understand each other. . . . I could see how it doesn't always work."

In fact, another fourth-grade teacher at Morrison, who had recently been reassigned from another grade, had no colleague to work with regularly. She explained, "You always grab a minute to speak to someone. . . . I'm always banging on the fourth-grade teacher's door to ask for help: 'What does this mean? Can you help me, please?'" Her account was consistent with that of a third Morrison teacher, who regretted that teachers' use of CPT was not better organized: "We don't have what other schools call 'common planning time,' or at least what it should look like, which is teachers with their plan books or computers and materials saying, 'We prioritize this' or 'No, let's look at this.'" Therefore, although scheduling CPT created possibilities for collaboration, there was no assurance that all teachers or their students would benefit.

In contrast, Thoreau High School teachers had three hours of CPT weekly within their small learning community (SLC). Unit leaders (who were also teachers) then decided with their colleagues how to use that time. One SLC designated a period for individual preparation, a second period for shared instructional planning, and a third to review students' progress. A teacher explained how they used that time: "During common planning time, one meeting a week, we do presentations on a topic [teachers] feel they do well. It might be technology in the classroom or helping special ed students access the curriculum. . . . So the unit leader will ask for volunteers. . . . He has a list of suggested topics, or you can do whatever you want. This has been new this year. And then the other meeting [focuses on] student support."

Like many of her peers, this teacher valued her SLC meetings and appreciated that teachers could decide how that time would be used. Another said that "having those small groups of teachers and working with them and meeting with them all the time has probably been the thing that makes me most want to stay here, as opposed to going somewhere else."

The principal's role in directing teachers' use of CPT at Thoreau and Stowe

Thoreau's principal, Ms. Thomas, who could direct how teachers used one period of CPT each week, required them to meet schoolwide by subject area. As we saw in chapter 3, many teachers thought their time in those departmental meetings was not well spent. One said he would prefer to have "more time to meet" with SLC colleagues, adding that teachers would "definitely" put additional time to good use.

Because Stowe Middle School had an extended learning program with extra compensation for teachers, Ms. Sterling could direct much more of her teachers' CPT, and she scheduled them to meet in different configurations throughout the week. On Mondays they conferred with colleagues who taught the same subject. On Tuesdays they discussed individual students with teachers at the same grade level. On Wednesdays they met as subgroups within grade levels to review their instructional practices under the supervision of an external consultant. On Thursdays they met again by grade level to review the behavior of their student cohort, focusing on discipline and recent student suspensions. Every other Friday teachers met again by grade level to, as one teacher said, "have our own time."

Some of Stowe's teachers welcomed the chance to have, in one teacher's words, "so much time to foster relationships within our faculty and to support the students." However, many complained that they actually had few opportunities to plan curriculum with other teachers or to prepare individually for class. One expressed her frustration:

> I don't know what's happened. When I first came here, we had time to meet with our coteachers and collaborate, and now we don't and I don't really know why. People say that they think the administration is eating up our time with tasks that don't really help us do a better job. It seems to a lot of people that these are tasks that are extraneous and take away [from the] time that we used to have and the time that we need to have to collaborate.

When we posed an open-ended question to Stowe's teachers about how to improve their school, many said that there should be fewer meetings and that teachers should have more say in how CPT was used. One contended that, despite daily meetings, "we haven't been able to meet as much as we would like. We meet a lot at lunch time, informally." Another agreed: "We love meeting with each other to discuss what's happening with our students and to plan special events. We have not had the time to do that, except if we do it literally outside of school time." In organizing CPT as she did, Ms. Sterling had a schoolwide purpose in mind—

increasing the regularity and efficiency of teachers' meetings—although many teachers suggested that her efforts to regulate their time were counterproductive.

These examples from Thoreau High School and Stowe Middle School illustrate the potential benefits that teachers saw in CPT and the opportunities it could provide. However, both cases also suggest that the value of CPT can be augmented or diminished depending on whether administrators understand teachers' professional needs and engage them in deciding how best to use the available time.

How the Successful Schools Organized CPT

In 2014–2015 when we studied six successful schools, we found that both district and charter schools provided CPT for teachers and that teachers had a substantial say in how they used that time. Teachers widely reported that collaborating during CPT paid off for them and their students.

The amount of CPT ranged from approximately five hours per week at Dickinson Elementary, the traditional WCSD school, to eight to ten hours per week at Naylor Charter School. Dickinson's staff included many veteran teachers who had taught at the school for twenty or thirty years and, therefore, remembered a time when they had only one or two hours a week for preparation. They generally viewed CPT as "their" time, which the principal might direct once a week, as their contract allowed. In contrast, Naylor's administrators had built CPT into the schedule when the school opened in 2005, and current teachers assumed that administrators were entitled to decide how they should use it. Despite these different histories, administrators and teachers at both schools regarded their school's scheduled time for collaboration as central to their success.

Dickinson's efficient use of CPT

Dickinson's principal, Ms. Davila, had organized her school's schedule so that groups of teachers in contiguous grades (K–1, 2–3, and 4–5) had one period of CPT every day. As we saw in chapter 3, she convened teachers in paired grades to review students' academic progress during one period each week. Teachers found these sessions worthwhile, although Ms. Davila said that having only one hour to examine student performance data and plan how to respond was "not enough; it really isn't." Still, teachers had easy access to their grade-level colleagues on other days and many met to plan curriculum, prepare lessons, share materials, and seek advice. Ms. Davila acknowledged:

If I walk around during their common planning time, they're usually sitting in each other's classrooms, talking about planning or something else. . . . They have lunch together and they don't talk about "Oh, what did you do last Saturday night?" They talk about, "I'm really having a hard time with Sally. Can anybody help me here? She's really not getting her high-frequency words, or she can't do her sibilant sounds." They're an amazing faculty. . . . They are a very hard-working staff.

Teachers' accounts confirmed Ms. Davila's. For example, Dickinson departmentalized reading and math instruction in grades 3 through 5. Two very experienced third-grade teachers shared responsibility for forty-eight third-grade students by switching classes for part of each day. One explained, "I teach reading; she teaches math. We get along very well. We cooperate in everything. We help each other. We do everything together, which is great." The math teacher said that she benefited from her colleague's "wealth of knowledge." In addition to sharing planning time, these teachers ate lunch together and talked by phone in the evening. Although other teachers described less extensive collaboration, they also appreciated and took advantage of the opportunities that CPT provided.

Ms. Davila said that, although she expected teachers to "give 110 percent," she did "not ask them to come in early or stay late, or anything like that." Here, too, she complied with the contract. Teachers were required to work 8:15 a.m. to 2:45 p.m., but as one teacher said, "Come on, who works 8:15 to 2:45? I'm okay working ten hours a day. I really am. That's what I do. I'm here early in the morning." She explained that "people here don't really follow the contract" but rather do things "to make the school successful." This was especially notable in a school with so many veteran teachers.

Therefore, Dickinson's teachers saw CPT as an essential arrangement that made collaboration possible. Their formal workday was shorter than others in the Successful Schools study, yet virtually all teachers said they spent longer than they were required at school and additional time at home exchanging ideas and materials by email and preparing for class. The teachers' respect for Ms. Davila and appreciation for how she managed their school, their shared stake in the school's success, and deep confidence in each other, and the school's strong professional norms that encouraged hard work by all combined to ensure that Dickinson's students were well served.

Naylor's expansive use of CPT

Teachers at Naylor Charter School were not unionized and had a required workday of 9.25 hours (7:15 to 4:30), nearly three hours longer than Dickinson's. Even so, many teachers said they came earlier than 7:15 and left well after 4:30. The principal's debriefs following classroom observations were scheduled before school, beginning at 6:30 a.m. The fact that many teachers stayed until 6:00 p.m. or later suggested that their administrators' expectations, bolstered by professional norms, encouraged them to spend many hours at the school.

Teachers' time at Naylor was carefully structured so that they met regularly with colleagues from their homeroom or grade level to monitor individual students' progress and plan activities for the cohort. They also met with colleagues from their subject area to coplan curriculum and lessons. Primary school teachers, who taught all subjects, met with the same group of teachers to carry out both activities. Elementary and middle school teachers, who each taught one or two core subjects, met regularly with their homeroom partners to plan activities for the twenty-five or thirty students in their cohort, but spent most of their CPT with colleagues who taught the same subject to different groups of students.

Although Naylor's administrators had created a highly differentiated and deliberately organized schedule, they didn't monitor how teachers used their grade-level or curriculum planning time. Importantly, it was teams, not individuals, who made those decisions. For example, a team might spend the entire block from 2:05 to 2:45 reviewing lesson plans for the following week, or they might decide to spend twenty minutes sharing feedback on lessons they all had taught earlier that day before breaking off individually to prepare for their next class.

In addition to these blocks of CPT during the regular school day, all Naylor teachers met for professional development every Wednesday from 1:00 p.m. to 4:00 p.m., after the students' early dismissal. The principal led the first session, which focused on an instructional topic relevant to everyone in the school. When we visited, that topic was teaching standards; earlier in the year it had been "positive narration—how to have and convey a positive vision for classroom culture." Typically during that time, teachers closely analyzed a video-recorded lesson recently taught by one of their colleagues. During the second session of the afternoon, teachers met for approximately two hours in grade-level or content teams to review and improve their approach to a common challenge. A fourth-grade teacher said that during the prior year the challenge focused on "reading—how to get more student buy-in and excitement about reading. This year, it's been focused on math—what is rigor in a math discussion and how do you lead a productive math discussion?"

Overall, Naylor's teachers thought that the allocated CPT was sufficient for teams to develop units and review lessons. However, most teachers—especially new ones—needed more time to write individual lessons and prepare for their classes, which they did after their formal workday, either at school or at home. Professional norms encouraged hard work and long hours for everyone, and all teachers we interviewed stayed at school substantially longer than the required workday. Although shared lesson planning reduced the demands on individual teachers for preparation, it increased expectations about the quality of those plans, which administrators reviewed and their colleagues taught. As a result, Naylor's teachers held high standards for the work they produced. Many spoke about the challenge of managing their responsibilities and maintaining the standards that those in the school expected.

The challenge of sustaining and retaining teachers

Naylor's teachers often discussed the stress they experienced as they speculated about how long they could sustain the current intensity of their work. Each year approximately nine of its forty-five teachers left the school, an annual turnover rate of 20 percent. Some teachers were promoted to other positions in the Naylor network, others left for graduate school, some left for teaching jobs in other schools, and some became parents who chose to stay home. Individuals offered various explanations for this high level of turnover, but most mentioned the school's long hours and high standards.

Teachers often suggested that they were caught between feeling proud of their accomplishments and being overwhelmed. One said: "Everybody is so high achieving and wants to do so well and we all care so much and we're so hard working. It's really easy to burn yourself out. The days are really long." Another echoed, "It's really hard, really exhausting, really time-consuming, but on the other side, really professionally fulfilling." She found herself thinking, "Well, I could maybe work less hard if I went someplace else, but I also wouldn't be able to see the same success from my kids. I have a hard time envisioning that." Another teacher said that Naylor "strikes a great balance between being very urgent [and] very focused on results, [having] very high expectations, without taking it to an extreme" and becoming "a joyless place." However, many more of those we interviewed would probably have agreed with this teacher's assessment: "You're churning through teachers at a much faster rate because it's just so intense." Ironically, CPT, which created valuable opportunities for teachers to collaborate as they planned and reviewed their work, sometimes raised standards and intensified expectations about what they should accomplish to the point that some teachers talked about leaving because of the pressure.

Naylor's network director said, "We want to retain teachers who are excellent, who want to be career teachers," but she also observed that "retention in and of itself" was not their goal. As a group, Dickinson's teachers were far more experienced than those at Naylor and only one or two left the school each year. Many of those we interviewed recited a similar mantra: "Teachers don't leave Dickinson, they retire from Dickinson."

With higher rates of turnover, Naylor had nine or ten new teachers each year who needed to learn how the school worked and then develop the skills and practices required to meet its demands. These novices appreciated having ample time to work with and learn from their more experienced colleagues. One novice said, "It's intense; it's draining. But you're surrounded by amazing, amazing coworkers who are way smarter than you and better at their job than you." However, the school's very few experienced teachers said that repeated turnover took a toll. One reflected that it "gets old." Another said, "Counting next year, for four years in a row, I'll have had a new [homeroom] coteacher and a new math planning person every single year." She said that "at this point in [her] life," she no longer wanted to be responsible for closely mentoring two new colleagues every year, "new to the school, new to trying to figure things out, or new to teaching math."

Naylor's teachers also repeatedly raised time as a concern—both the 9.25 hours they were required to be present and the additional time that they felt they were expected to be there. In contrast, Dickinson's workday for teachers formally ended at 2:35 p.m., when individuals could stay or leave without feeling judged. All Dickinson's teachers felt obliged to complete their work, but whether they did that at school or at home was up to them.

Differences in curriculum planning also affected the time that each school required of teachers. Most teachers at Dickinson had developed their curriculum over many years. If they adopted a new district-approved text or program, they would modify its use to meet their students' needs, usually with the advice of peers. However, as we saw in chapter 2, Naylor did not use an established curriculum and teachers were continuously developing new units and lessons that aligned with state standards. Although the CMO made all lessons from its three schools available to teachers online, those who took advantage of that resource found that they still had to rework (and often rethink) those lessons before using them. When teachers were new or lacked experience at the grade level or in the subject for which they were responsible, preparing detailed lessons for others' use proved to be very time-consuming. And with so many changes in staff, it was difficult for teams to build a curriculum that lasted for even two or three years.

Ms. Davila said that Dickinson benefited from having so many experienced teachers and practices refined over many years. At Naylor, as in many start-up schools, administrators had more teachers with youthful energy than with seasoned expertise. Generous CPT made it possible for the school to deal with the annual arrival of new teachers, who could be incorporated quickly into the school's professional culture and collaborative planning structures. However, doing so required a long and intense workday that discouraged many teachers from staying long-term at the school. If Naylor's administrators chose to maintain this high level of performance without adjusting its schedule, demands, and professional norms, it seemed likely that staff would continue to leave, undercutting the accumulated expertise that the school might acquire over time.

The challenge of scheduling collaborative time for specialists

Another related challenge that both Dickinson and Naylor faced was how to provide collaborative opportunities for the specialists who taught the art, music, or physical education classes and, in doing so, freed up CPT for teachers of core subjects. At both schools, these specialists carried a heavy workload, teaching every Dickinson student every week. The art teacher acknowledged, "Teaching seven classes a day can be really hard sometimes." She had planning time during first period and then taught seven classes in succession each day, from 9:35 until 2:35 with a break for lunch.

Further, specialists often had no colleagues in their content area. For a time, Naylor's specialists met on Wednesday mornings (when the core teachers all were instructing students) with their counterparts at other Naylor CMO schools. However, they found that it took too much time to travel and meet with those colleagues. And as one specialist pointed out, "Wednesday morning is really our only chunk of time to prep. . . . Now [we go to the other school] just once a month."

Dickinson's art and music teachers, who both were very experienced, expressed no concern about being the sole teacher in their content area. Given the long-term stability of the school staff, these specialists knew the other teachers well and didn't feel isolated. All teachers contributed to the school's annual fifth-grade musical—a defining ritual at Dickinson that integrated the arts and engaged everyone in the production.

Special education teachers had a related challenge. Dickinson had an inclusion program that relied primarily on push-in services, where special education teachers taught alongside the regular classroom teacher. Those special education teachers sometimes had CPT both with colleagues who had similar expertise and with their relevant grade-level team. However, this wasn't always possible because of their teaching schedule. At Naylor, where most special education services were separate or pull-out, specialists met only with one another, not with the core teachers. At both schools, special education teachers suggested that they felt somewhat removed from the collegial opportunities afforded to regular classroom teachers during CPT.

REFORM IN THE STUDENTS' SCHOOL DAY

As international comparisons showed US students lagging behind students in other developed countries, some critics raised concerns about what they believed was a short US school day and recommended more instructional time for students. Ambitious targets for improving students' test scores under federal and state accountability policies also drove such proposals, especially in schools serving low-income communities, where failure to make AYP under NCLB was common. Meanwhile, enrichment classes in art, music, and physical education, which had been staples in many school programs, often were cut back or eliminated, both because they claimed time that otherwise might be spent teaching tested subjects and because they were relatively easy targets for budget reductions following the 2008 recession. As a result, in many urban schools, classes in the arts were replaced by additional hours of direct instruction in math and ELA.

Stowe's Expanded Learning Time Falls Short

Two decades earlier, a funded initiative in Massachusetts prompted schools in several districts to expand their students' school day. Stowe Middle School participated in that program, lengthening the students' school day by two hours and compensating teachers for the extra time at their contractual hourly rate. At the time of our Teaching in Context study twenty-four years later, that program was still in effect at Stowe and teachers were earning additional annual stipends of approximately $10,000.

For many years, Stowe's expanded learning time was seen to meet its goals of improving students' learning and enriching their lives with opportunities they might not otherwise have. However, by 2010, Stowe's test scores were falling and enrichment opportunities had been cut back. A few teachers still endorsed the longer instructional blocks because they accommodated learning opportunities, such as science experiments that took more than a single period. However, other teachers said that administrators' anxiety about declining test scores was driving demands to use that additional time for more teacher-centered instruction. Many who had long supported the program began to say that they and their students were getting tired and that so-called enrichment activities, which once had included activities in the arts, debate, or chess, now were limited largely to athletics.

Extended Day in Lawrence Shows Promise

Meanwhile, extending the school day for underperforming, low-income schools was gaining support in other urban districts of Massachusetts, including Lawrence, a former mill town and the state's poorest community.[7] When the state commissioner placed the Lawrence Public Schools (LPS) in receivership for chronically low performance, he required every school to have a workday for teachers of at least 7.75 hours, more than an hour longer than WCSD's requirement. Jeffrey Riley, who was appointed by the state to serve as the district's receiver, had virtually complete authority to change local policy, including the school calendar and schedule. However, when the commissioner required LPS to increase instructional time and provide at least fourteen hundred hours annually for students, Riley allowed each school to decide the length of its school day within the state's parameters. Most schools adopted the minimum 7.75-hour day (7:45–3:30), although one remained in session until 4:00 and another until 5:00. Lawrence teachers received additional pay for this time, but their hourly rates fell far short of those their contract once guaranteed.

Lawrence schools used federal grants to hire additional teachers in the arts, while also partnering with community organizations, such as the YMCA, to provide enrichment activities and classes for students throughout the day. The schools' longer daily schedules also included more time for teachers to collaborate during CPT.[8] After five years in receivership, LPS had shown improvement in student performance, attendance, and graduation rates. However, a persistent 25 percent turnover rate among teachers remained an ongoing concern. In interviews, teachers and principals described being intensely committed to providing the best possible education for their students, but they also said that the longer school day was driving teachers away. They echoed concerns voiced by Naylor's teachers about the stress of trying to meet both the professional responsibilities of the longer school day and their personal needs, including family responsibilities.

These experiences implementing an extended school day at Stowe Middle School, Naylor Charter School, and in the Lawrence Public Schools raise an important question: is it possible for an urban public school to provide and sustain a challenging, rich program for students while supporting and retaining teachers? What we learned from studying Hurston K–8 School suggests that the answer is yes, but that the reform calls for creative planning and flexible practices.

Hurston K–8 Implements CPT and Extended Learning Time

Since 2003, when Hurston K–8 first opened as a new school in a new building, it had special status within the district, which gave the school autonomy to set its own schedule. Among the many changes the principal, Mr. Hinds, and his planning team implemented under turnaround were CPT for teachers and an extended day for students and teachers.

Abundant collaboration during CPT at Hurston

Before the school entered turnover, Hurston's teachers had noninstructional time daily for planning and preparation, as required by the WCSD contract. However, those blocks were not always aligned to permit or promote regular collaboration among teachers. As we saw in chapter 3, under turnaround, Hurston introduced CPT for grade-level teams in kindergarten through second grade and for both content teams and grade-level cohort teams in grades 3 through 8.

Like their counterparts at Naylor Charter, two Hurston teachers in grades 3 through 5 each taught two different subjects to the same group of students. In the middle school, however, core academic teachers specialized in a single subject. Depending on their assignment, Hurston's teachers could count on 2.5 to 4 hours of CPT each week and three additional periods to prepare individually for class.

During team meetings, the teachers planned instruction, although few prepared common lesson plans as Naylor's teachers did. In their meetings, Hurston's teachers also explored new topics about how to teach in their content area and tracked the progress of students in their cohort. A middle school math teacher was thrilled with how their time was organized: "We now have schedules that are like a dream. It's arranged so that our content and grade-level meetings are two consecutive hours a week. That uninterrupted time is so precious that we can actually get a whole lot of work done." A fourth-grade teacher said that, despite the school being sanctioned and placed in turnaround status, the experience of having enough time to work with his peers "felt like there was meaning behind the fresh start. It wasn't just platitudes. . . . Collaboration was encouraged and it was expected. It was like, why wouldn't we work together?"

Hurston's specialists in the arts (including visual arts, theater, dance, chorus, band, strings, and media) didn't meet with grade-level teams, because they, like specialists at Naylor and Dickinson, were teaching during the core teachers'

CPT. Instead, they met weekly as a separate team. Individual teachers then maintained contact with their relevant grade-level teams. As at Dickinson and Naylor, the arts teachers had demanding schedules. One visual arts teacher said that her schedule was "not sustainable. . . . We teach six classes a day, back to back, and lunch is short. . . . Time is everything." Although she said the rush was "definitely the number one disadvantage" of teaching art at Hurston, she still considered the opportunity to work there "one of the best experiences of my life." The school featured an annual art show that drew support from other teachers and enthusiastic attendance by members of the community. She also joined each year with other arts teachers to produce the school's very popular musical production. These activities ensured that, despite their packed teaching schedule, the arts teachers were not marginalized.

Integration of the teachers' workday and students' school day at Hurston

Whereas the standard WCSD workday for teachers was 6.5 hours, Hurston teachers were required to be at school for 7.5 hours (7:10 a.m. to 2:40 p.m.). Its professional development and data inquiry director, Mr. Hanover, observed: "We do have long hours, which for some veteran [teachers] is not attractive. We start early but don't end that late. If you're looking to get out to go pick up your kids, it's still a good deal. . . . We're a young faculty. We've had a dozen or more babies born to faculty members in the last two years and maternity leaves are constantly ongoing. We haven't lost, I don't think, any of those people."

Mr. Hinds had permitted two teachers to adjust their schedules so that they could arrive after the start of the official workday yet still fulfill the required number of in-school hours by staying later in the afternoon. One of these teachers, whose son's school started later than Hurston, said Hinds allowed her to arrive at 7:25, rather than 7:10. She was grateful for the fifteen-minute accommodation: "In general, when you ask him for something, if it's reasonable, he does it. If he can do it, he'll do it, and it's just that simple."

Several teachers explained that all teachers were present at school during the official hours, but then decided individually whether to also arrive early or leave late. One explained: "There are some teachers who are—their cars are here at 6:00 at night—who are just going at it really, really hard. I worry about that and I'm sure they worry about that. That's not driven by the administration. [The administrators] are not saying, 'If you're not here, you're not working.' It's understood that there are many ways to get a job done and the results are what we care about."

This teacher went on to speak about the "stability" that could be achieved in schools that find a way to effectively support new teachers while also retaining experienced colleagues who have "not burned out." He reflected, "There's got to be a sweet spot in there somewhere." He was confident that educators at Hurston would "figure it out," and he viewed Hurston's program as a promising "model for what [urban] schools could look like."

Hurston's middle school students had a seven-hour instructional day (7:30 a.m. to 2:30 p.m.), attending courses in core academic subjects as well as art, music, and physical education—all taught by Hurston teachers. Then, from 2:30 p.m. to 4:30 p.m., the nonprofit organization Citizen Schools continued the students' school day with what one Hurston administrator described as "a combination of academics and enrichment. . . . We've tried to make it more fun and less like more school." Citizen Schools staff, many recent college graduates who were considering teaching as a career, supervised students' homework time, tutored individuals, and sponsored sports teams, clubs, and apprenticeships for enrichment.

Extended learning time at Hurston was not an entirely separate afterschool program that started once the regular teachers were done. Instead, it was deliberately integrated with the school's core academic program, and Citizen Schools staff kept in close touch with Hurston's teachers. As one Hurston middle school teacher explained, a staff member from the extended-day program regularly attended his grade-level team meetings "to check in, saying, 'What are you guys working on? What issues are you having? Do you have any concerns for us?' There's always open communication." An administrator described how student cohorts in grades 6 through 8 carried a "clipboard with a travel tracking sheet" throughout the day. By the end of the day, it included the students' homework assignment for each class and an overall performance grade for the cohort, assigned by each teacher. He explained that when the cohorts arrived at the extended-day program, they gave their Citizen Schools teacher the clipboard, so he could see all their homework assignments and performance grades for the day. This let the Citizen Schools staff know "what [kind of] class they're getting for that day. If they have all A's, they're having a great day, keep it up! If they're getting Ds and Fs, the Citizen Schools teacher might be in for a rough road and kind of know what's ahead of him."

Hurston's regular teachers also participated periodically in the extended-day program. For example, during time designated for students to do homework, a science teacher from the regular school conducted a review for his students prior to an upcoming test. In addition, several teams of classroom teachers offered to identify and tutor small groups of students whose test data suggested that they had similar needs. An administrator recalled readily agreeing to these offers, responding with encouragement: "We would say, 'Yes, and we can pay you [for your time].'"

The Citizen Schools staff also served as a recruitment pool for the school. Two current Hurston teachers had first worked in the extended-day program. One had wanted to become an elementary teacher, but lacked formal preparation. When she applied to Citizen Schools, she was looking for what she called "sideways entry points" into teaching, "to get my foot in the door." In addition to teaching in the extended-day program, she was assigned to work in a math teacher's class, where she hoped to "find out whether I really want to work in a school. . . . It's a low-stakes way to try it. I really liked working here and I really liked this teacher and had a good sense about the people [on] the seventh-grade team." When a science teacher left for medical leave midyear, she stepped into his position.

These programs and experiences at Hurston illustrate how schools can productively use more time to serve both students and teachers. Unlike Stowe, where the rich experiences of extended learning time had gradually been eroded and replaced by direct instruction designed to raise students' test scores, Hurston's longer day supported students academically and socially, giving them access to enrichment activities they otherwise would not have. Meanwhile, teachers had more time to prepare and collaborate during their in-school workday. If they had young children, they could leave in time to meet them after school, before completing their work in the evening or on weekends.

CONCLUSION

The basics of teachers' time—how much they have, how it is used, and who decides—vary widely among urban schools serving low-income students, even those in the same city. Critics conclude, often based solely on teachers' required in-school work hours, that teachers have it easy, even though most of them are present at school one to three hours longer than they are required, arriving earlier than they must, leaving later than they can, and continuing to work at home. The length of the workday is important because it signals a school's expectations about minimal obligations. But far more important are teachers' actual practices and the norms and systems within the school that shape them. When teachers and administrators decide together how time can best be used, the decisions they make not only are likely to be sound, but also probably will be genuinely endorsed by those who implement them.

Whatever teachers' practices might be, our research suggests that a very long workday for teachers can be as problematic as a very short one. Teachers who hope to find a balance between teaching and other personal responsibilities and interests may decide over time that a long workday with steep demands makes teaching untenable for them. A school that depends on a steady stream of young and dedicated teachers who stay for only two or three years may well benefit from their energy and enthusiasm, but remain in a perpetual state of churn as early-career teachers are replaced year after year by novices. Such schools will never achieve the depth and stability they could if they had the autonomy, resources, and will to organize time in ways that simultaneously meet the needs of their students and teachers. Meaningful improvement cannot be done on the cheap or, as many warn, on the backs of teachers.

If all students are to benefit from the knowledge, skills, and cumulative experience of teachers, then time must be well administered and carefully protected for its intended purposes. The goal of effectively managing the schedule is not to monitor individuals, but to ensure that they can use their time well, both on their own and with their colleagues. In chapter 3 we saw how valuable and productive teacher teams could be, and chapter 6 discussed how much teachers can contribute to leading change. However, those benefits cannot be realized unless teachers have sufficient, regular time to meet. As the experiences described here illustrate, this depends on effective leadership by both teachers and principals, a strong and positive school culture, and professional values that endorse collaboration. If teachers don't have the time they need to work together and with administrators, then students will fail to benefit from the expertise of anyone but their assigned teacher. Therefore, providing CPT for teachers is essential if all students are to have the opportunity to learn that they deserve. Arguably, the value of that time will increase if teachers play a lead role in deciding how it should be used.

As the case of Hurston K–8 illustrates, it is indeed possible to provide both common planning time for teachers and an extended school day for students. Combined, these reforms provide students with a strong, rich academic and extracurricular program. But to have such an integrated program calls for a new perspective on time and how it can be used. The schedule need not be uniform or inflexible. The entire faculty does not have to be present in the building for exactly the same hours. What matters is that teachers do their work and do it well, both individually and together. During the course of the school day, students can benefit from instruction by professional teachers as well as learning opportunities provided by staff from partner organizations. Those approaches can mix and match in different ways at different times, while ensuring that the adults remain well informed and engaged in jointly progressing toward achieving the school's goals. Just as the school is more productive when it functions as an integrated organization rather than a collection of cellular classrooms, it will be more productive and satisfying if educators work together to use the time they have deliberately, efficiently, and creatively.

Although teachers' scarce time must be allocated wisely if students are to be well served, teachers also depend on sufficient, timely pay so that they can do the work they've chosen. That is the topic of chapter 8.

CHAPTER EIGHT

What Pay Means to Teachers

TEACHERS SEIZED NATIONAL HEADLINES in early spring 2018 when they marched by the thousands on state capitols in West Virginia, Kentucky, Arizona, and Oklahoma, protesting low pay and their state's failure to adequately fund schools. The teachers' numbers, vehemence, and persistence took both politicians and the media by surprise.

Although these seemingly spontaneous strikes in largely "red" states were un-expected, they should not have been. Teachers' annual pay in the states where teachers went on strike averaged between $45,292 (in Oklahoma) and $47,403 (in Arizona), while teachers in the nation's highest paying states earned on average far more—$81,902 (in New York), $79,128 (in California), and $78,100 (in Mas-sachusetts). When annual pay is adjusted for the cost of living, the states where the strikes occurred rank in the bottom quarter of all fifty in the US.[1]

Evidence of stunning state-to-state differences in teachers' earnings were hard to ignore. Polls conducted at the time of the strikes revealed that over 78 per-cent of the public believed that teachers are not paid enough, and 52 percent sup-ported those on strike.[2] Subsequently, Arizona, Kentucky, Oklahoma, and West Virginia approved raises to end the strikes, which lasted six to nine days and closed many schools. However, even when Oklahoma increased teachers' aver-age pay by $6,100, their wages still fell behind those of teachers in thirty other states. Writing in the *New York Times*, Paul Krugman captured the disappoint-ment and desperation that triggered these strikes: "So we're left with a nation in which teachers, the people we count on to prepare our children for the future, are starting to feel like members of the working poor, unable to make ends meet unless they take second jobs. And they can't take it anymore."[3]

The strikes, which were generally viewed as successful, may not have eliminated disparities, but they did focus policy makers' attention on teachers' pay. Is it sufficient? Is it fair? Compared to what? Arkansas school board member Robert Maranto asserted in the *Wall Street Journal* that teachers are underpaid and deserve a 40 percent raise, which he said "would lift the median teacher's pay far above that of accountants ($68,000) and into the same ballpark as civil engineers ($84,000)." Maranto further argued, "Surely educating the nation's children is as important as balancing books or building bridges." However, he also urged that the increases he proposed be made "in exchange for real reforms to improve teacher quality." He recommended recruiting the most talented graduates, making certification more competitive, and firing ineffective teachers, all human capital strategies that focus on the individuals who teach, but do not address shortcomings in the schools where they teach.[4]

HOW PAY AFFECTS THE PROFESSION

Teacher' pay unquestionably is a pressing and contentious professional issue. Critics argue that teachers already make a very reasonable wage, given their short hours and school year. Research findings on this issue are contradictory, largely because analysts begin with different assumptions about how best to measure teachers' work and pay. Some use an hourly wage based on teachers' required workday; others use weekly earnings based on time spent in school according to the school calendar; and still others simply compare annual salaries. As we saw in chapter 7, the time that teachers must work in order to do their job well far exceeds the hours of their formal workday and the days of the school calendar, making it nearly impossible to accurately calculate an hourly, daily, or weekly wage.

Teachers Earn Less Than Other College Graduates

Economists Sylvia Allegretto and Lawrence Mishel compared teachers' weekly earnings with those of other college graduates and found what they call a "pay penalty" for teachers. Their analysis showed that the gap in pay between teachers and other college graduates has been steadily growing for two decades. In 1994, teachers made only 1.8 percent less than others with a college education. By 2017, that pay gap had increased to 18.7 percent. Female teachers made 15.6 percent less than comparable female workers, and male public school teachers earned 26.8 percent less than comparable male workers. When these analysts considered pay and benefits together, the total "compensation penalty was a record high of 11.1 percent in 2017."[5]

In their 2018 report on teacher salaries, researchers at Education Resource Strategies note that in twenty-seven states, teachers' average pay now falls below the state's living wage. Further, they concluded that states where teachers are paid the least have more teacher shortages, a higher teacher turnover rate, and more uncertified and novice teachers than states that pay the most. Teacher shortages, these analysts argue, are increasingly exacerbated by low pay as the "value proposition" of becoming a teacher becomes less and less attractive.[6] Although the 2018 strikes highlighted state-to-state discrepancies in teachers' pay, the Paris-based OECD reveals that teachers' pay also should be viewed as a national concern. Of all its member countries, the US has the biggest salary gap between teachers and others with the same level of education.[7]

The Hidden Subsidy of Low Wages Is Gone

This raises the question of whether schools can attract and retain the teachers they need if their teachers earn substantially less than others with similar education and those gaps persist or widen. During the 1960s, teachers' pay was artificially suppressed by a job market that all but barred both women and men of color—teaching's traditional recruits—from pursuing higher paying careers, such as medicine, law, and engineering. If they wanted to be professional employees, these teachers had no choice but to be paid far less than they could have earned if other fields had been open to them. This created what is often called the "hidden subsidy" of public education, which enabled schools to attract and retain highly qualified teachers at low rates of pay. However, that subsidy began to disappear in response to legal and social changes during the women's and civil rights movements of the 1960s and 1970s. By 2000, when all fields were open to education's traditional recruits, the public schools' hidden subsidy had virtually disappeared. The average SAT scores of entering teachers had declined over time as many of the "best and the brightest" college graduates chose other careers.[8] Although many school officials failed to realize it, for the first time in history public schools would have to compete with many other fields for the talented, committed teachers they needed.

At that time, many reformers called for increasing teachers' pay in order to once again attract talented candidates. However, few districts today offer pay that successfully competes with compensation in other professional fields. As the strikes demonstrated, teachers deeply resent the growing pay penalty, especially as other resources for schooling also decline. National survey data analyzed by the US Department of Education in 2018 show that, overall, 55 percent of teachers are dissatisfied with their salary. Notably, there is scarce difference between the views of teachers in traditional public schools (55 percent) and charter schools (54 percent).[9]

Many think that the obvious answer to this problem of teacher supply is to increase pay for all teachers, which theoretically would attract stronger applicants and enable school districts to be more selective. However, addressing pay without improving the teacher's workplace will not likely deliver the benefits its proponents count on, because, as we'll see shortly, higher pay is unlikely to compensate for poor working conditions. Using pay as the sole or primary lever for improving teacher quality will be unsuccessful and wasteful unless policy makers and administrators understand what pay means to teachers and how it influences their work and their career decisions.

Good Pay May Attract Candidates Already Committed to Teaching

If states were to take teachers' protests seriously and grant the 40 percent raises that Maranto proposes, would they succeed in attracting strong and promising candidates who want to teach, but choose other work because of low pay? The answer is probably yes. However, it seems unlikely that salary hikes alone would attract and retain other promising candidates to teaching who were not compelled by the work itself and the intrinsic rewards it offers. Even if pay is high, teaching is very demanding, exhausting, and sometimes thankless work, with relatively low status, long hours (not short, as some argue), and, at best, average working conditions.

In 1998, Massachusetts created a $20,000 signing bonus (awarded over four years) to attract "high achieving" candidates who would not otherwise consider a teaching career. Recipients were required to complete a fast-track preparation program during the summer and begin teaching in a high-need urban school district in September. We interviewed thirteen of the fifty-nine original recipients and found that this substantial bonus had little influence on their decision to enter teaching. Many had prior experience in education and were attracted to this program not by the bonus, but by the brief summer training program that led to initial certification and promised access to a teaching position. Eight of the thirteen recipients we interviewed (62 percent) left teaching well before the four years they were required to remain on the job in order to receive the full bonus. In further research, Clarke Fowler found that after three years, twenty-seven of the fifty-nine recipients (46 percent) had left teaching.[10]

That research and interviews I've conducted with teachers over many years have convinced me that higher pay, in itself, will not likely attract and retain strong teachers, unless they already are familiar with schools and committed to working closely with students. Pay would, at best, be a secondary incentive for teachers, for there are far easier ways for a college-educated professional to make good money. Maranto argues, "Higher pay would attract talented college graduates who have other employment options but might prefer to teach, all other things being equal." It's those details, "prefer to teach" and "all other things being equal," that make all the difference.

Good Pay Can Make Teaching an Affordable Career

Many teachers who enter the classroom despite low salaries eventually find that, although they love their work, their wages don't keep pace with the growing financial demands of living a middle-class life, raising children, or buying a house. Teachers who manage to continue teaching, despite low salaries, often can do so only because they live alone, moonlight at a second job, or depend on a partner's higher income to subsidize their own.[11]

Having children is "a complete game-changer," as one teacher we interviewed explained. The needs of a teacher's children compete not only for her scarce time, as we saw in chapter 7, but also for scarce dollars in the family budget. Good day care, which makes teaching possible for a new parent, is increasingly expensive. In fact, some teachers view it as a luxury they can't afford and decide to stay home with young children. During the 2018 strikes, the media ran stories about teachers in low-paying states, such as West Virginia, who qualified for food stamps, which they in fact needed to feed their family.[12] Competitive pay would allow those teachers to contribute to the public good without having to rely on public assistance.

Therefore, pay alone is very unlikely to attract outstanding, committed candidates to teaching unless they are already motivated by the intrinsic rewards that the work promises. However, schools must provide adequate pay so that teachers who choose to teach because they love the work can afford to do so, both initially and over time.

HOW PAY INFLUENCES TEACHERS' DECISIONS ABOUT WHERE TO TEACH

The 2018 strikes highlighted the role of the legislature in determining a state's starting salary for new teachers and the overall state average in teacher's pay. However, it's important to keep in mind that wages can vary widely within states, largely reflecting differences in local commerce and industry as well as property values. With the growth of charter schools, which receive state funding and additional resources from corporations, nonprofit organizations, and individual donors, some public school teachers may be paid substantially more than others, not only from one district to another, but also from school to school within cities and communities.

Pay Differences Within the Walker City Job Market

Our study of six successful schools in Walker City allowed us to explore whether and how teachers responded to different pay options within a single, small job market. We explored the role that pay played both in teachers' decisions to accept an initial job offer and, subsequently, in deciding whether to remain in their position, transfer to another, or leave teaching altogether. As noted earlier, these schools often were competing for the same pool of candidates.

Teachers' pay in three WCSD schools was determined largely by the single salary scale established through collective bargaining with the local teachers union. In the three charter schools, pay and working conditions (including hours and the school calendar) could, for the most part, be independently set. WCSD's wages were higher than those of most other school districts and charter schools within commuting distance. In 2014–2015, the district paid first-year teachers with a bachelor's degree $51,099. In comparison, three other urban school districts within thirty miles paid novices $40,047, $41,718, and $44,292.

Many early-career teachers we interviewed said that they had accepted their job without knowing how the salary offer compared with what they might earn in nearby districts or schools. Some would have settled for any job, but most were looking for a position in a school they thought they would like. Only after they received a job offer—and for some, not even then—did they consider whether their salary would cover their bills. For example, one teacher with two years of experience had moved from a charter school in California and "was in desperate need for a job." However, because he had experienced "basic administrative incompetence" in his last school, he explained that he was "really looking" for a school "not only . . . where I would get a paycheck, but also where everyone was just professional enough in the administration and supportive enough that good teaching could happen." He chose Naylor Charter School, where he was happy to learn that his pay would be "something like" $5,000 more than in his previous school: "I was going to be a new, starting teacher here. I expected to maybe even dip a bit [in salary]. The pay was actually nice. I don't know how it really compares with other [schools in the Walker City area]. I've never done a search. I think maybe just for my own peace of mind, I don't really want to know."

It's not unusual for teachers to remain intentionally ignorant about their salary as this Naylor teacher did. During my earliest years of teaching, I knew many things about my job, but I couldn't have answered the straightforward question, "How much do you make?" In contrast, some teachers in our study who had grown up locally said they had considered only WCSD schools, because they knew from their family and friends that pay would be higher there than in other nearby districts. In no case, though, did any of these teachers suggest that the prospect of high pay had led them to teaching, even in Massachusetts, where teachers earn more than in most other states. Of course, we have no way to know whether other applicants who received an offer chose not to accept it because of low pay.

Pay influences teachers' decisions to stay or leave

For many early-career teachers, pay did not become an issue of real concern until they had been teaching three or four years. Then, as they anticipated or experienced changes in their life—marrying, having children, wanting to buy a house—they began to consider other positions that would pay more. For example, although Rodriguez Charter School experienced little turnover, some teachers did leave, as one veteran teacher explained, "because of money. . . . We get paid less than the Walker City School District, significantly less. And I think some people just need more money . . . you know, they're having families or they're—they need more money." Her colleague, who had five years of experience but was in his second year at Rodriguez, said that he also gradually had begun to think about pay: "I didn't become a teacher because I thought it was going to be, like, the most lucrative thing. I don't know. I don't know. I haven't thought that much about it. With my wife at school and having a daughter, we definitely don't have as much money as we used to have when she was working and I was working, too."

A third Rodriguez teacher with similar concerns about pay had been teaching primary school for ten years and was actively exploring other options. He said that Rodriguez administrators had assured him that he had "a job down at the end of the hall until I don't want it anymore." They valued his contributions to the school's young students, but he said they also supported his job search: "They know that I need more [money] . . . that I don't want to rent for the rest of my life . . . that I'm going to get married and we want to have a kid. . . ." He realized that the school couldn't pay more: "If there was more money, I know that they would pay us more, because even though they don't always say it, they definitely recognize how much we all work and they know that we're considerably underpaid for what we're doing."

This teacher was looking not only for a new teaching position he could afford, but also one that would provide increasing professional opportunities over time, such as becoming an instructional coach or department head. "I'm very happy teaching in the classroom and I'm thirty-three. I'm sure that I'm going to be teaching K–2 when I'm forty-three, but when I'm fifty-three, I'm probably going to want some sort of exit strategy out of the classroom." Although many schools and districts would welcome a successful male primary teacher, he was considering only schools in WCSD because of "salary, which is huge." After ten years at Rodriguez, he earned $67,000; if he had been teaching in WCSD, his pay would have been $92,000.

Working conditions often trump pay

However, high pay alone is not enough to sustain a successful teaching career. After state officials intervened because of poor performance in one WCSD middle school, Kincaid CMO restarted the school as Kincaid Charter Middle School. Under the terms of the agreement, Kincaid paid teachers at least the same salary they would have earned in a traditional WCSD school. Therefore, Kincaid Charter's teachers earned much more than their counterparts at Rodriguez Charter.

Most of the teachers we interviewed at Kincaid had fewer than four years of experience at the school and earned between $51,099 (with no prior experience and a bachelor's degree) and $68,449 (three years of experience and a master's degree). Mr. Kaplan, Kincaid's founder, explained that, although he was obliged to match salaries with those of regular WCSD teachers, Kincaid set its own calendar and schedule. Teachers worked a nine-hour day and all of August, far more than other WCSD teachers. Therefore, they earned substantially less per hour and per day than WCSD teachers. Mr. Kaplan explained: "They do not receive extra compensation for that time. . . . They are paid the same amount that they would be [paid] at any other district school . . . but they're not paid incremental hourly wages in any way, shape, or form."

Kincaid's teachers said they were glad to earn more than they could in most other charter schools, but some also expressed dissatisfaction with both the time that was required and the quality of their work environment. Teachers worked long hours, which some found overwhelming. Most who complained did not mention their low hourly rate, which compared poorly with that of other WCSD teachers. One exception was a teacher who planned to leave at the end of the year, saying he was "a parent and part of a family of four, who matter in this equation." After teaching four years at Kincaid, he was no longer overwhelmed by his job: "I know the deal. I know the drill. I'm comfortable. I have the systems down. I know what to expect. I know what they're looking for from me. Nothing's a huge surprise anymore." Nonetheless, he was looking for a school "that has better hours than this, where I could potentially be home to pick up my kids before I have to pay for afterschool care. That would be a huge savings to us. . . . We're talking $600 a month." He was indignant that the stipend he earned for being a teacher leader at Kincaid was going to be cut the following year from $6,000 to $2,500, and he role-played what he would like to say to the administration: "Well, so now you've docked me $3,500. I could probably make that up by being home at 3:25, and then some. I'd probably actually make out better."

Another Kincaid teacher said she earned much more there than she had at her previous school. Yet she described herself as "a very disgruntled employee right now" and went on to list the disadvantages of the school: "No one smiles. The leadership team has very little experience. All the deans, across the board, this is their first year." She also found the work overwhelming: "People here work so hard. When I leave here at 9:00 . . . there are [other] teachers here and they're busting tail. It's like they can never get [the job] done, because there's always something else." She had begun applying for jobs in nearby districts and was encouraged by a "great interview" the day before.

Salaries at both Rodriguez and Kincaid Charter Schools were much higher than those paid in Oklahoma or West Virginia. We heard of no teacher in Walker City who relied on public assistance to feed his family, despite the city's high cost of living. However, these charter school teachers compared not only their earnings, but also their hours, with those of teachers in WCSD schools. Sometimes, the demands of a longer school day or the stress of an unfriendly or punitive work environment intensified their financial worries. A nine-hour day meant not only spending less time with one's children, but also paying more for child care. Therefore, pay was certainly not the only important factor in these teachers' career decisions, but it did come into play, especially when teachers were dissatisfied with the demands and quality of their work environment.

THE SINGLE SALARY SCALE: A PRIMER

The single salary scale is currently used by more than 97 percent of public school districts with two or more schools, as well as by many independent and charter schools.[13] On it, pay is arrayed on a grid. From the bottom to the top of that grid run a set of ascending "steps," each representing an additional year of teaching experience. From left to right run a set of intersecting columns, each designating additional academic degrees and credits, such as "master's" or "master's +30 hours." The entire pay scheme of a large school district fits easily on a single sheet of paper and a teacher can quickly find his new salary by locating the box on the grid where his years of experience intersect with his highest academic qualifications. During my final year of teaching, I might not have been able to say what I was earning, but I did know where to find it—the box on the pay scale where nine years of experience intersected with having a master's degree.

The single salary scale is often criticized for being "rigid" or "lockstep." Despite its reputation for uniformity, though, the format accommodates many variations. The total number of steps (or years of experience) that a district credits with annual raises varies from district to district. If the pay scale "tops off" at eight steps, teachers move far more rapidly to the highest pay level than they would on an eighteen-step scale. That may be advantageous to early-career teachers, but disadvantageous to veterans, because once they reach the top of the scale, they usually receive no raise except an intermittent cost-of-living adjustment. Also a district may reward teachers for a master's degree or for a master's degree plus additional credit hours (+15, +30, +45), or a master's degree plus certification by the National Board for Professional Teaching Standards, or a doctorate. If a district grants an annual raise for many years of experience, the scale will be tall. If it recognizes many academic degrees and additional course credits or specializations, it will be wide. Whatever its shape, it is explicit, transparent, and even-handed, in that everyone with the same level of experience and credentials is paid the same.

In districts that bargain collectively, school officials and representatives of the local teachers union negotiate other rules that apply to the scale. For example, when new teachers with previous teaching experience are hired, the contract may limit the number of years that school officials can credit the teacher and, therefore, where he will be placed on the salary scale. Because a teacher's initial salary placement affects his pay in all subsequent years, this provision can make it difficult for schools to attract more experienced teachers. Newly hired teachers in WCSD could receive credit for no more than three years of prior experience, which would place them at step 4 on the scale, even though they might have ten years of experience in another district.

Further, if a district grants teachers a pay raise as a result of collective bargaining—say, 3 percent—the agreement also may call for the new money to be distributed so that every teacher's base pay increases by the same percentage or all receive the same dollar increases. Salary scales also can be adjusted to address staffing problems. For example, if a district wants to reward loyalty among mid-career teachers in order to retain them, it might successfully bargain to allocate more dollars to the paychecks of teachers on steps 7 to 15 of the salary scale and fewer dollars to veteran teachers, who are far less likely to leave. Therefore, the single salary scale can be used to address a variety of current issues or concerns, but it does so based on objective criteria that can be easily measured and verified.

The Single Salary Scale Has Advantages and Disadvantages

Despite its poor reputation, the single salary scale has notable advantages. The first is its objectivity. Adopted in the 1920s to eliminate favoritism and discrimination by race and gender, it continues to serve that even-handed purpose.[14] Second, it is stable, enabling teachers to anticipate their earnings and school districts to predict their costs far more accurately than if compensation were continuously reset or renegotiated in response to various qualifications, behaviors, performance assessments, and subjective judgments. Third, the single salary scale is efficient; once it is adopted, administrators and teachers spend virtually no extra time haggling about how to interpret or apply it. They can all get on with their work.

The scale also has disadvantages. First, in practice, its primary incentive is for teachers to stay put. Although that serves the school well if the teacher is skilled and productive, it is not helpful if the teacher is mediocre. Because teachers who transfer to a new district often lose credit for prior years of experience, a salary scale may discourage them from searching for better pay or working conditions, especially those who have extensive experience. Second, because salary scales do not take performance into account, a teacher who decides to coast by doing the minimum often can do so without financial consequence. Third, a salary scale invests a large share of the district's resources for professional development in continuing payoff for the academic degrees and credits that teachers have earned. Although teachers may be motivated to enroll in additional coursework because of the ongoing pay increase such studies guarantee, few districts monitor the courses teachers choose or the topics they study. There is no evidence that, on average, such additional coursework benefits students or that what teachers learn one year will be relevant five years later, especially in fields that change rapidly, such as physics or computer science.

AN ALTERNATIVE: MERIT PAY

Paying teachers for their performance is an old idea that gradually regained prominence in school reform agendas after 2000. In the 1920s, a period when reformers were captivated by the promises of "scientific management," and again in the 1960s, when policy makers were alarmed by the Russians' launch of *Sputnik*, school districts across the US enthusiastically adopted various merit pay plans, only to drop them after several years in response to a legion of technical, organizational, and financial problems: difficulties finding time to evaluate teachers, failure to apply criteria fairly, opposition by teachers unions, poor morale among teachers, charges of favoritism, funding shortfalls, the overall expense of the program, and the failure of pay bonuses to provide teachers the intended incentives and rewards.[15]

By 2000, proponents of merit pay—increasingly called *performance-based pay*—were convinced that new value-added methods (VAMs), which purportedly calculate the unique contribution that individual teachers make to their students' learning (as measured by standardized test scores), would solve the measurement problem that had vexed merit pay reformers in the past. The rationale of this reform was that successful teachers could be rewarded financially for achieving higher VAM scores, and therefore all teachers would be motivated to work harder. The prospect of earning such rewards was expected to attract strong candidates for job openings, making hiring more competitive. Those who succeeded in earning a bonus were expected to stay, while those who didn't receive the bonus would be discouraged and leave.

Implementing Merit Pay Remains Challenging

History and research about merit pay for teachers, as well as lessons gained from research about compensation in other sectors, raise many cautions about using pay to reward differences in teachers' performance. First, standardized tests, which are used to determine teachers' value-added scores, address only a few of the many goals that the public, parents, and educators themselves have for their schools. Teachers are expected not only to raise students' test scores, but also to develop their curiosity, creativity, critical thinking, democratic values, and an array of practical life skills. However, no test assesses so many aspects of students' development, and thus it would be impossible to reward teachers for all their accomplishments or penalize them for all their shortcomings. Also, a state often requires teachers to cover topics and skills that are not assessed by the standardized tests their students take. Moreover, VAM scores are currently available only for teachers of tested subjects and grades, making it impossible to use this method to assess every teacher. When districts persist in relying on standardized tests, VAM scores, and pay bonuses to motivate teachers, they risk generating serious, unintended consequences, including efforts by some teachers to game the test or even cheat by coaching students during the test or later changing their written responses.[16]

Second, using pay effectively as an incentive for better performance requires having a "clear line of sight" between the individual to be motivated and the behavior to be rewarded.[17] That is, if the prospect of higher pay is to serve as a potent incentive for teachers, then they must know how to achieve the desired outcome. This is especially challenging in schools, given the wide variation among students and competing beliefs about how best to educate them. As Richard Murnane and David Cohen report in their 1984 study of merit pay plans, teachers seldom knew the answer to two key questions: "Why is 'worker X' paid more than I am?" and "What can I do to earn higher pay?"[18] VAM scores may provide an answer, however disputed, about how much a teacher contributes to students' learning, but they never offer an explanation about what a teacher can do to improve his score.

Third, individualized merit pay fails to account for the complex, interdependent process of educating a student. Although it may be an effective means of motivating a worker when the task to be completed is relatively simple, short-term, and dependent on a single employee—for example, piecework or sales—it is not well suited for improving practice in an extended, complicated process, such as education, where a student's progress depends on many teachers' contributions over time. Why should a sixth-grade teacher be credited with his students' success or failure solving word problems when the reading skills they need to understand those problems were taught by language arts teachers in grades 3 to 5? Or why should a math teacher be rewarded for the efforts of a science teacher who taught her students basic algebra so that they could interpret the results of a lab experiment? It is virtually impossible to tease out the contributions made by each teacher to students' learning in any single subject, let alone all subjects. Clearly, this complicates the task of measuring merit and certainly undermines teachers' confidence in the process.

Finally, by basing teachers' pay—even a small part of it—on narrow evidence of their success or failure, reformers may compromise the school's potential to serve all its students well. Because the incentives embedded in most merit pay plans focus on the individual, not the group, they can unintentionally lead to increasing isolation and generating unproductive competition among teachers, rather than promoting more collaboration. Further, they can dissuade teachers from investing effort and time educating the students who are least likely to make rapid, testable gains, such as those with disabilities or English language learners, even though the school may be held accountable for those students' performance.[19]

Merit Pay Plans Vary Widely

In 2009, John Papay and I created a framework for analyzing merit pay plans.[20] It accommodates different types of programs, including those that are geared to individuals and groups, as well as those, such as evaluations, that use measures of teachers' performance other than test scores (see table 8.1). Our framework categorizes programs by whether top performers are identified by relative or standards-based rankings; whether performance is measured by student achievement, performance evaluations, or both; and whether awards are made to individuals or groups. Combined, these three dimensions yield twelve potential types of performance-based pay plans.

We then interviewed administrators to learn about thirteen distinct plans sponsored by four school districts. Our inquiry and analysis revealed that the process of designing and implementing a performance-pay plan is exceedingly complex and subject to many factors that may distort the purpose of the plan or derail it altogether. In the end, reconciling competing incentives for individual and organizational success may be impossible. Also, rewarding outcomes that yield extrinsic financial gains for teachers may interfere with practices that lead to the very intrinsic rewards they seek and that serve students well. Even a well-designed plan that takes many factors into account is often complicated by financial uncertainty and conflicting political preferences. Further, there is no way to know whether students actually benefit from financial incentive plans that are designed to motivate their teachers. Overall, we concluded that, although these local districts invested considerable resources and effort in designing their merit

Table 8.1 How to measure performance

		Student achievement	Professional evaluation	Mixed measures		
HOW TO IDENTIFY TOP PERFORMERS	Relative rankings				Individual	LEVEL AT WHICH TO PROVIDE AWARDS
					Group	
	Standards-based				Individual	
					Group	

Source: John Papay and Susan Moore Johnson, "Teacher Pay-for-Performance: A Framework for Program Design," in Johnson and Papay, *Redesigning Teacher Pay: A System for the Next Generation of Educators* (Washington, DC: Economic Policy Institute, 2009), 16–21.

pay plans, each had shortcomings and all encountered problems during implementation. None offered a sufficiently promising model that could be confidently adopted widely by other districts.[21]

THE PAY PLANS OF SIX SUCCESSFUL SCHOOLS

Teachers in four of the six successful schools we studied in 2014–2015 were paid according to WCSD's negotiated salary scale, while Rodriguez and Naylor Charter Schools had designed and were in the process of refining their own approaches to compensation.

The Single Salary Scale in WCSD

The story about pay in WCSD is that there is no story, beyond the fact that teachers and administrators generally were satisfied with their union-negotiated single salary scale. Virtually all teachers viewed their pay as adequate, even though many still thought that they and their peers remained underpaid for the work they do. As we saw in chapter 7, the teachers we interviewed often spoke about the stress of not having enough time to do their job well and live their life as they wanted, but none suggested they would rather have had merit pay than the single salary scale.

Early-career teachers often say that, because they work longer hours than some of their more experienced peers, they deserve to be paid more. They confidently assume that if their school offered merit pay, they would receive it. But no teachers in these successful schools made that argument or complained about their peers. One teacher who had taught in a WCSD high school for five years before transferring to Hurston K–8 suggested that, because he and his current colleagues put enormous effort into their jobs, the prospect of gaining a merit-based bonus would not likely motivate them: "Anyone who's worked at a high school in this district, I'm sure, has countless examples of teachers who have really no business being in a classroom, and certainly not being paid what we're getting paid. . . . At other high schools I've seen I would be like, 'Why is this person being paid money, the same amount of money as me?' I've never felt that here. Everyone here works hard."

His explanation suggests that the single salary scale might be problematic in schools where low effort is tolerated, but at Hurston, where administrators' expectations and professional norms supported sustained effort and accomplishment, no one thought that pay should serve as an incentive. It simply made teaching affordable work.

Several of these successful schools' interrelated practices, which were introduced in earlier chapters, combine to explain why teachers had such confidence in their peers. First, each school hired teachers carefully so that new entrants would anticipate and endorse their school's expectations about hard work. Second, administrators supervised teachers closely during their early years, helping them to improve their instruction and dismissing them if they failed to measure up. As a result, few, if any, slouches remained. Third, collaborative teams of teachers met regularly to deliberate about students and instruction, making it virtually impossible for teachers to remain isolated or ignore their colleagues' needs and expectations.[22]

Rodriguez and Naylor Charter Schools, which did not use the WCSD pay scale except as a point of comparison, were continuing to revise their approach to pay in response to the views of both administrators and teachers. Both had earlier used bonuses to reward effective teachers, but eventually dropped them. When we studied these schools, both were implementing a new salary scale. Rodriguez's scale incorporated no performance measures, while Naylor's did.

Rodriguez Charter's tailored single salary scale

Twenty years earlier, when Rodriguez Charter opened, administrators negotiated pay individually with every new teacher. Compensation was considered a confidential matter that teachers should not discuss among themselves. However, an experienced teacher recalled an incident some years later when Rodriguez administrators offered what he said was a "really, really high salary" to a "smooth talker" from out of state who taught special education. He said that the new teacher then "screwed up because he told someone how much he made." As a result of the complaints that followed, "that next year we implemented a pay scale." Reviews of past merit pay initiatives often report that performance-based pay plans collapse when teachers discover such pay inequities within their school, especially if they think a higher-paid teacher is lazy or ineffective.

Then, in 2007, Rodriguez adopted a new salary scale after analyzing pay in neighboring urban and suburban districts. The school couldn't match WCSD's pay, but it did base compensation on the average pay of other districts in the metropolitan area. Over time, however, finances at Rodriguez became tight when high mortgage interest rates on its new building limited the funds available for teachers' pay and the state reduced its per-pupil funding following the economic recession of 2008.

By 2013, school officials at Rodriguez found that they could no longer afford their current pay scale. In part, this was a consequence of their own success in retaining experienced teachers, whose salaries continued to rise. Also, however, administrators had sometimes ignored the single salary scale of 2007 when negotiating initial pay with a new teacher. An administrator observed, "There used to be a lot of flexibility. . . . We're trying to be much more standardized. I think, still, if there's somebody that's really, really wonderful, and we really want them, we would think about fudging that a little bit, counting something." Administrators were keenly aware that they were competing with WCSD schools to recruit new teachers and retain current ones, who would have been making much more if they had been teaching in a WCSD school.

In 2013–2014, Rodriguez appointed a compensation committee composed of teachers and administrators who then developed yet another salary scale that they were implementing when we visited. The school's director, Ms. Rowland, explained that, when Rodriguez had expanded eight years earlier, they hired many new teachers with little experience, resulting in a teaching staff with an average of only 2.5 years of experience. Gradually, that climbed to its current average of 6.7 years, with "easily a dozen people who are at ten years or more."

However, the school then encountered a new problem: retaining early-career teachers. In response, administrators created a salary scale designed to maintain teachers' commitment for at least four or five years. The steps of the new scale were deliberately uneven. Rather than granting substantial raises during each of a teacher's first four years, they held off until after the teacher had demonstrated success for three years. As one administrator explained, "It doesn't make sense to always give people step increases if they're only here for two years and then leave—and they weren't very good." The new scale awarded modest cost-of-living raises of .5 percent for the teacher's second and third years and then provided what one administrator called a "big boost" of 2 percent in the fourth year, followed by two more years of cost-of-living raises, before a second "big boost."

Increases based on this salary scale were never withheld because of a teacher's performance. Between 2007 and 2012, Rodriguez also had awarded merit bonuses. Each year, teachers received either no bonus, a small bonus ($150), a medium bonus ($300), or a large bonus ($500), based on a combination of what one administrator called "real data" (test scores), "objective data" (classroom observations), and "subjective data" (personal judgments). However, the school polled teachers in 2013 and, as one administrator explained, they "overwhelmingly voted not to have bonuses. They felt they were not transparent enough and a little capricious."

When we interviewed Rodriguez teachers in 2015, they offered very similar assessments of their pay. Early- and mid-career teachers expressed concern that their salary failed to keep pace with their financial needs, saying that over time it fell far short of what they would have made in WCSD. One noted that the school provided day care for teachers' children, which she found "really helpful." Yet she went on to characterize the problem of pay "from the teacher's standpoint: 'I don't know how to make this sustainable for me in a way that makes [teaching here] possible.'"

All teachers expressed confidence in their administrators' efforts to support and retain them. One who had been on the school's compensation committee said that in reviewing the budget, she was surprised that the administrators' salaries were so low, given their responsibilities. "We're like 'No way!' If this is what the top whoever is making, it's got to be a labor of love." The teachers appreciated efforts to ensure equity and provide transparency in pay. This seemed to be especially important, given the substantial demands on their time and Rodriguez's ambitious expectations for success—that 75 percent of students score at the proficient level on the MCAS.

Most veteran teachers at Rodriguez suggested they had figured out how to live on a modest paycheck, but still they had concerns. One explained that she had been at the school for "a very long time" and intended to stay: "I like it here. I like the quality of life that I have right now. I like my job. . . . [But] I have some salary issues." A less experienced teacher reflected: "I think the majority of us are here because we want to be teachers. I always find it fascinating when I meet people who are doing a job for the money. That just doesn't compute with me. I would do this even if I didn't get paid because this is what I do. I think for a lot of teachers here, that's how it is."

However, most of those we interviewed simply couldn't contemplate teaching for no pay—or even for less pay. Some, who also loved teaching at Rodriguez, said that they would have to leave if they could not make more money. Yet no one suggested that performance-based pay might solve the problem, and no one recommended reinstating bonuses or any other individualized approach to pay.

Naylor Charter School's performance-based career tracks

Before 2014, salaries for current teachers at Naylor Charter School had three components: a base salary, a standard percentage raise, and a bonus of up to

$10,000 that rewarded performance and retention. Ms. Nelson, the CMO's co-director, explained that these bonuses were "a pretty significant part of people's salaries." However, they were not awarded until October of the school year after they were earned. "If you didn't come back, you didn't get anything." Ms. Nelson said that new teachers, who were supremely confident and expected to receive the highest bonus, were the most ardent supporters of the bonuses. However, experienced teachers, who had come to realize that the bonuses fluctuated due to unexpected factors, agreed "the least" with this approach.

Like Rodriguez, Naylor had spent the prior year reviewing its approach to compensation. It held informational sessions and focus groups with teachers, asking them whether performance assessments should be based entirely on students' test results, entirely on evaluations, or a mix of both. Ms. Nelson said, "Most people really believed that it should be a mix." However, administrators also learned that the bonuses they awarded sometimes discouraged collaboration among teachers, because the money available to fund them was fixed and, therefore, "if everyone did better, then your raises were a little lower for the next year."

As at Rodriguez, Naylor's new salary scale did not grant teachers substantial annual increases until they had successfully completed their third year. Ms. Nelson explained that, in setting a new teacher's pay level, the school began with a base salary of $48,000 and an additional "$2,000 for every year of experience. We don't pay for master's, doctorate, coursework, anything like that." She said that a teacher's starting pay was "negotiable—not super-negotiable, but negotiable within a few thousand dollars. If someone wants double what we offered, it's not *that* negotiable." Then, for their first three years, teachers received only a cost-of-living raise. Those who returned for a fourth year received a promotion to one of three salary tracks and received a substantial pay raise.

The school decided to end bonuses in light of teachers' concerns that the awards did not reliably reflect their accomplishments. Instead, administrators incorporated performance measures into a simple career ladder with three tracks. All teachers who were invited back after their third year were assigned to one of these tracks, based primarily on their students' performance during the prior two years. In calculating the teachers' contribution to students' learning, the school relied on the state's measure of student growth, based on MCAS scores.

The "veteran track" included most of Naylor's teachers with at least three years of experience. They received a pay increase of 8 percent for 2014–2015. A second small group of teachers was placed on the "master teacher track," reserved for those few teachers with consistently high student growth scores. Administrators informally referred to them as the "rising superstars" and granted them a pay increase of 11 percent for 2014–2015.

Finally, a very few were selected as "master teachers." They had achieved what Ms. Nelson called "insane results," based on "very clear metrics" that the CMO administrators had "benchmark[ed] from our best Naylor teachers." The requirements were stiff. She said that in addition to having "their students achieve very high scores in three out of [their] last four years, [teachers] have to receive fours on [their] teacher evaluation in several categories: collaborates well with others, [being] a thoughtful and active participant in professional development, [and having] a growth mind-set for yourself and your kids."

Ms. Nelson emphasized that high test scores alone were not enough: "If your results are high, but you don't work well with others, we actually let you go. If you work okay with others and your results are high, you still can't be a master teacher. You have to really be exceptional." Once teachers became master teachers, they were guaranteed raises of at least 10 percent annually until they reached $120,000. The school's two master teachers had received 15 percent raises that year.

No more than 10 percent of a school's teachers could be on the master teacher track. Ms. Nelson explained that administrators set this quota both because their budget couldn't support more teachers at that level and because they wanted most teachers to remain on the veteran track so that no one would feel like "a failure" for not being promoted. Ms. Nelson gave principals a list of teachers who were eligible for the master teacher track, based on their test results, and the principals then decided which teachers to promote.

Therefore, Naylor had incorporated measures of performance into a salary scale with three tracks. As Ms. Nelson said, career teachers [on the veteran track] would have "a comfortable income, that they can do fine and raise their family on." She went on to explain the school's rationale for the master teacher track: "We really want Naylor to be a place that rewards excellence so that [prospective teachers] think, 'I can actually have a good, well-paid career here, if I'm awesome.'" However, it wasn't yet clear to the teachers we interviewed whether or how they could move from the veteran track to the master teacher track, making them eligible to eventually become a master teacher and earn a $120,000 salary. Also, teachers in the primary grades wondered whether they could ever be promoted to the master teacher track, since their students did not take the MCAS and so they had no value-added performance measures.

Also, the role that master teachers would play in the school remained undefined. Several teachers suggested that master teachers would mentor new teachers.

Another had heard that they would help develop the CMO's interim assessments. Other teachers seemed uncertain about whether the master teacher track was intended primarily to recognize and compensate exceptional teachers or to elevate and support them as active leaders within their school. One teacher on the master teacher track, who expected to be promoted to master teacher for the following year, speculated about what role he might have: "I think that I would just take on more leadership roles around the school in whatever way. I think they would just ask me to step up for more things and just ask [me] to do more stuff, like go to different conferences, panels."

It wasn't clear how Naylor's new performance-based pay scale would fare over time. Teachers generally said that they were pleased with their pay increase, although several regretted not having negotiated a higher base salary when they were hired. Because many teachers were new and most were still early in their teaching careers, there was little talk of the financial strains that come with day care costs, mortgages, or college tuition. No one mentioned missing merit bonuses of the past, and most who spoke about pay seemed to approve of Naylor's compensating all teachers in the veteran track with the same percentage raise each year. For them, the new pay plan functioned much like a simple salary scale. Research about performance-based pay suggests that setting quotas on advancement, as Naylor did for teachers in the master teacher track, may compromise collaboration, but the issue had not come up, possibly because so far it applied to so few teachers.

THE CHALLENGE OF DESIGNING A CAREER LADDER

Single salary scales and merit pay are not mutually exclusive, as Naylor's three-track pay plan with annual raises illustrates, nor are they the only approaches used to pay teachers. Another option is a well-designed career ladder that, in addition to setting forth a salary scale, provides a framework for individuals' career advancement. From the time they start their job, employees can progress up the career ladder to higher levels of skill, responsibility, and authority in the organization, while earning higher pay. Advancement on a career ladder is earned, not automatic. It can be designed to integrate performance assessments with a pay scale, motivating and rewarding teachers with promotions, while also encouraging their loyalty and retention. However, past efforts to create career ladders have been short-lived due to many of the same problems presented by performance bonuses.

Those who design a performance-based career ladder for teachers must decide which of teachers' many responsibilities and contributions matter most and then devise ways to encourage and assess them. They must ensure that their plan will be affordable over time, while also providing sufficient incentives so that all teachers see the financial and organizational benefits of improving their practice and moving up the ladder. In order for the plan to gain widespread support throughout the school, CMO, or district, the process for determining which teachers progress must be rigorous, thorough, and even-handed. Finally, one of the fundamental assumptions embedded in a career ladder model is that teachers who reach its higher rungs assume responsibilities and roles that improve the capacity and performance of the school or district. Defining what those responsibilities are in a profession that is traditionally very flat, and where teachers have long had a great deal of autonomy, requires a careful analysis of the organization's need and potential. Despite these complex challenges, teachers generally view the prospect of having a career ladder positively, as a fairer and more promising option than merit bonuses.

A Tiered-Pay and -Career Plan

In 2009, John Papay and I proposed a model for a career ladder that was informed by prior research about pay.[23] We envisioned an approach that would attract strong candidates to teaching and steadily support them in developing instructional skills. We also designed our model to offer substantially higher pay to those who progressed through its performance levels and then assumed responsibility for improving instruction beyond their classroom.

The model we designed would replace a school or district's current salary scale. It has four tiers, each requiring teachers to know and do more, while rewarding those who progress with expanded opportunities and substantially higher pay (see table 8.2).

Initially, all probationary teachers would be placed on Tier I and then move to Tier II once they achieved permanent professional status or tenure. Teachers who failed to pass their tenure review in Tier I would be dismissed. We reserved Tiers III and IV for teachers who achieve notable success in their teaching, acquire advanced levels of knowledge and skill, and prepare to become teacher leaders within their school or district. In all cases, movement from tier to tier would require informed, deliberate review.

Each tier has several levels and teachers would advance one level annually within that tier as long as they received a satisfactory performance evaluation and continued to demonstrate success with their students. Those reaching the top step in Tier II could remain there as long as they continued to perform ef-

Table 8.2 A tiered-pay and -career structure

Tier IV School and district leaders
Tier III Master teachers and school-based leaders
Tier II Professional teachers with tenure
Tier 1 Probationary teachers

Source: Susan Moore Johnson and John Papay, "Pay and Career Development: A Proposal for a New Generation of Teacher," in Johnson and Papay, *Redesigning Teacher Pay: A System for the Next Generation of Educators* (Washington, DC: Economic Policy Institute, 2009), 43–77.

fectively. Their salaries would increase as a result of cost-of-living allowances or across-the-board raises. If Tier II teachers failed to perform effectively, they could be dismissed, in keeping with their state's laws. Notably, teachers would not have to pass through each level before moving to a higher tier, but could apply for promotion whenever they thought they met the selection criteria.

The pay structure would thus maintain key advantages of the single salary scale by continuing to provide stable and predictable salaries for teachers. However, those who demonstrated strong performance over time and sought to influence their school or district more broadly could be rewarded for their initiative and success.

Importantly, this salary structure called for creating new roles for teachers promoted to Tiers III and IV. Most Tier III teachers would continue to instruct students full-time, but also open their classroom to others who could learn from their practice. They would be eligible for specialized roles within the school, such as grade-level team leader, department head, or data analyst, for which they would be compensated with released time or additional stipends. Teachers in Tier IV would assume roles designed to influence practice throughout the school or district, such as coordinating induction for new teachers, coaching teachers in particular subjects, overseeing the implementation of a new curriculum, coordinating lesson study groups, or conducting performance assessments as peer evaluators. Tier IV teachers could move in and out of specialized roles, returning to full-time teaching periodically. Whether on special assignment or teaching full-time, Tier IV teachers would be expected to exercise pedagogical and organizational leadership among their peers.

Although our proposed plan addresses the needs of both the individual and the organization, it gives priority to the organization—in this case, the school. That is because, although research has shown that the teacher is the single most important school-based factor in students' success, the school remains the key unit of instructional improvement.[24]

Two urban school districts (Baltimore City, Maryland, and Lawrence, Massachusetts) have designed and implemented career ladders that closely resemble the model we created. Although we don't know if our proposal influenced their designs, we're encouraged that a similar career ladder has been adopted and successfully implemented by two urban school districts.

Career Ladders in Baltimore City and Lawrence

Teachers in both Baltimore City and Lawrence had long been unionized and worked under a traditional, single salary scale that provided raises for every year of their experience and additional supplements for academic degrees and coursework. The scale in Baltimore had twenty-one steps; the one in Lawrence had ten. In reforming their pay systems, both districts entirely eliminated their single salary scale and replaced it with a career ladder. Thus, their approach differed fundamentally from those of districts that retain a single salary scale and attach bonuses to it, such as the well-established ProComp pay system in the Denver Public Schools.[25]

In Baltimore, the reform was led by Superintendent Andrés Alonso, who worked closely with local teachers union leaders to design the district's four career pathways (Standard, Professional, Model, and Lead), by which teachers could progress to specialized leadership roles and higher pay. Each pathway included five to fifteen "intervals" through which teachers advanced, based on their performance. When it was adopted in 2010, teachers' salaries ranged from $46,773 to $99,316 (see table 8.3).

In Lawrence, Jeffrey Riley, appointed by the Massachusetts Commissioner of Education to be the Lawrence Public Schools (LPS) "receiver," had the combined authority of a superintendent and school board. He could unilaterally impose a new pay plan. Nevertheless, he developed the new career ladder for the district with advice from local union leaders, although he moved ahead with implementation when they withheld their endorsement. The LPS career ladder, implemented in 2013, replaced the district's traditional salary scale, which had ten steps for ex-

Table 8.3 Career pathways, Baltimore, Maryland, 2012–2013

Interval (12 AUs = 1 interval)	Standard pathway[a]	Professional pathway[b]	Model pathway[c]	Lead pathway[d]
1	46,773	58,434	85,337	92,916
2	48,176	60,984	86,837	94,516
3	49,621	63,534	88,337	96,116
4	51,110	66,084	89,837	97,716
5	52,643	68,624	91,337	99,316
6		71,384		
7		74,234		
8		75,734		
9		76,739		
10		77,744		
11		78,749		
12		79,754		
13		80,759		
14		81,764		
15		82,769		

Source: Baltimore City Public Schools, "Career Pathways," https://www.baltimorecityschools.org/Page/14091.

[a]Focus on instruction; professional development.

[b]Focus on classroom success; active in school-based roles. Earned by moving through five standard pathways.

[c]Serve as a model of excellence; play leadership roles. Can be earned only by going through the Professional Peer Review Committee (PPRC).

[d]Serve as lead academic teacher at a school; collaborate with the principal to improve academic performance. Process for achieving lead pathway still under development.

perience and eleven columns for additional education. The new ladder had five tiers (Novice, Developing, Career, Advanced, and Master), each with one to four levels. Teachers' salaries ranged from $44,000 for novices to $85,000 for master teachers (see figure 8.1).

Moving up the career ladder

Baltimore City's career pathways had several unique features. Teachers moved up intervals within their current pathway by earning achievement units (AUs), a new professional currency that teachers could acquire as a result of their annual evaluation, coursework, professional development, contributions to student learning, contributions to colleagues, and overall contributions to the school district.

Figure 8.1 Lawrence Public Schools career ladder, 2013

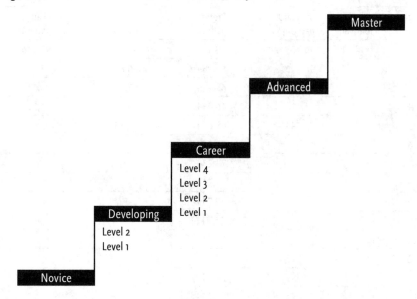

Transition to the career ladder: Effective July 1, 2013, all current teachers will be assigned to one of the tiers based on the teacher's salary placement on the previous salary schedule as of June 30, 2013, without regard to the teacher's rating on the end-of-year evaluation, as follows:

Current step	Career level placement	2013–2014 salary
	Novice	$44,000
1	Developing Level I	$46,000
2	Developing Level II	$47,500
3	Career Level I	$55,000
4	Career Level I	$55,000
5	Career Level II	$59,000
6	Career Level II	$59,500
7	Career Level III	$64,000
8	Career Level IV	$68,500
9	Career Level IV*	$68,500*
10	Career Level IV*	$68,500*

Source: Lawrence Public Schools, https://www.lawrence.k12.ma.us.

Teachers who accumulated twelve AUs moved up one interval on the ladder and received the accompanying salary increase. Teachers were not required to progress through every interval as they advanced in their pathway, but could skip intervals during a year of unusual accomplishment. Those who reached the top of the professional pathway could apply to become a model or lead teacher by submitting an electronic portfolio, which included evidence of their students' progress and a video of their teaching. Model and lead teachers were selected for advancement by a committee of peers who already had been promoted to that pathway.

Though less elaborate than Baltimore's, Lawrence's career ladder had similar features. LPS teachers moved up through the first three tiers of the career ladder (Novice, Developing, and Career) at different rates, depending on their principal's evaluation of their work. It might take two or more years for a teacher to improve sufficiently to advance a level. However, a principal also could move an unusually effective teacher more rapidly up the ladder by skipping one or two levels.

The fourth and fifth tiers (Advanced and Master) were reserved for exceptionally skilled teachers who held specialized roles as "schoolwide models of excellence." As in Baltimore, they were selected through a process requiring them to submit videos of their teaching and evidence of their students' performance. Applicants had to receive their principal's endorsement and were reviewed for promotion by a districtwide committee of administrators and peers.

Roles for advanced and master teachers in Lawrence were developed and proposed at the school level, with the principal's advice and endorsement. Therefore, the roles varied widely, from mentoring and curriculum development to coordinating intramural athletics and creating new programs, such as one in restorative justice for middle school students.

Implementing the career ladder

Both Baltimore City and Lawrence invested substantial resources in implementing their new career ladders. In order to maintain teachers' support for the program, it was essential to place each individual appropriately on the new scale during its first year and ensure that everyone initially received at least a modest pay increase.

Baltimore created several committees to oversee implementation of its Pathways Program. One, the Joint Governing Panel, was composed of eight teachers (four appointed by the union and four appointed by the district) who were released from teaching full-time to support implementation for the first two years of the program. This group of teachers assumed substantial responsibility for decisions such as defining a model teacher and developing a rubric for selecting one.

Both districts worked through the initial challenge of creating a peer review system to select their teacher leaders, given that as yet they had no current teachers at the higher levels of their ladder. Baltimore solicited the expertise of teacher leaders from Toledo, Ohio, for its first review and subsequently turned that responsibility over to its own model and lead teachers. Central administrators in Lawrence initially selected their advanced and master teachers, but subsequently included teachers who already held those positions to review proposals.

Anecdotal evidence suggests that the financial and professional incentives built into the career ladders of both Baltimore and Lawrence have been successful in retaining effective teachers and encouraging them to assume new responsibilities that increase the instructional capacity of their schools. However, both districts also encountered the initial challenges of defining meaningful leadership roles for teachers who were promoted to advanced positions. It was not that teachers or administrators in either district thought that such leadership was unnecessary. Rather, these educators were steeped in the assumption that teachers should work full-time with their students in a classroom, rather than assuming responsibility for their peers. In addition, professional norms of egalitarianism continued to dampen some teachers' interest in the advanced roles.

After two years Baltimore was still defining roles for its lead pathway, and after three years Lawrence had appointed only seven master teachers. As at Naylor Charter School, which had appointed few master teachers and had yet to define their role, this remaining process was both challenging and crucial to their program's success. Nevertheless, the steady progress each district made in implementing its career ladder suggests that this approach to teachers' development and pay has far more promise than past efforts by other districts to award pay bonuses based on students' test scores. However, because these career ladders entirely supplanted the districts' established salary scale, the reforms had to be planned in detail and implemented with care, allowing for adjustments over time.

CONCLUSION

Pay is a professional issue with implications for both individual teachers and their schools. Ideally, pay serves the interests of both, compensating teachers so that they can afford to teach and live a reasonably comfortable middle-class life, while also contributing to a better, more successful school. In considering how to improve compensation for teachers, reformers must recognize that pay functions differently depending on the work to be done and those who choose to do it. If individuals are not attracted by the intrinsic rewards of teaching, higher pay will not likely draw them in, at least not for long.

Yet good pay is essential because it makes teaching affordable and respected work, both on entry and throughout a teacher's career. If teachers find their pay inadequate, they may be distracted from their responsibilities, discouraged, or demoralized. As we saw in chapter 7, successful schools depend on teachers committing extra hours well beyond their defined workday for activities such as planning their curriculum, preparing for classes, grading papers, and maintaining contact with parents. However, if their paycheck fails to cover their bills, they may have to take a second job, reducing the time they otherwise might invest in teaching. Alternatively, they might feel burdened or poorly rewarded and decide to leave the profession altogether.

In their effort to create incentives for better performance, some districts and schools have introduced bonuses to reward teachers for their students' performance. Yet, despite serious efforts by policy makers, administrators, and teachers, these initiatives invariably fall short of proponents' expectations, largely because schools have many complex goals and the mechanisms used as measures of success, such as standardized test scores and VAMs, remain insufficient and primitive, given the demands. Therefore, most districts and schools continue to rely on some version of a standardized salary scale, which rewards loyalty and longevity but not successful teaching.

As we learned from considering the successful district schools in Walker City, a standardized salary scale can work well if a school's other systems and practices—hiring, evaluation, and teams—play their role in maintaining high standards and promoting steady improvement. It appears that when such systems are integrated and coupled with a standardized salary scale, educators can be confident that teachers will work hard, learn new skills, and contribute to their colleagues' development. However, counting on a compensation scheme to substantially influence teachers' performance is misguided, especially in a field of human service that relies primarily on intrinsic rewards to motivate its key employees. Of course, this does not mean that teachers should go unrecognized or uncompensated for the responsibilities and roles they assume. Rather, their sense of obligation and commitment should follow largely from the work they do, rather than what and how they're paid.

Yet if schools—especially urban schools—are to steadily improve, then teachers surely must be key players in making that happen. As we saw in chapter

6, formal roles for teacher leaders who served as team facilitators at Hurston, Fitzgerald, and Kincaid were powerful sources of change. The teachers' accounts also suggested that the role might be compromised if pay were substantially reduced or eliminated, as it was at Fitzgerald.

Positions for teacher leaders, such as instructional coaches, peer reviewers, or department heads, can be created and paid separately, but they can also be incorporated into a career ladder, like those introduced in Baltimore and Lawrence. Career ladders are a promising approach for paying and promoting teachers based on both experience and performance. If they are well implemented, career ladders incorporate the transparency of the single salary scale with rewards for exemplary performance and initiative. They also provide opportunities for teachers to advance in their career while working to improve their school or district. When they are carefully planned and implemented, career ladders can succeed in serving the interests of both the individual teacher and the school organization.

It is no small matter to replace a conventional, established salary scale with the much more complicated and dynamic career ladder, which simultaneously rewards teachers' loyalty, development, and contributions. As the experiences in Baltimore and Lawrence demonstrate, no model can be applied in every setting. If new approaches to pay are to succeed in the short run and last in the long run, they must be tailored to the local needs and realities of the teachers and their schools.

Districts or schools that want to have an integrated system for assessing, advancing, and compensating teachers can learn from the experiences of Baltimore and Lawrence. Importantly, it takes skilled and dedicated teachers and administrators to maintain a career ladder over time and to ensure that related practices, such as hiring, evaluation, team activities, and student support services, are interdependent and coherent. Pay can never compensate for deficient leadership and management.

Having closely considered the key components of teachers' work and how they affect students' learning and school success, we now move on to the conclusion, which draws lessons for policy makers, practitioners, and others who care about the future of US public education.

Conclusion

Wʜᴇɴ ʀᴇsᴇᴀʀᴄʜᴇʀs ᴄᴏɴᴄʟᴜᴅᴇᴅ at the turn of the century that the teacher is the most important school-based factor in students' learning, many policy makers and local school officials seized on this singular finding as an all-purpose fix for public education. They saw in it an obvious solution for improving schools, especially underperforming urban schools that enroll large numbers of students from low-income and high-poverty communities of color. This strategy called for administrators to hire, reward, and retain effective teachers, while rejecting, dissuading, and dismissing ineffective ones. Over time, the theory of action goes, as a school swaps out weak teachers for strong ones, the overall human capital of the school will increase and students will be better educated.

In June 2018, as I was finishing this book, the RAND Corporation issued its detailed evaluation of the Bill & Melinda Gates Foundation's six-year, $575 million intervention that put this human capital strategy to the test. Participants included three large urban school districts (Hillsborough County, Florida; Memphis/Shelby County, Tennessee; and Pittsburgh, Pennsylvania) and four CMOs in California (Green Dot, Alliance, Aspire, and Partnership to Uplift Communities). The primary strategy of the intervention was to improve the overall quality of the schools' staff by acting on information about their teachers' effectiveness. School officials would recruit and hire teachers with high potential; evaluate their performance based on observations and students' test scores; place the most effective teachers in schools with the most low-income, minority students; and reward and retain effective teachers while dismissing ineffective ones.[1]

Despite all the money and effort invested in this reform, RAND concluded that it failed to achieve its goals, having no appreciable benefits for students' achievement on standardized tests or their graduation rates. Nor did the low-income minority students in these schools have better access to more effective teachers. Administrators had conducted regular evaluations using the reform's measures of teaching effectiveness, which were the fulcrum of this reform, but evaluations had not paid off as the Gates reformers expected.

WHY THE TEACHER-CENTERED HUMAN CAPITAL STRATEGY FAILED

How should we explain this outcome? Although it was ambitious, the strategy itself was too narrowly conceived, focusing on individual teachers while ignoring the schools in which they worked. Although the levers built into this change strategy—recruitment, selection, evaluation, individualized professional development, and performance-based compensation—are all important, they are not enough. This strategy does nothing to improve how those teachers do their work together in the context of the school—for example, ensuring that goals for students' learning are understood and shared by everyone, recognizing how their interactions with students both inside and outside class affect the school's culture, considering how well their curriculum and instruction align with what children experience within and between grades, establishing ways to track students' progress through the school's program over time, and interacting with parents in ways that contribute to a better home-school relationship. If educational reform neglects these organizational concerns, students will experience their schooling not as a sustained process of learning, but as a series of disjointed activities and events. And the public will declare it a failure.

In designing our study of successful schools, we took an inductive approach to school improvement, figuring that by looking closely at schools where low-income students succeed, we might learn more about the role that school context plays in teachers' work and the contributions teachers make to their school's improvement both within and beyond their classrooms. We knew we would come to understand more about the challenges these schools encountered and how they interpreted and addressed them. We hoped to identify promising practices that could inform the work and decisions of others who have a stake in public education, including policy makers, administrators, teachers, parents, and the public itself.

We found more convergence of key practices in the successful schools than we expected. For example, each school had a clear, compelling mission to effectively educate students who in the past were ignored or poorly served. This was not a generic mission statement hanging framed on the wall, but a widely shared commitment that motivated and guided these educators. We found that teachers collaborated in all six successful schools and that professional norms fostered joint efforts to improve practice within and across classes.

Other researchers have found similar schoolwide values and practices in exemplary schools. For example, in their recent book, *The Ambitious Elementary School*, Elizabeth Hassrick, Stephen Raudenbush, and Lisa Rosen carefully track and describe the instructional and organizational practices of two successful elementary schools serving low-income students living on the South Side of Chicago. They conclude that meeting those students' needs called for "a new conception of teachers' work and a fairly radical reorganization of the school and its leadership. It required new tools and practices, new relationships among teachers, new partnerships with parents, and mobilizing time in highly strategic ways. Above all, it meant keeping close track of every child's progress and taking pains to ensure that every child got on track for academic success." These authors also found that in order for instruction to be effective it had to be grounded in a deliberately structured, supported, and sustaining school organization that focused on learning.[2]

Starting with the Challenges School Face

In Ronald Heifitz's terms, reformers who advance a narrow human capital solution to solve the schools' complex problems target what they think is a technical problem—that schools do not have enough effective teachers—and address it with what they imagine is a reliable solution: hire, assign, reward, and dismiss teachers based on their evaluations and student test scores. However, the challenges that educators faced in the fourteen schools of the three major studies we've discussed went well beyond staffing. They were complex and involved many parts of the school and a wide range of participants, including teachers, administrators, staff, students, parents, and professionals working in community agencies. These challenges related directly and indirectly to students' learning and development, but not all of them centered on teachers' instruction. For example, educators in one school were concerned about an academic program that favored a small number of high achieving students while neglecting the needs of others; in another school, the teachers disagreed with their principal, but superficially complied with her directives because they feared retribution; and students in a third school showed little sense of responsibility for their actions, while adults tolerated their disruption and disrespect.

Heifitz would call such problems "adaptive challenges," because they have no surefire solution. Instead, they require careful, collaborative analysis by many participants throughout the organization, who then work together to devise strategies that address them—organizational strategies that are, in themselves, complex. To make any real progress throughout the school, teachers must join administrators as active agents of change rather than being treated as subordinates required to implement the changes that others prescribe.

We concluded that teachers indeed matter, but not solely as instructors within their own classrooms. As students move from class to class and grade to grade over time, they experience their schools as organizations. Compartmentalized, fragmented schools where the adults disagree about purpose, hold conflicting professional standards, and contradict one another in their actions and words will never educate students equitably and well. However, in coherent school organizations where teachers and administrators continuously confront and address adaptive problems in all their complexity, students throughout the school can and do succeed.

Adaptive challenges can be solved

It's important to emphasize that, although difficult and complex organizational problems lack a standard solution, they are not insoluble. We and other researchers have studied many schools that made steady progress in addressing such challenges. It's not that good solutions don't exist, but rather that no solution is applicable in all settings and no single response is a match for the complex challenges that any school faces. However, once the organization's participants accept and understand their problems, they are in a position to choose from promising approaches that they and others devise. They can then tailor and combine them in novel ways to address their particular challenges. And as they implement their solutions, they can monitor and refine their approach.

With this larger perspective in mind, what have we learned from the fourteen schools we studied? What was happening in schools where students' progress was slow or stagnant and teachers reported being dissatisfied both with their school's response and their own work environment? And what did we find in schools that were making steady improvement, where teachers expressed confidence in the changes they were implementing?[3]

HAVING AN EFFECTIVE PRINCIPAL IS A MUST

The role that principals played was, not surprisingly, significant in all the schools we studied. In those that were failing or foundering, many teachers viewed their principal as either ineffectual or high-handed. Those they thought were high-handed treated teachers instrumentally, ignoring or rejecting their capacity to diagnose problems, develop solutions, and then implement and refine them. In response, teachers resisted either openly or covertly, sometimes feigning compliance while withdrawing to their classrooms. Some chose to leave their school in search of another where their views and voice would matter.

However, in schools where principals approached leadership inclusively, teachers continuously reinvested in efforts to better organize their school for learning. These principals were active, engaged leaders who made their views known, elicited teachers' opinions and ideas, and learned along with them as they adopted and adapted new approaches. Notably, each principal was respected not only for being a responsive and inclusive leader, but also for being an instructional expert whose knowledge, skills, and priorities teachers widely respected.

Among the six successful schools, we found some notable variation in how the principals approached leadership and school improvement. Some were more responsive to teachers' recommendations than others. Teachers at two charter schools, Kincaid Middle School and Naylor K–8, had less influence on school-site policies than their counterparts in other schools, largely because the CMO defined those policies. In all cases, though, teachers reported feeling respected and being able to exercise influence beyond their classroom in the day-to-day life of the school.

Through their words and actions, the principals in the Successful Schools study expressed their commitment to equity and their belief that providing a good public education for all students is an act of social justice. Teachers widely adopted this mission as their own. Overall, they respected their principal as a school leader who worked hard, understood instruction, and held high standards for himself or herself and others.

To the extent that the schools' MCAS performance is informative, it's worth noting that across all our studies, student growth scores were higher in schools where teachers described inclusive leadership by their principal, frequent collaboration among colleagues, and broad participation by all parties in the school's improvement than they were in schools where teachers described instrumental or authoritarian leadership by principals. This was true even though these schools served demographically similar groups of students.

SUCCESSFUL SCHOOLS RELY ON SOCIAL SYSTEMS

In none of the six successful schools we studied were individual teachers expected to decide entirely on their own what and how to teach; what rules to enforce and how to discipline students; or how to assess students' progress. Despite the differences in these schools' educational philosophies, each had adopted a set of systems to guide and manage such practices. In no school were teachers encouraged—or in some cases, even permitted—to adopt one-off approaches that might undermine or conflict with those of other teachers who upheld the tenets and practices of an explicit schoolwide strategy.

Early in this book, I alerted readers to the tension that teachers across the fourteen schools experienced between the priorities and needs of those involved in their schools (the administrators, teachers, staff, students, and parents) and the rules and practices that policy makers, central office administrators, or consultants imposed in an effort to influence and regulate what the educators did (for example, scripted curricula and pacing guides, standardized tests, interim assessments, zero-tolerance discipline measures, merit pay bonuses, and an array of standardized reporting requirements).

However, we also found that teachers supported, often enthusiastically, a constellation of practices that they and their colleagues adopted after careful consideration. They endorsed a strategy when they believed it fit their needs and would work well to address their challenges and achieve their goals. These effective systems included sets of deliberately selected, sequenced, and linked practices intended to achieve a desired outcome. For example, a hiring system that is likely to succeed over time involves many practices—ambitious recruitment, clear job definition, careful screening, visits to the school, meetings with the principal and prospective colleagues, teaching demonstrations, and feedback. When such practices are implemented as a complete system, both the school and newly hired teachers can be reasonably sure that they are making good decisions. The newly hired teacher will begin her job with realistic expectations, and current teachers are apt to support their new colleague's entry into the school. As a result, the school is far less likely to experience the churn of turnover.

When a robust hiring system then is linked to a system that supports collaboration among teachers, both gain strength. Teachers who work together on teams that are based on their subject, or on the cohort of students they teach, can assume responsibility for many parts of the school's important work—planning curriculum units and lessons, experimenting with ways to improve their instruction, monitoring the needs of individual students, and gauging the responses and progress of student subgroups. But these activities do not occur simply because teachers assemble regularly in a room. If teams are to yield schoolwide benefits, they must be deliberately supported by the school's schedule and have an explicit, worthwhile purpose. Further, they can be informed and guided by schoolwide goals, curriculum maps, classroom exit tickets, surveys of parents, recommendations from instructional coaches, active engagement by administrators, and planned facilitation and follow-up of the meetings. Again, these components are thoughtfully, deliberately combined so that they yield the outcomes educators seek: a curriculum that is aligned from grade to grade, students who have the extra supports they need to do well, and an orderly, purposeful learning environment. Meanwhile, that new teacher who was so carefully hired now has an opportunity to learn from her new colleagues in an experience that is far more likely to support her than intermittent meetings with an assigned mentor, who may not even teach her subject or grade level.

What became clear in our studies was that teachers objected not to systems that worked on behalf of them and their students, but to systems that were imposed by outsiders, were static and mechanistic, or did not respond to the varied needs of their students. Teachers wanted to work in an organization that had achieved a sensible balance between order and autonomy. With very few exceptions, those we interviewed did not suggest that they should teach what and how they wanted. Instead, they sought to exercise reasonable autonomy in a school organization where its educators adopted, devised, and developed systems they could rely on. The systems these schools adopted to guide their work were *social* systems in that the people using them had chosen, implemented, and adapted them to meet their needs. It took the people to make them work, and they worked well because of those people.

Systems Used by All Successful Schools

Across our three studies, schools faced similar challenges. Eight of the fourteen had recently experienced similar alarming problems—plummeting test scores, low graduation rates, chaos in classrooms and corridors—which gave them a reputation for being dysfunctional and dangerous schools. Many of their students were far below grade level in most or all subjects. Several were continuously disrupted by high rates of turnover among teachers and principals. Many students across all of these schools experienced poverty, racial and ethnic discrimination, and the threat of violence or homelessness, which teachers found limited their learning. Often students and their parents did not trust the school or its educators because of its chaotic or punitive past.

As we explored the past and present of the six successful schools in our third study, we were impressed to find that they all had adopted schoolwide systems to address their challenges. These were not singleton practices that were currently popular, such as school uniforms, Chromebooks, or breaks for exercise or meditation, but rather sets of practices that were deliberately selected, developed, and sequenced to address a need. Although we found remarkable similarity across the six schools in some of these systems, we found notable differences in others. This suggested that the widely adopted systems—those for hiring, teachers' collaboration on teams, supervision and evaluation, and monitoring students' progress—were sufficiently sturdy and reliable to serve as models for other schools to consider. They were not proven technical solutions to technical challenges (such as arranging teachers' bus duty so that students would be safe as they arrived and left school), but they had survived careful scrutiny, refinement, and testing. Most educators in the successful schools that used them vouched for their value. Let's consider these before moving on to systems that varied across the sample.

Hiring systems were robust and refined

Hiring was the most consistent and fully implemented system we found across all the successful schools. As we learned in chapter 1, the principals of these schools widely viewed decisions about hiring as the most important they made, reinforcing beliefs about the importance of increasing human capital and supporting interventions to improve staffing. All posted jobs early to be sure that they could compete with suburban schools for the strongest candidates, then screened applicants carefully to assess their qualifications and commitment to the school's mission. They sponsored school visits to ensure that prospective teachers would have a good preview of what it would be like to work in their school. Then the principals interviewed all candidates, not simply in an effort to sell their school, but also to ask hard questions so that they could judge whether applicants were likely to withstand the pressures of the work ahead.

But three additional practices distinguished these schools' hiring systems. First, they involved current teachers in the process, either as participants working with the principal during interviews or at a team meeting, where the teachers might ask their prospective colleague to discuss data or help plan a lesson. Second, they required candidates to demonstrate their instructional skills by teaching a lesson, either in their own class or one at the hiring school. Third, following the teaching demonstration these schools held debriefs with the applicants and provided feedback about their instruction. In such sessions, principals, sometimes joined by teachers, gauged whether the candidate truly was committed to improving his practice and could learn from constructive criticism. These three practices proved to be valuable not only in selecting the right candidate, but also in convincing that candidate that the school would be the right one for him. Thorough hiring required time and effort from many people, but principals and teachers were convinced that their investment paid off.

Teacher teams had a clear purpose and established, predictable practices

Systems for teacher teams also were well developed in five of these schools. They scheduled teachers so that they would have common planning time for their meetings. Within these schools, teachers dedicated separate sessions or segments to discuss both content (curriculum, unit and lesson planning, and group assessments to gauge the effectiveness of instruction) and the student cohort (individual students' performance, group behavior, and norms). Scheduled team time was inviolable, not to be interrupted or appropriated by others. In most cases, teacher leaders facilitated the teams either formally or informally, although administrators remained engaged and informed about their work. The teams had a clear purpose and explicit goals. They often were settings where teachers could be candid and take risks in order to learn and improve their instruction and their school.

Systems for evaluating teachers promoted development over dismissal

One of the most troubling challenges that teachers face, often silently and on their own, is how to become a better teacher, given that they receive scarce feedback about their instruction. Teachers may be hopeful about the promise of new classroom management routines or pedagogical practices that they learn at workshops, but when they try them out, find them less useful than they had hoped. In some schools literacy or math coaches occasionally observe classes, but few offer teachers personalized responses with advice.

All schools in this study were implementing the state's new evaluation policy, which was intended to support teachers' development and ensure that they would be held accountable for their practice. However, of those two purposes, all principals in these successful schools gave priority to developing their teachers. As we saw in chapter 3, what distinguished this system most was the frequency of observations with feedback, which on average far exceeded the number required by the state. Notably, teachers appreciated this concentrated attention and regularly reported that they were becoming better teachers because of it.[4] The fact that these principals were all known to have been effective teachers in the past increased the value that teachers saw in the process. Other administrators supported this system, either by freeing up time for the principal's observations or by expanding the team of evaluators. Yet finding time continued to be a challenge, along with the need to match teachers and evaluators by subject matter and grade level. These schools had not yet solved this problem of match, but they were working on it.

Systems That Differed Widely Among Successful Schools

A second group of systems differed notably across the six schools. These addressed curriculum, rules and discipline, personal supports for students and families, how time was used, and how teachers were paid. To be clear, every school had a system to deal with each of these issues, but the schools' choices and practices varied much more within the sample than did the systems just discussed. In part, this was because the schools differed philosophically about how to address fundamental challenges. Also, however, these remaining systems tended to be less developed and refined than those used for hiring, evaluation, and teams.

Philosophical differences influenced systems for curriculum development

We saw the most variation among the successful schools in their approach to the content of their curriculum, which arguably is at the core of teachers' work with students. The state's learning standards influenced their strategies, and the annual MCAS scores and interim assessments provided some evidence of their progress. But as we saw in chapter 2, the schools had different expectations and used different means to assist and guide teachers in deciding what and how to teach.

At Rodriguez Charter, individual teachers were expected to develop their own curriculum in keeping with the school's commitment to active, project-based learning. In contrast, teachers at Fitzgerald Elementary, Naylor Charter K–8, and Kincaid Charter Middle School developed curriculum as members of grade-level or subject-based teams. The teams at these three schools could rely on units and updated lessons developed in the past, but most spent their time creating new approaches and materials, often in response to their students' recent performance on interim assessments. When Hurston was in turnaround, teams used the district's approved curriculum in math but developed their own multigrade language arts curriculum, having concluded that no single program available through the district was effective. In contrast to this organized process of team-based curriculum development, Dickinson's teachers worked on their own, in pairs, and sometimes as grade-level teams to selectively adopt and adapt prepared curriculum that had been approved by the district.

Therefore, we found no prevailing system for creating, choosing, or adapting curriculum across the successful schools. Nevertheless, there was wide agreement among teachers and administrators that a good curriculum was not one that prescribed precisely what teachers and students should do, but rather one that provided an organized, well-conceptualized approach to the subject and an engaging process for learning and using its basic principles. The teachers and administrators we interviewed did say that they had not yet arrived at a common, adequate, and reliable system that supported teachers in deciding what and how to teach, although they were continuing to explore new approaches and refine those they had adopted.

Discipline systems reflected different beliefs about what worked

The schools also differed in how they approached discipline for students. Two charter schools (Kincaid and Naylor) relied on detailed rules and penalties coupled with explicit expectations and procedures for teachers to use in administering them. Underlying those systems was the belief that students were best served when the school set detailed requirements for individuals' behavior and then rigorously enforced them. The other schools relied on a combination of rules, norms, and incentives to promote discipline and order in their school. Educators in these schools believed that students were more responsive to expectations and norms than to detailed prescriptions and prohibitions.

The six schools all had orderly environments, but notable differences existed among them in how students behaved in classes, corridors, and the cafeteria. Teachers generally appreciated and supported their school's system, although a few objected. For example, some teachers at Dickinson, which had the most flexible, least uniform approach, complained that responding to students' misbehavior consumed too much time, while some teachers at Kincaid and Naylor thought their discipline system was too rigid and suggested that it made students dependent on rules and penalties, rather than self-reliant and responsive to others.

Schools viewed their relationship with students and parents differently

The schools also viewed their responsibility to students and families differently and, therefore, provided varying kinds and levels of services. Educators at Kincaid and Naylor—both self-described "no excuses" charter schools—deliberately limited their responsibility to what happened with students when they were at school. They did not point to racism, poverty, violence, or abuse to explain students' academic performance, and they discouraged teachers from taking those factors into account while working with students. Parents were viewed as partners in the process of educating students, but not clients who themselves deserved the school's attention and services. Parents were expected to support the goals and expectations the school held for students, such as attending school regularly and punctually and completing their homework.

The other four schools viewed their responsibilities much more broadly. They saw students standing at the center of their work, and all had systems for identifying and dealing with personal problems that compromised those students' academic performance and personal growth. Several schools addressed those problems in both their supports for students and teachers' professional development. At either grade-level or student support team meetings, teachers, administrators, and staff systematically reviewed every student's academic progress, behavior, and apparent well-being. In response to those assessments, they variously provided support for students with one-to-one or small-group counseling; referred parents who needed help to community agencies; created special events for parents to learn about their children's courses and classes; encouraged families to participate in workshops on effective parenting practices; and hosted local food banks where parents might pick up the food they needed while also talking with their children's teachers, who reliably showed up to meet them.

Overall, the six schools provided a different range of services, depending on their resources and philosophy. Both groups of schools had developed systems for responding to the needs of students and parents, but those were minimal at Kincaid and Naylor and extensive at the other schools.

Schools efficiently organized teachers' noninstructional time within different constraints

The schools also approached teachers' noninstructional time differently—both how much was available and who decided how it could be used. Most obvious were differences in the teachers' workday, which ranged from 6.25 hours at Dickinson Elementary to 9.25 hours at Naylor Charter. Schools with longer workdays incorporated regular, substantial blocks of time for team meetings and professional development, while schools with shorter workdays relied primarily on teachers' daily prep and planning periods for team meetings and informal collaboration. At charter and former turnaround schools, administrators directed how teachers used their noninstructional time, while at the traditional WCSD school, Dickinson, Ms. Davila was authorized to direct how teachers used only one period a week, when she convened them in grade-level teams.

Therefore, each school had a system for efficiently using the time available. There was a case to be made for a longer workday that incorporated more time for teachers' professional learning and collaboration. Compared with top-performing systems internationally, US teachers have far less in-school time for collaboration.[5] However, a longer in-school workday came with disadvantages for teachers who were parents and needed or wanted to be home with their own children after school. Many early-career teachers we interviewed in schools with long workdays said that their teaching career there would necessarily end once they had children. Therefore, policies that required long workdays raised concerns about increasing turnover and doubts about whether schools with both high expectations and long workdays were sustainable.

Different approaches to pay were grounded in different assumptions about its purpose

Finally, these schools also approached teachers' pay differently. In the three WCSD schools—Hurston, Fitzgerald, and Dickinson—teachers were paid according to the district's negotiated pay scale, which compared favorably with those of surrounding districts and charter schools. Although teachers sometimes criticize such pay scales because they don't promote effort or reward accomplishment, teachers in these WCSD schools didn't voice these complaints and seemed confident that all their colleagues worked hard and deserved credit for their students' learning. As a restart school within WCSD, Kincaid Charter also paid teachers according to the district's scale and its teachers appreciated earning more than teachers in other charter schools. It's important to note that some complained about their long hours, but not their hourly wage or the fact that they received no bonuses for exemplary performance.

In contrast, Naylor and Rodriguez Charter Schools continued to experiment with differentiated pay scales designed to reward teachers after three years of effective work. Both had recently abandoned paying merit bonuses because teachers had little confidence in the validity of the judgments they were based on and some said they sowed discontent among teachers. Naylor also recently had instituted a simple career ladder that permitted a few master teachers to earn very high pay. The school had not yet defined the roles that these master teachers would play.

None of the schools in our studies had adopted a comprehensive career ladder that included performance-based progression and roles for exemplary teachers who advanced to its highest steps. However, examples of such career ladders from Baltimore City, Maryland, and Lawrence, Massachusetts, illustrate that, with careful planning, it's possible to develop and implement a comprehensive career ladder that teachers support.

WHAT TO DO WITH WHAT WE KNOW

By now it is clear that this is not a book with a simple punch line or a slam-dunk solution. Instead, based on case studies that offer rich stories and illustrations, it explains how organizational context shapes practice, why a schoolwide stance on improvement is essential, how teachers can contribute their knowledge and expertise to address their school's challenges, how collaboration among teachers and administrators increases a school's capacity to solve problems and serve students, and how social systems adopted and refined by the school can support and advance its mission.

Together, these cases provide insight into the many ways that teachers and administrators in schools that serve students from low-income and high-poverty communities address the complex challenges they face. These cases include examples of efforts that failed because of inadequate or authoritarian leadership, insufficient or inaccurate diagnoses, and strategies that were poorly matched to the challenge they were meant to address. Many more examples illustrate success. Often, celebratory descriptions of effective urban schools single them out as extraordinary, but somewhat mysterious and beyond replication. That's a mistake. Although the work these schools undertook was demanding and complex, it is not unknowable or undoable.

With that in mind, I'll conclude with some key observations and recommendations for teachers, administrators, policy makers, and the public.

Remember, Teachers Do Matter

When researchers reported what to me seemed obvious—that teachers are the most important school-level factor in students' learning—I was initially reassured. It seemed that teachers, who Ted Sizer said are often treated like "hired hands," were finally going to receive their due recognition.[6] However, as policy makers enacted changes that narrowly limited the organizational space where teachers could act, it looked as if their true potential to take up and guide schoolwide reform beyond their classrooms might be dismissed rather than fostered. The experiences of teachers in the successful schools we studied show that this approach was neither wise nor inevitable.

Teachers do matter, but if they're to join with their colleagues and principals to lead, they must do so with a schoolwide perspective on their work and then collaborate with others to diagnose complex challenges and devise ways to address them. Principals, too, must recognize how much teachers can offer, once they have the space, opportunity, and encouragement to contribute what they know and can do. Admittedly, this means working in ambiguity and managing uncertainty. There are many promising paths, but few lead with assurance to predictable outcomes. However, if schools are to effectively serve students, that search and the subsequent efforts to effectively implement new approaches are certainly worthwhile.

Rely on Teachers, but Count on the School

Although accountability policies, such as NCLB, have set expectations and imposed sanctions over the past two decades based on a school's accomplishments and failures, those very policies have caused administrators and teachers to remain focused on students' performance within single classrooms. This largely results from basing judgments in accountability schemes on students' standardized test scores and value-added estimates of individual teachers' performance, rather than broader assessments based on other schoolwide measures.

However, let there be no question: the school is the place that warrants sustained attention and effort from policy makers, researchers, administrators, and teachers. It is well past time to recognize the school as the pivotal organization it is. The school is where students can experience a coherent curriculum, a supportive and inspiring school culture, and consistent expectations from class to class and year to year. It is there that teachers can set common goals and pursue practices that, though distinctive, work in sync on behalf of their students. It is there that teachers can thrive.

Once they've recognized the importance of the school, policy makers can initiate and fund efforts to build the capacity of their schools as organizations. This means going well beyond efforts to hire and retain an effective teacher in each classroom. It involves expanding those teachers' influence with peers and administrators, while developing principals' skills as collaborative leaders. Rather than devising experiments to test with districts and schools, researchers can work with practitioners in research-practice partnerships to help identify and assess systems that not only establish effective practices, but also support their ongoing improvement.[7]

If schools are to become the engine of change that public education needs, then their educators must have sufficient autonomy as a group to make key decisions about staffing, budgeting, curriculum, and the schedule. Whereas school districts have long controlled such matters, schools will inevitably be limited in what they can achieve if they are needlessly bound by uniform regulations and expectations. District and CMO officials should continue to have a legitimate role in setting broad policies that ensure equity, monitor schools' performance, and maintain efficient use of resources. However, increasingly we should assume that schools deserve at least what Baltimore City CEO Andrés Alonso called "guided autonomy" so that they can do their work well.[8]

Rediscover the Principal (Teacher)

If policy makers and school officials actually take the school seriously, then the principal will certainly deserve close attention. Each time I study teachers and their work I learn more about principals—their importance, their role, and their widely varying skills and approaches to leadership and management. As policies and practices that affect the school change, so, too, must our expectations and support for principals. This is obviously a big agenda and one that many scholars have examined and organizations have invested in. However, our studies, especially those in successful schools, lead to a few important conclusions.

First, if principals are to be the instructional leaders their schools need, they must bring to their position deep expertise as teachers. In all the schools we studied that demonstrated success, the principal was known to have been a skilled teacher before becoming an administrator. Knowing good instruction and how to help teachers develop their skills is, in my view, essential for all principals. Such expertise is acquired over time through teaching, not by practicing to reliably score instruction while watching videos of teaching.

Currently, the principal's role includes many responsibilities that require a wide range of skills—managing finances, overseeing facilities, enforcing discipline, monitoring grants, responding to district requirements, ensuring safety, and more. As the schools we studied demonstrate, many of those tasks can be assumed by other administrators, while principals who are instructional experts concentrate on the systems and practices that have the most direct effect on students' learning: recruiting and hiring promising candidates, supporting and guiding teachers' growth, and overseeing the curriculum and its development.

Originally, the principal was known as the "principal teacher" of the school. We need to again put good teaching (which inevitably requires good leading) first on the list of qualifications to become a principal. State and local policy makers should require principals to have substantial experience as an effective teacher before they qualify for the role. Superintendents who hire principals might ask them to demonstrate their skills as teachers and coaches—for example, by observing a lesson, providing feedback to the teacher, and then modeling exemplary instructional practices in an area identified for improvement. Surely, there is more to be learned about a principal's potential as an instructional leader in this kind of demonstration than in the typical inbox exercise often used for hiring. If principals are going to become the instructional leaders that schools need, then central office and CMO administrators will have to pare back and reassign the management responsibilities that detract and distract principals from focusing on teaching and learning.

Policy makers and district officials could also create more attractive and effective pathways so that teacher leaders who are inclined toward school leadership can prepare for and move into the principal's role or serve in related academic leadership positions.[9] If the responsibilities of the principal were focused tightly on improving teaching and learning rather than being scattered across a myriad of managerial tasks, the role would become far more attractive to talented and knowledgeable teacher leaders, who are reluctant to take the job as it is currently conceived and structured.

In addition to being first-rate teachers, principals need to develop sophisticated skills as organizational analysts and leaders. The conventional top-down organization chart not only is inadequate for identifying opportunities to improve the school, it is also misleading. The most successful principals we studied relied on a much more dynamic, complicated, three-dimensional map of their school organization and led collaboratively with teachers, administrators, and staff from everywhere, all at once.

Create Social Systems That Provide Structure and Support

It takes systems—social systems that link the efforts and practices of educators—to meet the complex challenges of schools. Such systems, which are grounded in the school's mission and philosophy, can be designed to plan curriculum, provide supports for students, hire new teachers, or organize how time is used. They provide support and guidance for teachers and administrators as they work together to educate their students and improve their school from their various roles. The many examples in earlier chapters illustrate how systems can create the kind of flexible order that makes progress possible.

Good systems can contribute to a strong, interdependent organizational culture. When individuals have confidence that others will do their part in a joint effort to improve their school, trust builds among colleagues. In his book *Checklist Manifesto*, Atul Gawande highlights the importance of procedures, such as regular hand washing, that increase safety and improve outcomes in medicine. However, he also stresses that it's "not ticking boxes" that matters, but the personal and professional relationships that develop as the organization "embraces a culture of teamwork and discipline."[10] So, too, in schools.

Start small and go from there

Before adopting or creating a system, it's important to be clear about what problem that system is meant to address. It might be unaligned math classes, lack of visible support from parents, teachers' apprehension about new standards, reports that older students are bullying younger ones, an unexpected drop in reading scores at the second grade, or one of many other challenges large and small. There are many possible starting points. But unless the identified problem is truly small, such as students being assigned the same novel in different grades, it's likely to be complex and include many subchallenges within it. For example, the perceived need to develop more support among parents will probably require gaining a better understanding of the kinds of support that teachers are looking for; the opportunities for parental engagement that already exist, and whether some are more effective than others; and the role that factors such as scheduling, child care, transportation, and language differences might play in parents' reluctance to attend conferences, events, or meetings. If teachers and administrators begin with their favorite solution, practice, or system, rather than a deep understanding of the challenge they face, they'll find that the changes they make won't deliver the results they hope for and, in the meantime, they will have wasted precious resources and time.

It's also important to learn about any current practices that relate to the challenge. Tony Bryk and his colleagues remind us that we must know the system we have so that we can understand why it's failing to provide the results we want. Once educators understand what the components of their current system are and how they work (or fail to work), they can begin to make adjustments or create a new approach that better fits their school's needs.[11]

Obviously, investigating challenges and current practices in this way takes time that no single administrator has. Therefore, teachers should be engaged in leadership early and often; efforts to get their buy-in after the fact are meaningless and counterproductive. The real value of having teachers deeply engaged in this work comes from their detailed insider's knowledge about the school and how it works, what their students experience day to day, and why their colleagues respond as they do. Ultimately, genuine discussions among teachers—as they work on teams, talk while on recess duty, participate in departmental or schoolwide faculty discussions—are likely to spark the best ideas and build the strongest consensus about how to move ahead.

In developing new ways to address a school's challenges—both the technical and adaptive ones—it's worth considering approaches and models that work for others. A school that wants to make better hiring decisions would do well to closely consider the components of the hiring systems that we found in all the successful schools. But it would be a mistake to settle for a practice that works somewhere else without testing it out and tailoring it to one's own school. With so much recent emphasis on the importance of scaling up practices, some might think it's sensible to quickly and completely replace a faulty system with a new one. However, running very small pilot tests of possible changes can be enormously informative and ultimately save a great deal of time.

Because systems have many parts, it makes sense to introduce new ones gradually, paying close attention to how they are connected or where they should be linked. It's important to test not only how well each component works, but also how well they all work together. Tracking progress over time and documenting what is being learned for everyone to see keeps those with an interest in this system informed and engaged. When something goes awry, as it inevitably does, teachers who have been involved throughout the process are sure to have plausible explanations for what's gone wrong and good suggestions about what to do differently. They'll appreciate having their views taken into account.

It's important to remember that as a school's educators systematically explore and address even one aspect of an important problem, they are developing and refining essential skills, such as how to gather, record, and interpret data; how to get quick feedback or facilitate a focus group; how to use Google Docs to keep minutes and set agendas; or how to recognize and verify when a decision has been made. Once practiced, these techniques can then be applied to the next challenge. As those in the school increasingly share information with their colleagues about what seems to be working, the school's capacity to address the next challenge or refine another system grows. Lessons learned in adopting a single practice will have implications for how best to add a second practice or begin work on an entirely new system. Meanwhile, those participating in the process will become more open-minded, astute, and efficient. Bryk and colleagues explain that, as the school's educators solve problems, they also "get better at getting better."

It Can't Be Done on the Cheap

Improving schools for students from low-income and high-poverty communities calls for new resources, often far beyond what is currently available in low-income district schools. We should not imagine that this work will be easy or inexpensive.

New efficiencies can save only so much before they begin to compromise students' learning. Eventually, public officials—from the federal government to the mayor's office to the school board—must invest much more in their schools, particularly those that have been neglected.

Unfortunately, too many in our society seem to believe that schools can always do more with less. When Hurston and Fitzgerald successfully emerged from turnaround, their principals had to find new sources to fund stipends for teacher leaders who facilitated their very effective teams. Mr. Hinds secured a small grant to fund a scaled-back program, while Ms. Forte convinced teachers to continue in their position without pay, although teachers doubted that this would be enough to sustain that valuable practice.

In other events—from the teacher strikes at state capitols to individual teachers' accounts of inadequate materials and broken copy machines—we see evidence of underfunded public education. If students are to get what they deserve in any school, then teaching must reliably be an affordable career, where it's possible to pay one's bills and enjoy life without having to hold a second job or lie awake worrying about finances at night. Only when our society acknowledges and funds the costs of a first-class education system will our schools and teachers succeed in providing it.

Study Methods

SECOND-STAGE TEACHER STUDY

Research team:

- Susan Moore Johnson
- Megin Charner-Laird
- Cheryl Lynne Kirkpatrick
- Stacy Agee Szczesiul

We conducted this study in 2008 in order to learn more about how second-stage teachers (SSTs), who had been teaching four to ten years, experienced their work in low-income schools. We had studied teachers from this same broad cohort between 1998 and 2004, when they were novices or early-career teachers. In that research, we learned that teachers of this new generation hoped to work in collaboration with their peers, expected curricular support from their school, were disappointed with the mentoring they received, and had made only a tentative commitment to a career in teaching. Over time, they gradually replaced a very large cohort of retiring veteran teachers, most of whom had spent their entire career in the classroom. These novices entered teaching just as accountability policies were becoming central to teachers' work.

Our study of SSTs was designed to consider teachers from that same cohort once they had overcome the challenges that all new teachers face and had achieved a level of competence and confidence in their work, which we reasoned might allow them to decide where to invest their nonteaching time and whether to pursue roles as teacher leaders. At the time of our study, SSTs made up approximately one-third of the teaching force in the US and, though more experienced than novice teachers, the cohort was still experiencing high rates of turnover.

Our earlier studies at the Project on the Next Generation of Teachers focused on individuals as the unit of analysis. We had learned from the teachers we interviewed and surveyed that school context played a very important role in teachers' experience, but we had not directly studied the relationship between teachers and their school context. In this study we used a nested design to study teachers within schools that were located in three urban districts of Massachusetts. The state had adopted a new set of curriculum frameworks, a comprehensive assessment (the MCAS), and a school-based accountability system in its Education Reform Act of 1993, amended in 2006 to be compliant with NCLB requirements. When we conducted the study, Massachusetts officials determined whether schools achieved AYP under NCLB by analyzing performance and improvement data for each school and district. This included students' MCAS scores and attendance and graduation rates for every subgroup of students.

Our unit of analysis for this study was teachers within schools. We were especially interested in four aspects of the SSTs' experience: (1) how they engaged in their work and used their time as SSTs, and whether administrators and peers influenced those decisions; (2) what opportunities they had to learn and improve their practice, especially with colleagues; (3) whether they supported or participated in leadership roles within their school; and (4) how they experienced the demands of test-based accountability policies. We wanted to understand each of these themes both independently and in interaction.

Site Selection

We chose to study teachers working within low-income districts because their schools often face great challenges in achieving success with their students, especially in the context of accountability. Although these districts were not the lowest performing in the state, each had been sanctioned and continued to be under state officials' watch. We selected a sample of three to six schools in each district, depending on the district's size and specific characteristics of the schools, for a total of fourteen schools. The state had identified all but one of these schools for improvement, corrective action, or restructuring.

Participants

After gaining permission to conduct the study from district officials, we received lists of teachers at each school, which included their years of experience and teaching assignment. In selecting participants, we began by choosing a group of teachers at each school, which included individuals who had different levels of experience (between four and ten years) and taught different grades and subjects. Based on their names, we included both women and men. We hoped to interview three to five teachers in small schools and eight to twelve teachers in larger schools.

We invited teachers by email with follow-up phone calls. If we failed to contact them, if they declined to participate, or if the district had incorrect information about their experience, we substituted new names. The final sample included eighty-five teachers (twenty-two from elementary schools, twenty-nine from middle schools, and thirty-four from high schools).

School Visits and Interviews

We scheduled interviews at each teacher's convenience and conducted them using a semistructured protocol, which asked teachers to describe and assess their experience in each of the four areas of our inquiry—engagement, professional learning, leadership roles, and accountability. Teachers also completed an information form that asked for demographic data about their age, race, and gender; their years of experience as a teacher; the courses and grades they had taught; and the size of their student load. Interviews, which lasted between forty-five and ninety minutes, were audio-recorded and transcribed.

Data Analysis

After each interview, we wrote a thematic summary of the individual's responses to questions about each of our four main areas of interest as well as any other important points raised during the interview. We then drew up a list of topical codes that were drawn from the relevant literature or emerged during the interviews. For example, we coded for "colleagues" and "off-site learning" because research showed that teachers commonly report that they learn from both. However, we were also struck by the participants' comments about how they experienced teaching differently at their current career stage, leading us to introduce the code "SST-ness" into our list.

After reaching agreement about the meaning of each code and practicing using them reliably, we coded the interviews topically using *ATLAS.ti*. The software made it possible to draw and analyze data systematically as we investigated various codes. We created matrices to examine the responses of individual teachers within and between schools. We found that teachers within the same school provided similar accounts of specific topics, leading us to track patterns of responses by school throughout the study. We then drew up tentative findings, which we reviewed, critiqued, and revised as a team.

Each of the four researchers then took responsibility for writing about one of the key themes in the study. Chapter 2 of this book focuses on how teachers chose what and how to teach within the context of accountability. The chapter includes detailed descriptions of two schools from this study—one elementary (Lane) and one middle school (Deer Park)—both located in the same district. Information about the demographic makeup of the students in those schools and their student growth scores are included in table I.1.

TEACHING IN CONTEXT STUDY

Research team:

- Susan Moore Johnson
- Megin Charner-Laird
- Matthew A. Kraft
- Monica Ng
- John P. Papay
- Stefanie K. Reinhorn

We designed and conducted this study in 2010–2011 in an effort to learn how teachers and administrators in six high-poverty schools of the Walker City School District (WCSD) defined and addressed the challenges their school faced and how teachers experienced their work there.

Site Selection

In selecting our sample of six schools, we were guided by two basic principles. First, using data from the 2007–2008 school year, we identified high-poverty schools as those that fell above the district median in the proportion of students who qualified for federal free and reduced-price lunch, a proxy that researchers frequently use to identify low-income schools. Because the proportion of students who apply for federal lunch subsidies decreases as students age, we stratified by school level and calculated median rates of participation across the district of 80 percent (elementary), 82 percent (middle school), and 64 percent (high school).

From among those schools, we selected a purposive sample of six schools that exhibited different levels of student achievement growth (as measured by state officials) and teacher satisfaction, as reflected in responses to the statewide TeLLs survey. We averaged the Student Growth Percentile (SGP) measures over two years (2007–2008 and 2008–2009) in mathematics and language arts. We then created a plot of the high-poverty schools in the district, arrayed by their average SGP (horizontal axis) and their average working conditions measure (vertical axis). Our possible schools fell into four quadrants: high-growth schools with strong work environments, low-growth schools with strong work environments, low-growth schools with weak work environments, and high-growth schools with weak work environments. We used this analysis to inform our site selection. We wanted to study a set of schools that fell into different quadrants, while also including elementary, middle, and high schools from various locations. We also hoped to select a sample of schools with some variation in the principal's race, gender, and administrative experience. Although we intended to include at least one low-growth school with a weak work environment in our sample, WCSD was in the process of closing or reconstituting many of those schools; several had been closed by the time we began data collection. The principal of one we invited to participate declined and the school was subsequently closed. Therefore, we did not include a school from the quadrant that combined low student growth and low scores on the work environment survey. The principals of all other schools that we recruited agreed to participate.

Our final sample included two traditional elementary schools, one K–8 school, one middle school, and two high schools. Basic information about the schools can be found in table I.1. All schools served large proportions of low-income students and would be labeled "high-poverty" schools according to the Institute of Education Sciences' criteria (>75 percent low-income). The schools enrolled large proportions of students of color, although the demographic subgroups of students within the schools varied considerably. The median SGP percentiles within the sample ranged from as low as the 20th and 35th percentiles in mathematics and English language arts to as high as the 65th and 60th percentiles, respectively. However, the schools generally clustered around the 50th percentile.

Data Collection

Two- and three-person teams took responsibility for data collection at each site and the lead researcher participated in data collection at all six. Each researcher conducted interviews at two or more schools, which informed cross-case analysis. We collected data concurrently during the 2010–2011 school year.

We first conducted a two-hour, semistructured interview with the principal in order to learn about the school's general characteristics, organization, and programs, as well as the principal's view of the school's challenges and his or her perspective on school leadership. We interviewed a wide range of teachers and, where they were present and available, other administrators. We solicited teachers' participation in various ways, including written requests sent by email, flyers placed in the teachers' mailboxes, principals' recommendations, and professional networking. We also relied on recommendations from teachers we interviewed about others in their school whose views might differ from their own. Interviews with teachers lasted thirty to sixty minutes and included questions about their experiences with hiring, instruction, evaluation, discipline, the administration, and other factors of the school's environment.

We interviewed eighty-three teachers and twelve administrators. In each school, we interviewed new teachers, mid-career teachers, and veteran teachers; teachers in different grades and subjects; teachers who were hired new to the school and those who had transferred in from other schools; and teachers with differing views of the school. The racial composition of teachers and administrators included in our sample was broadly representative of the schools and the district as a whole—59 percent were white, 20 percent were African American, 10 percent were Hispanic, 8 percent were Asian American, and 3 percent were of mixed or another race.

Although interviews were the main source of data for our study, we learned about programs and practices by reading and analyzing various documents, such as formal plans for reform, curriculum guides, memoranda from the principal and district office, and posted standards for student behavior. Also, during our many school visits to conduct interviews, we observed day-to-day practices as teachers taught classes and interacted with colleagues; students enjoyed recess, worked in the library, or changed classes; and parents arrived to drop off their children, meet with a counselor, or make inquiries at the main office. We paid attention to what we saw on the walls of classrooms and corridors—student work, recognition of achievement, rules, and graffiti—as well as how students, teachers, and administrators treated one another. Thus, we interpreted teachers' and administrators' comments during interviews within this larger context of ongoing activity that we observed while in the schools. After many visits and interviews, we had gained a nuanced picture of each school.

Data Analysis

Following each interview, we wrote a structured thematic summary, highlighting the views of each participant on a standard set of topics. During the process of data analysis, we relied on these thematic summaries to write memos that captured emerging themes at each school and, subsequently, across schools. These documents informed our ongoing analysis and discussion of findings.

We coded interview transcripts topically using both a priori codes drawn from the literature about teachers' roles, working conditions, leadership, satisfaction, and retention, as well as codes that emerged from our data, such as demands on teachers, accountability, and discipline. Team members then coded a small subset of transcripts individually using this list of codes and then compared and discussed our decisions in order to improve the reliability of our ratings. We repeated this process and then finalized our list of codes. We then coded each transcript using the software *ATLAS.ti*. We developed data analytic matrices to explore each case separately and then created cross-site matrices to identify patterns across cases. Throughout this process, we sought to identify and understand variation as it became apparent both within and across schools. We considered patterns of responses in subgroups of teachers identified by experience (novice, mid-career, and veteran), subject, clusters, or grade levels. As we developed tentative findings and explanations, we often returned to the data to review our coding and to test our explanations against the full range of interviews.

SUCCESSFUL SCHOOLS STUDY

Research team:

- Susan Moore Johnson
- Stefanie K. Reinhorn
- Nicole S. Simon

We conducted this study in 2014–2015 in order to better understand human capital practices in urban schools and the relationship between school context and teachers' work. Previously, we had studied the effects of context in six WCSD schools, all serving large proportions of students of color living in high-poverty environments. Based on measures of student growth provided by the state, those schools varied in performance from high to low achieving and in teachers' satisfaction, based on a state-level survey. For this study, we were interested in learning about successful schools, rather than schools exhibiting a wide range of performance. We hoped to identify and describe promising and exemplary practices. Further, we wanted to explore how differences in policy affect what successful schools can do. Therefore, we included in our sample different types of public schools operating in the same locality, including traditional district schools, state charter schools, district turnaround, and restart schools.

Site Selection

At the time of our study, Massachusetts education officials rated all public schools based on their students' MCAS performance and their progress in reducing or eliminating achievement gaps among racial and economic subgroups of students. Therefore, we decided to study schools that the state had rated at Level 1 and that were widely viewed as high performing. So that the schools would all be located in the same context, we decided to study only schools within the limits of Walker City. We chose to consider only elementary or middle schools so that we could draw more meaningful comparisons across the sample.

In seeking to identify schools that met our criteria (Level 1 schools serving high-poverty, high-minority student populations), we found a relatively short list of candidates. We realized, however, that among these relatively few district and charter schools, further variety existed, because each was also affected by a particular set of policies, including local school board and administrative requirements, the WCSD teachers' contract, state accountability regulations, and state charter laws. Therefore, as we selected the six schools for our study, we also deliberately incorporated variation in school-based policy contexts. We then reviewed available reports and websites about the schools we were considering and consulted our professional networks in order to confirm that the state's ratings were consistent with these schools' reputations. We drew up a proposed sample that included one traditional district preK–5 elementary school, two former turnaround schools (one K–8 and one preK–5), two state charter schools (one K–8 and one preK–8), and one restart charter middle school (6–8), all operating within the Walker City limits. The schools enrolled between 72 and 88 percent low-income students; between 82 and 99 percent were students of color. We invited the principals and heads of these schools to participate in our study and all agreed. Information about the demographics and performance of these schools can be found in table I.1.

Data Collection

We conducted 142 semistructured interviews with teachers, administrators, and other staff, including instructional coaches and program coordinators. We first interviewed the principals and CMO heads and then solicited teachers' participation by email and flyers. We also followed up on recommendations of those we interviewed about others we should contact. We interviewed between 33 and 56 percent of the teachers at each school, depending on its size and complexity. We asked participants about an array of practices that might affect teachers and their work, including recruitment and hiring, collaboration among colleagues, curriculum and instruction, student discipline and supports, teacher leadership, professional responsibilities, and pay. We recorded and transcribed all interviews. In the course of visiting the schools to conduct interviews, we informally observed practices in classrooms, corridors, and offices, which we recorded in field notes. We also gathered and analyzed relevant documents, including teacher evaluation frameworks and rubrics, teacher handbooks, school policies for students and families, lesson planning templates, and examples of observation feedback for teachers.

Data Analysis

Before closely analyzing our interview data, we wrote structured thematic summaries of each, organized according to a common set of topics, including personal background, school overview, school culture, recruitment and hiring, induction, professional development, curriculum supervision, evaluation and dismissal, student supports, pay and benefits, retention, and teacher voice. We reviewed these summaries to identify common themes and differences within and across the sites. We created a list of forty-five topical codes including those drawn from the literature and others that emerged from our study, such as "sustainability." We then independently coded a subset of transcripts and met to refine our definitions and calibrate our use of codes. To code the data we used the software *Dedoose*, which allowed us to attach multiple codes to a single segment of interview data and then to systematically review participants' responses not only by topic, but also by descriptors such as role, school, gender, and years of teaching experience.

Next, we created analytic matrices so that we could closely examine our emerging findings about practice within and across schools. As we proceeded to write about specific practices, we relied on this combination of thematic summaries, coded interviews, and matrices, often moving back and forth among them to clarify and document our conclusions. We conducted member checks by sharing our initial findings with principals from all schools and providing all participants with online links to our working papers. In each case, we invited participants' responses.

ADDITIONAL STUDIES

The methods used in other studies conducted by the Project and referred to in this book can be found at http://projectngt.gse.harvard.edu.

Notes

Introduction

1. This finding is often stated incompletely, without the important qualifier "school-level," as if the teacher is *the* most important factor in students' learning; in fact, individual and family characteristics have far more influence. However, of the factors that are within the control of the school, these researchers have found that the teacher ranks first. Jonah E. Rockoff, "The Impact of Individual Teachers on Student Achievement: Evidence from Panel Data, *American Economic Review, Papers and Proceedings* 94, no. 2 (2004): 247–52; Steven G. Rivkin, Eric A. Hanushek, and John F. Kain, "Teachers, Schools, and Academic Achievement," *Econometrica* 73, no. 2 (2005): 417–58.

2. Raj Chetty, John N. Friedman, and Jonah E. Rockoff, "Measuring the Impacts of Teachers II: Teacher Value-Added and Student Outcomes in Adulthood," *American Economic Review* 104, no. 9 (2014): 2633–79.

3. Eric A. Hanushek, "Teacher Deselection," in *Creating a New Teaching Profession*, ed. Daniel Goldhaber and Jane Hannaway (Washington, DC: Urban Institute Press, 2009), 165–80. Chetty et al. make the same recommendation in "Measuring the Impacts."

4. Edward Liu, Susan Moore Johnson, and Heather G. Peske, "New Teachers and the Massachusetts Signing Bonus: The Limits of Inducements," *Educational Evaluation and Policy Analysis* 26, no. 3 (2004): 217–36.

5. For descriptions of policies in Houston, Texas; Hillsborough County, Florida; Charlotte-Mecklenberg, North Carolina; and Minneapolis, Minnesota, see John P. Papay and Susan Moore Johnson, "Pay-for-Performance in Practice," in *Redesigning Teacher Pay: A System for the Next Generation of Educators*, Susan Moore Johnson and John P. Papay (Washington, DC: Economic Policy Institute, 2009), 23–42.

6. Jill Barshay, "National Test Scores Reveal a Decade of Educational Stagnation," *Hechinger Report*, April 10, 2018, https://hechingerreport.org/national-test-scores-reveal-a-decade-of-educational-stagnation/; Michael Hansen et al., *Brookings Brown Center Chalkboard* (blog), April 17, 2018, https://brook.gs/2rb7RiR.

7. Brian M. Stecher et al., *Improving Teaching Effectiveness: Final Report: The Intensive Partnerships for Effective Teaching Through 2015–2016* (Santa Monica, CA: RAND Corporation, 2018), https://www.rand.org/pubs/research_reports/RR2242.html.

8. David Tyack, *The One Best System: A History of American Urban Education* (Cambridge, MA: Harvard University Press, 1974); Dan C. Lortie, *Schoolteacher: A Sociological Study*

(Chicago: University of Chicago Press, 1975); see also Judith Warren Little, "The Persistence of Privacy: Autonomy and Initiative in Teachers' Professional Relations," *Teachers College Record* 91, no. 4 (1990): 509–36.

9. Helen F. Ladd and Lucy C. Sorenson, "Returns to Teacher Experience: Student Achievement and Motivation in Middle School," *Education Finance and Policy* 12, no. 2 (2017): 241–7; Tara Kini and Anne Podolsky, *Does Teaching Experience Increase Teacher Effectiveness? A Review of the Research* (Washington, DC: Learning Policy Institute, 2016).

10. James S. Coleman, "Social Capital in the Creation of Human Capital," *American Journal of Sociology* 94 (1988): S95–S120. Andy Hargreaves and Michael Fullan introduced the concept of "professional capital," which integrates teachers' individual, social, and decisional capital, in *Professional Capital: Transforming Teaching in Every School* (New York: Teachers College Record, 2012). Other scholars have conducted research that informs our understanding of how social capital works. See, for example, James P. Spillane et al., "The Social Side of Capability: Supporting Classroom Instruction, and Enabling Its Improvement" in *Teaching in Context: The Social Side of Education Reform*, ed. Esther Quintero (Cambridge, MA: Harvard Education Press, 2017), 95–111; Carrie R. Leana and Frits K. Pil, "Social Capital: An Untapped Resource for Educational Improvement," in Quintero, *Teaching in Context*, 113–129.

11. For an explanation of the features that the teacher's workplace comprises, see Susan Moore Johnson, *Teachers at Work: Achieving Success in Our Schools* (New York: Basic Books, 1990), 11–23.

12. Heather G. Peske et al., "The Next Generation of Teachers: Changing Conceptions of a Career in Teaching," *Phi Delta Kappan* 83, no. 4 (2001): 304–11; Susan Moore Johnson and Sarah E. Birkeland, "Pursuing a 'Sense of Success': New Teachers Explain Their Career Decisions," *American Educational Research Journal* 40, no. 3 (2003): 581–617.

13. Susan Moore Johnson and the Project on the Next Generation of Teachers, *Finders and Keepers: Helping New Teachers Survive and Thrive in Our Schools* (San Francisco: Jossey-Bass, 2004).

14. Michael T. Luekens et al., *Teacher Attrition and Mobility: Results from the Teacher Follow-up Survey, 2000–2001* (Washington DC: National Center for Education Statistics, 2004).

15. Richard Ingersoll and Thomas Smith, "The Wrong Solution to the Teacher Shortage," *Educational Leadership* 60, no. 8 (2003): 30–3.

16. Susan Moore Johnson et al., "The Support Gap: New Teachers' Early Experiences in High-Income and Low-Income Schools," *Education Policy Analysis Archives* 12, no. 61, (2004): 1–24. The separate survey studies summarized here are discussed in subsequent chapters.

17. Susan Moore Johnson, Matthew A. Kraft, and John P. Papay, "How Context Matters in High-Need Schools: The Effects of Teachers' Working Conditions on Their Professional Satisfaction and Their Students' Achievement," *Teachers College Record* 114, no. 10 (2012): 1–39.

18. The original TeLLS survey was developed by Eric Hirsch of the New Teacher Center. It included eighty-seven multiple-choice or Likert-scale questions about the teacher's experience, satisfaction, and career intentions. Forty-six percent of all teachers in Massachusetts completed the TeLLS online survey in 2008. Currently, it is called the Teaching, Empowering, Leading and Learning Survey (TELL), https://newteacher center.org/approach-old/teaching-empowering-leading-and-learning-tell/.

19. Eric A. Hanushek, John F. Rivkin, and Steven G. Kain, "Why Public Schools Lose Teachers," *Journal of Human Resources*, 39, no. 2 (2002): 326–54; Nicole S. Simon and Susan Moore Johnson, "Teacher Turnover in High-Poverty Schools: What We Know and Can Do," *Teachers College Record* 117, no. 3 (2015): 1–36.

20. Helen F. Ladd found a similar relationship between working conditions and student performance, using the TeLLS survey in North Carolina. Helen F. Ladd, "Teachers' Perceptions of Their Working Conditions: How Predictive of Policy Relevant Outcomes?" (Working Paper No. 33, National Center for Analysis of Longitudinal Data in Education Research, Washington, DC, 2009), https://www.urban.org/research/publication /teachers-perceptions-their-working-conditions-how-predictive-policy-relevant -outcomes. Ladd also found that teachers' predictions about their own career decisions were accurately reflected in a school's subsequent turnover rates. Helen F. Ladd, "Teachers Perceptions of Their Working Conditions: How Predictive of Planned and Actual Teacher Movement?" *Educational Evaluation and Policy Analysis* 33, no. 2 (2011): 235–61.

21. Drawing upon four years of teachers' responses to the NYC School Survey, Matthew Kraft and colleagues analyzed the relationship between middle school contexts, teacher turnover, and student achievement in New York City. They found that improvements in school leadership, academic expectations, teacher relationships, and school safety all were independently associated with reductions in teacher turnover, while increases in school safety and academic expectations were associated with student achievement gains. Matthew A. Kraft, William H. Marinell, and Darrick Shen-Wei Yee, "School Organizational Contexts, Teacher Turnover, and Student Achievement: Evidence from Panel Data," *American Educational Research Journal* 53, no. 5 (2016): 1411–49. In a 2017 study, Richard Ingersoll and colleagues analyzed the relationship between teachers' responses to the TELL survey in sixteen states and student achievement data. They found that schools with higher levels of both instructional leadership and teacher leadership have higher student achievement. Also, they found lower levels of both instructional leadership and teacher leadership in high-poverty schools, which they observed that these organizational consequences could put their students at an academic disadvantage. Richard M. Ingersoll, Philip Sirinides, and Patrick Dougherty, "School Leadership, Teachers' Roles in School Decisionmaking, and Student Achievement" (CPRE Working Paper, Consortium for Policy Research in Education, Philadelphia, 2017), http://www.cpre.org/school-leadership-teachers-roles -school-decisionmaking-and-student-achievement.

22. The New Teacher Project, "Teacher Experience: What Does the Research Say?" March 2012, https://tntp.org/assets/documents/TNTP_FactSheet_TeacherExperience_2012 .pdf.

23. Charles T. Clotfelter, Helen F. Ladd, and Jacob L. Vigdor, "Teacher-Student Matching and the Assessment of Teacher Effectiveness," *Journal of Human Resources* 41, no. 4 (2006): 778–820; Ladd and Sorenson, "Returns to Teacher Experience"; Douglas Harris and Tim Sass, "Teacher Training, Teacher Quality and Student Achievement," *Journal of Public Economics* 95, no. 7–8 (2011): 798–812; John P. Papay and Matthew A. Kraft, "Productivity Returns to Experience in the Teacher Labor Market: Methodological Challenges and New Evidence on Long-Term Career Improvement," *Journal of Public Economics*, 130 (2015): 105–19.

24. Birkeland and Curtis also found that the replacement costs (including hiring and professional development) totaled $10,546 for a first-year teacher, $18,617 for a second-year teacher, and $26,687 for a third-year teacher. Sarah E. Birkeland and Rachel Curtis, *Ensuring the Support and Development of New Teachers in the Boston Public Schools: A Proposal to Improve Teacher Quality and Retention*, (Boston: Boston Public Schools, 2006). The Learning Policy Institute provides a useful tool for estimating the often-surprising costs of teacher turnover at https://learningpolicyinstitute.org/product/the-cost-of-teacher-turnover.

25. Elaine Allensworth, Stephen Ponisiack, and Christopher Mazzeo, *The Schools Teachers Leave: Teacher Mobility in Chicago Public Schools* (Chicago: Chicago Consortium for School Research, 2009), https://consortium.uchicago.edu/sites/default/files/publications/CCSR_Teacher_Mobility.pdf.

26. The authors found these effects to be particularly strong in schools that enrolled more black and low performing students. Matthew Ronfeldt, Susanna Loeb, and James Wyckoff, "How Teacher Turnover Harms Student Achievement," *American Journal of Educational Research* 50, no. 1 (2013): 4–36.

27. The National Center for Children in Poverty reports that 44 percent of children in the US lived in low-income families in 2013. "Low-income" is defined as less than 200 percent of the federal poverty threshold (FPT), which for a family of four was $23,624. At that time 22 percent of children were categorized as "poor," defined as living below 100 percent of the FPT. Schools do not report the income level of their students' families, but they do report students' eligibility for Free and Reduced-Priced Lunch (FRPL), which is used by researchers as a proxy for low-income families. High proportions of students in schools serving low-income and high-poverty urban communities are members of ethnic and racial minority groups. Most of the schools described in our studies enrolled very high proportions of students of color who also qualified for FRPL. Yang Jiang, Mercedes Ekono, and Curtis Skinner, *Basic Facts About Low-Income Children: Children Under 18 Years* (New York: National Center for Children in Poverty, Mailman School of Public Health, Columbia University, 2015), http://www.nccp.org/publications/pub_1100.html.

28. Clotfelter, Ladd, and Vigdor, "Teacher-Student Matching"; Kevin Carey, "The Real Value of Teachers: Using New Information About Teacher Effectiveness to Close the Achievement Gap," *Thinking K–16* 8, no. 1 (2004); Allensworth, Ponisciak, and Mazzeo, *The Schools Teachers Leave*; Ruth Heuer and Stephanie Stullich, *Comparability*

of State and Local Expenditures Among Schools Within Districts: A Report from the Study of School-Level Expenditures (Washington, DC: US Department of Education, 2011); Lisa Quay, "Closing the Revolving Door: Understanding the Nature and Causes of Disparities in Access to Effective Teaching," *Voices in Urban Education* 31 (Fall 2011): 7–16; Geoffrey D. Borman and N. Maritza Dowling, "Teacher Attrition and Retention: A Meta-Analytic and Narrative Review of the Research," *Review of Educational Research* 78, no. 3 (2008): 367–409.

29. Under Race to the Top, the US Department of Education provided substantial School Improvement Grants through the states to selected schools that were among the lowest performing 5 percent of all schools, based on their failure to achieve Adequate Yearly Progress on state standardized tests. To be eligible for these grants, the school district had to adopt one of four strategies—turnaround, restart, transformation, or closure—to improve these failing schools or reassign their students to different schools. Massachusetts earlier had assigned two schools in our study to turnaround and one school to restart. The turnaround model called for replacing the principal and 50 percent of the teachers, adopting a new instructional model, providing job-embedded professional development for teachers, adopting a longer instructional day for students, providing more time for teachers to collaborate, and using data to chart progress. The restart model called for closing the school and reopening it under charter management.

30. This case was made cogently over twenty years ago by psychologist Rob Evans, highlighted twelve years later by Tony Bryk and Barbara Schneider, and recently revisited by Esther Quintero of the Albert Shanker Institute and her colleagues. Robert Evans, *The Human Side of School Change: Reform, Resistance, and the Real-Life Problems of Innovation* (San Francisco: Jossey-Bass, 1996); Anthony S. Bryk and Barbara Schneider, *Trust in Schools: A Core Resource for School Reform* (New York: Russell Sage, 2004); Esther Quintero, ed., *Teaching in Context: The Social Side of Education Reform* (Cambridge, MA: Harvard Education Publishing, 2017).

31. Atul Gawande, *The Checklist Manifesto: How to Get Things Right* (New York: Holt Metropolitan Books, 2009), 21, 49, 65, 73.

32. These concepts, which are explained in detail in chapter 1, are drawn from Edward Liu and Susan Moore Johnson, "New Teachers' Experiences of Hiring: Late, Rushed, and Information-Poor," *Educational Administration Quarterly* 42, no. 3 (2006), 324–60.

Chapter 1

1. Daniel Weisberg et al., *The Widget Effect: Our National Failure to Acknowledge and Act on Differences in Teacher Effectiveness* (New York: The New Teacher Project, 2009), https://www.carnegie.org/publications/?q=Widget+Effect&per_page=25&per_page=25#!/publications/widget-effect/.

2. Dale Ballou, "Do Public Schools Hire the Best Applicants?" *Quarterly Journal of Economics* 111, no. 1 (1996): 97–113; Dale Ballou and Michael Podgursky, "Teacher Recruitment and Retention in Public and Private Schools," *Journal of Policy Analysis and Management* 17, no. 3 (1998): 393–417.

3. In 2002, Edward Liu found that 45.9 percent of new teachers in four states experienced a highly decentralized hiring process in which they applied directly to and were offered a position by their school. Another 30.9 percent experienced a moderately decentralized hiring process (they were screened first by the district office, but then interviewed and offered a position by a school). Finally, 23.2 percent experienced either a moderately or highly centralized hiring process in which district officials either assigned them to a specific position or offered a job and then required them to secure a position within a school. Edward Liu and Susan Moore Johnson, "New Teachers' Experiences of Hiring: Late, Rushed, and Information-Poor," *Educational Administration Quarterly* 42, no. 3 (2006): 324–60. Recently, Mimi Engel and colleagues reported that more than 90 percent of principals nationally hire their own teachers. Mimi Engel, Marisa Cannata, and F. Chris Curran, "Principal Influence in Teacher Hiring: Documenting Decentralization Over Time," *Journal of Educational Administration* 56, no. 3 (2018): 277–96.

4. Research on this issue is ongoing. Initially analysts and policy makers assumed that, when an effective teacher transferred to another school, his knowledge and skills would move with him and he would be equally effective there. However, subsequent studies suggest that the teacher's effectiveness in a new school is influenced by that school's work environment and culture, including factors such as the quality of leadership and colleagues, the composition of the student body, and discipline and support for students' needs. Matthew A. Kraft, John P. Papay, and Manuel Monti-Nussbaum recently studied this issue using experimental data from the Talent Transfer Initiative study, conducted in ten districts across seven states by Steven Glazerman et al., *Transfer Incentives for High-Performing Teachers: Final Results from a Multisite Randomized Experiment* (NCEE 2014-4003) (Washington, DC: National Center for Education Evaluation and Regional Assistance, Institute of Education Sciences, US Department of Education, 2013), https://files.eric.ed.gov/fulltext/ED544269.pdf. High performing teachers from high achieving schools received a $20,000 stipend to move to a low achieving school within their district and remain there for two years. The researchers found that the teachers who transferred were, on average, substantially less effective in math and ELA during their first year than they had been in their prior school. That decline persisted in math, but not ELA, into the second year of the experiment. The transferred teachers were, however, more effective than the teachers they replaced. Kraft, Papay, and Monti-Nussbaum observe that these findings call into question the "assumption that teacher effectiveness is fully portable across contexts" in "Is Teacher Effectiveness Portable? Evidence from Randomized Transfer Incentives for High-Performing Teachers" (working paper, Brown University, Providence, RI, 2018).

5. DeArmond and colleagues studied and described the process of matching in hiring by charter management organizations. Michael DeArmond et al., *Managing Talent for School Coherence: Learning from Charter Management Organizations* (Seattle: Center on Reinventing Public Education, University of Washington, 2012), https://eric.ed.gov/?id=ED532634. Match also has been studied in fields outside of education. For a review of this research, see Liu and Johnson, "New Teachers' Experiences of Hiring," 327–33.

6. Susan Moore Johnson and Project on the Next Generation of Teachers, *Finders and Keepers: Helping New Teachers Survive and Thrive in Our Schools* (San Francisco: Jossey-Bass, 2004); Edward Liu, *Information-Rich, Information-Poor: New Teachers' Experiences of Hiring in Four States* (Ed.D diss., Harvard University, Cambridge, Massachusetts, 2004).

7. See, for example, James A. Breaugh, "Realistic Job Previews: A Critical Appraisal and Future Research Directions," *Academy of Management Review* 8, no. 4 (1983): 612–9; Daniel M. Cable and Timothy A. Judge, "Person-Organization Fit, Job Choice Decisions, and Organizational Entry," *Organizational Behavior and Human Decision Processes* 67, no. 3 (1996): 294–311, https://www.sciencedirect.com/science/article/pii /S0749597896900813; Jean M. Phillips, "Effects of Realistic Job Previews: Job Previews on Multiple Organizational Outcomes: A Meta-Analysis," *Academy of Management Journal* 41, no. 6 (2017): 673–90, https://journals.aom.org/doi/10.5465/256964.

8. Jessica Levin and Meredith Quinn explain the problem of late hiring in urban schools in *Missed Opportunities: How We Keep High-Quality Teachers Out of Urban Classrooms* (New York: The New Teacher Project, 2003), https://tntp.org/assets/documents /MissedOpportunities.pdf.

9. John P. Papay and Matthew A. Kraft, "The Productivity Costs of Inefficient Hiring Practices: Evidence from Late Teacher Hiring," *Journal of Policy Analysis and Management* 35, no. 4 (2016): 791–817.

10. Susan Moore Johnson and Sarah E. Birkeland, "Pursuing a 'Sense of Success': New Teachers Explain Their Career Decisions," *American Educational Research Journal* 40, no. 3 (2003): 581–617.

11. Susan Moore Johnson et al., "The Support Gap: New Teachers' Early Experiences in High-Income and Low-Income Schools," *Education Policy Analysis Archives* 12, no. 61 (2004): 1–24.

12. Carol Dweck, *Mindset: The New Psychology of Success* (New York: Ballantine, 2006).

13. Claire Cain Miller, "Does Teacher Diversity Matter in Student Learning?" *New York Times*, September 10, 2018, https://nyti.ms/2oXsE80; Thomas S. Dee, "Teachers, Race, and Student Achievement in a Randomized Experiment," *Review of Economics and Statistics* 86, no. 1 (2004): 195–210.

14. Michael M. DeArmond, Kathryn L. Shaw, and Patrick M. Wright, "Zooming In and Zooming Out: Rethinking School District Human Resource Management," in *Creating a New Teaching Profession*, ed. Dan Goldhaber and Jane Hannaway (Washington, DC: Urban Institute Press, 2009), 54.

Chapter 2

1. David Kauffman et al., "'Lost at Sea': New Teachers' Experiences with Curriculum and Assessment," *Teachers College Record* 104, no. 2 (2002): 273–300.

2. Japanese teachers often make such decisions collaboratively with colleagues who teach the same grade or subject within their school in a process called "lesson study." James W. Stigler and James Hiebert, *The Teaching Gap: Best Ideas from the World's Teachers* (New York: Free Press, 1999); Catherine Lewis and Ineko Tsuchida, "Planned Educational Change in Japan: The Shift to Student-Centered Elementary Science, *Journal of*

Educational Policy 12, no. 5 (1997): 313–31; Linda Darling-Hammond et al., *Empowered Educators: How High-Performing Systems Shape Teaching Quality Around the World* (San Francisco: Jossey-Bass, 2017).

3. David K. Cohen and Deborah Loewenberg Ball, "Reform by the Book: What Is—or Might Be—the Role of Curriculum Materials in Teacher Learning and Instructional Reform?" *Educational Researcher* 25, no. 9 (1996): 6–8, 14.

4. David K. Cohen and Deborah Loewenberg Ball write, "[Teachers] primarily work alone, with their own students, and their interpretations and decisions are tailored to the specifics of their situations." *Instruction, Capacity, and Improvement* (Philadelphia: Consortium for Policy Research in Education, University of Pennsylvania, Graduate School of Education, 1999), 11.

5. John W. Meyer and Brian C. Rowan, "Institutionalized Organizations: Formal Structures as Myth and Ceremony," *American Journal of Sociology* 83, no. 2 (1977): 340–63. Meyer and Rowan refer to institutions' reliance on structures that are largely symbolic as being based on a "logic of confidence." According to this theory, the society assumes that schools are effective because they employ widely accepted features and practices, such as grade-level structures, students' promotion from grade to grade, and formal adoption of curriculum and texts.

6. National Commission on Excellence in Education, *A Nation at Risk: The Imperative for Educational Reform* (Washington, DC: US Department of Education, 1983).

7. Susan R. Fuhrman, *Legislatures and Educational Policymaking from the Capitol to the Classroom: Standards-Based Reforms in the States: One Hundredth Yearbook of the Society for the Study of Education: Part II* (Chicago: University of Chicago Press, 2001), 1–12.

8. Bob Slavin's *Success for All* is one widely known scripted reading curriculum, which researchers found improved students' literacy, http://www.successforall.org/.

9. Sterling Lloyd, "Nation Earns C, Massachusetts Ranks First in 'State of the States' Report Card," *Education Week, Quality Counts*, January 7, 2016, https://www.edweek .org/media/qualitycounts2016_release.pdf; Thomas C. Frohlich, "States with the Best Schools," *USA Today*, January 15, 2015, www.usatoday.com/story/money/business /2015/01/15/247-wall-st-states-best-schools/21388041; 24/7 Wall St., "The States with the Best (and Worst) Schools," *Huffington Post*, January 26, 2017, https://bit .ly/2ioEchL; Judy Nichols Douglass, "Which States Have the Highest Standards for Students?" *Christian Science Monitor*, October 3, 2009, https://www.csmonitor.com /USA/2009/1030/p02s07-usgn.html.

10. Kauffman et al. "Lost at Sea," 281.

11. Susan Moore Johnson et al., "The Support Gap: New Teachers' Early Experiences in High-Income and Low-Income Schools," *Education Policy Analysis Archives* 12, no. 61 (2004): 13.

12. Fred M. Newmann, M. Bruce King, and Mark Rigdon, "Accountability and School Performance: Implications from Restructuring Schools," *Harvard Educational Review* 67, no. 1 (1997): 41–75. Newmann et al. contend that a school responds more effectively to external demands for accountability when it exhibits strong internal coherence among all its improvement efforts, including instructional programs and

materials, grant-funded initiatives, external partnerships, and professional development programs that focus on the goal of building instructional capacity and improving student learning. See also Richard R. Elmore, *School Reform from the Inside Out: Policy, Practice, and Performance*, especially chapter 4, "When Accountability Knocks, Will Anyone Answer?" (Cambridge, MA: Harvard Education Press, 2004), 133–99; Stacy Agee Szczesiul, *Decisions About Practice in Contexts of Strong External Accountability: A Qualitative Study of How Second-Stage Teachers Respond to External Accountability Policies and Reforms in Their Low-Performing Urban Districts* (PhD diss., Harvard University, Cambridge, MA, 2009). In analyzing all the schools in this study, Szczesiul distinguishes between schools with "strong" and "weak" internal accountability systems, based on whether or not teachers within the school expressed a shared understanding of how to improve their school and relied on coherent practices to make that happen.

13. This information is drawn from the school's 2005–2008 School Improvement Plan and the Deer Park website.

14. Among others, these foundational studies include Judith Warren Little, "Norms of Collegiality and Experimentation: Workplace Conditions of School Success," *American Educational Research Journal* 19, no. 3 (1982); Susan J. Rosenholtz, *Teachers' Workplace: The Social Organization of Schools* (New York: Longman, 1989); Judith Warren Little and Milbrey W. McLaughlin, eds., *The Teachers' Workplace: Individuals, Colleagues, and Contexts* (New York: Teachers College Press, 1993); Frederick Newmann, *Authentic Achievement: Restructuring Schools for Intellectual Quality* (San Francisco: Jossey-Bass, 1996); Joel Westheimer, *Among Schoolteachers: Community, Autonomy and Ideology in Teachers' Work* (New York: Teachers College Press, 1998); Milbrey McLaughlin and Joan E. Talbert, *Professional Communities and the Work of High School Teaching* (Chicago: University of Chicago Press, 2001); Anthony Bryk et al., *Organizing Schools for Improvement: Lessons from Chicago* (Chicago: University of Chicago Press, 2010); and Elizabeth McGhee Hassrick, Stephen W. Raudenbush, and Lisa Rosen, *The Ambitious Elementary School: Its Conception, Design, and Implications for Educational Equality* (Chicago: University of Chicago Press, 2017).

15. Linda Darling-Hammond et al. report similar findings about the benefits of collaboration based on TALIS, the OECD international survey, in *Empowered Educators*, 112–13.

16. Massachusetts standards were updated again in 2017.

17. See, for example, Lucy Calkins, *A Guide to the Reading Workshop, Grades 3–5* (New York: Heinemann, 2010); Irene Fountas and Gay Su Pinnell, *Guiding Readers and Writers (Grades 3–6): Teaching Comprehension, Genre, and Content Literacy* (New York: Heinemann, 2001).

Chapter 3

1. Darrel Drury and Justin Baer, eds., *The American Public School Teacher* (Cambridge, MA: Harvard Education Press, 2011).

2. Matthew Ronfeldt et al., "Teacher Collaboration in Instructional Teams and Student Achievement," *American Educational Research Journal* 52, no. 3 (2015): 475–514.

3. Richard M. Ingersoll, "Teacher Turnover and Teacher Shortages: An Organizational Analysis," *American Educational Research Journal* 38, no. 3 (2001): 499–534.

4. Susan M. Kardos et al., "Counting on Colleagues: New Teachers Encounter the Professional Cultures of Their Schools," *Educational Administration Quarterly* 37, no. 2 (2001): 250–90.

5. Susan M. Kardos and Susan Moore Johnson, "New Teachers' Experiences of Mentoring: The Good, the Bad, and the Inequity," *Journal of Educational Change* 11, no. 1 (2010), 23–44.

6. New teachers who continued for a third year in the mentoring program showed some improvement in student learning, but had no better retention rates. Steven Glazerman et al., *Impacts of Comprehensive Teacher Induction: Final Results from a Randomized Controlled Study* (Princeton, NJ: Mathematica Policy Research, 2010), https://ies.ed.gov/ncee/pubs/20104027/pdf/20104028.pdf.

7. We documented several comprehensive induction programs where mentoring was well integrated with other professional practices at the school, but these were unusual. See Susan Moore Johnson and the Project on the Next Generation of Teachers, *Finders and Keepers: Helping New Teachers Survive and Thrive in Our Schools* (San Francisco: Jossey-Bass, 2004), 193–224. See also Thomas A. Smith and Richard Ingersoll, "What Are the Effects of Induction and Mentoring on Beginning Teacher Turnover?" *American Education Research Journal* 41, no. 3 (2004): 617–714. Based on their analysis of national data from the 1999–2000 *Schools and Staffing Survey* and the 2000–2001 *Teacher Follow-Up Survey*, Smith and Ingersoll concluded that mentoring was more successful when it was accompanied by additional structured interactions with colleagues, especially common planning for instruction.

8. As educational sociologist Dan Lortie observed, "teachers attach great meaning to the boundaries [of classrooms]." Dan C. Lortie, *Schoolteacher: A Sociological Study* (Chicago: University of Chicago Press, 1975), 169.

9. Ronfeldt et al., "Teacher Collaboration"; Yvonne L. Goddard, Roger D. Goddard, and Megan Tschannen-Moran, "A Theoretical and Empirical Investigation of Teacher Collaboration for School Improvement and Student Achievement," *Teachers College Record* 109, no. 4 (2007): 877–96.

10. Lortie, *Schoolteacher*, 14.

11. Lortie, *Schoolteacher*, 195.

12. Lortie, *Schoolteacher*, 101.

13. Judith Warren Little, "The Persistence of Privacy: Autonomy and Initiative in Teachers' Professional Relations," *Teachers College Record* 91, no. 4 (1990): 509–36.

14. Morgaen L. Donaldson et al., "Angling for Access, Bartering for Change: How Second-Stage Teachers Experience Differentiated Roles in Schools," *Teachers College Record* 110, no. 5 (2008): 1088–1114.

15. Daniel Koretz, *The Testing Charade: Pretending to Make Schools Better* (Chicago: University of Chicago Press, 2017). Wayne Au conducted a metasynthesis of forty-nine qualitative studies in order to learn how high-stakes testing affects curriculum. The primary effects he found were that it narrowed the curricular content to tested sub-

jects, fragmented subject area knowledge, and increased the use of teacher-centered pedagogy. However, in a small number of cases, high-stakes tests had the opposite effect, expanding curricular content, integrating knowledge, and increasing student-centered, cooperative pedagogy. Wayne Au, "High-Stakes Testing and Curricular Control: A Qualitative Metasynthesis," *Educational Researcher* 36, no. 5 (2007): 258–67.

16. Jennifer O'Day explores the organizational benefits of accountability in "Complexity, Accountability, and School Improvement," *Harvard Educational Review* 72, no. 3 (2002): 293–329. However, Andy Hargreaves and Dennis Shirley caution that the demands of accountability might discourage, rather than support, collaboration in *The Fourth Way: The Inspiring Future for Educational Change* (Newbury Park, CA: Corwin Press, 2009).

17. Richard DuFour and Robert Eacker, *Professional Communities at Work: Best Practices for Enhancing Student Achievement* (Bloomington, IN: Solution Tree, 1998).

18. Little, "Persistence of Privacy."

19. Vivian Troen and Katherine Boles examine the challenges and opportunities that teacher teams encounter in *The Power of Teacher Teams* (New York: Corwin Press, 2012), 44.

20. Ronfeldt et al. also report high rates of participation in "Teacher Collaboration." Over 84 percent of the nine thousand teachers surveyed in Miami-Dade County reported that they participated on a team or had a group of colleagues who worked together.

21. Megin Charner-Laird et al., "Gauging Goodness of Fit: Teachers' Responses to Their Instructional Teams in High-Poverty Schools," *American Journal of Education* 123, no. 4 (2017): 553–84.

22. Andy Hargreaves, *Changing Teachers, Changing Times: Teachers' Work and Culture in the Postmodern Age* (London: A&C Black, 1994), 186.

23. Amy Edmondson, *Teaming: How Organizations Learn, Innovate, and Compete in the Knowledge Economy* (San Francisco: Jossey-Bass, 2012), 83–113 and 115–48.

24. Edmondson, *Teaming*, 100.

25. Jonathan A. Supovitz, "Developing Communities of Instructional Practice," *Teachers College Record* 104, no. 8 (2002): 1591–1626; Troen and Boles, *The Power of Teacher Teams*.

26. In an extensive study of their research-practice partnership to design and implement coherent mathematics instruction in four districts, Cobb et al. document the central role that teachers' collaboration played in the process. They found that school leaders were important in scheduling and protecting team time, providing skilled facilitators, and taking a "professionalizing" rather than a "surveillance" stance toward the teachers' work. Paul Cobb et al., *Systems for Instructional Improvement: Creating Coherence from the Classroom to the District Office* (Cambridge, MA: Harvard Education Press, 2018), 105–11. Other researchers have documented the important role that principals play in teachers' collaboration. See, for example, Anthony Bryk et al., *Organizing Schools for Improvement: Lessons from Chicago* (Chicago: University of Chicago Press, 2010).

27. Matthew Ronfeldt et al. report similar benefits when teams are effectively organized, in "Teacher Collaboration in Instructional Teams and Student Achievement," *American Educational Research Journal* 52, no. 3 (2015): 475–514.

Chapter 4

1. Dan C. Lortie, *Schoolteacher: A Sociological Study* (Chicago: University of Chicago Press, 1975), 101.

2. Susan Moore Johnson and Sarah E. Birkeland, "Pursuing a 'Sense of Success': New Teachers Explain Their Career Decisions," *American Educational Research Journal* 40, no. 3 (2003): 581–617.

3. Lortie, *Schoolteacher*, 133. For descriptions of new teachers' encounters with the uncertainty that students introduce, see Susan Moore Johnson and the Project on the Next Generation of Teachers, *Finders and Keepers: Helping New Teachers Survive and Thrive in Our Schools* (San Francisco: Jossey-Bass, 2004), 73–80.

4. Dinah Volk and Susi Long, "Challenging Myths of the Deficit Perspective: Honoring Children's Literacy Resources," *Young Children* 60, no. 6 (2005): 12–9.

5. Eric A. Hanushek, John F. Kain, and Steven G. Rivkin, "Why Public Schools Lose Teachers," *Journal of Human Resources* 39, no. 2 (2004): 326–54.

6. Richard Ingersoll and Henry May, *Recruitment, Retention and the Minority Teacher Shortage* (Philadelphia: Consortium for Policy Research in Education, 2012); Elaine Allensworth, Stephen Ponisciak, and Christopher Mazzeo, *The Schools Teachers Leave: Teacher Mobility in Chicago Public Schools* (Chicago: Consortium on Chicago School Research, University of Chicago, 2009); Susan Moore Johnson, Matthew A. Kraft, and John P. Papay, "How Context Matters in High-Need Schools: The Effects of Teachers' Working Conditions on Their Professional Satisfaction and Their Students' Achievement," *Teachers College Record* 114, no. 10 (2012): 1–39; Nicole S. Simon and Susan Moore Johnson, "Teacher Turnover in High-Poverty Schools: What We Know and Can Do," *Teachers College Record* 117, no. 3 (2015): 1–36.

7. This analysis builds on our earlier article about students in WCSD schools. Matthew A. Kraft et al., "Educating Amid Uncertainty: The Organizational Supports Teachers Need to Serve Students in High-Poverty, Urban Schools," *Educational Administration Quarterly* 51, no. 5 (2015): 753–90.

8. W. Richard Scott and Gerald F. Davis, *Organizations and Organizing* (New York: Pearson, 2007). Since the 1950s, organizational theorists have debated whether organizations operate as open or closed systems. Scott and Davis explain that some factories and businesses seek to function as "rational" systems, excluding outside influences that might disrupt their operations or corrupt their management. They view the organizational environment as "alien and hostile," something to be kept out, rather than brought in (p. 106). However, Scott and Davis conclude that "organizations are not closed systems, sealed off from their environments, but are open to and dependent on flows of personnel, information, and resources from outside. From an open systems perspective, environments shape, support, and infiltrate organizations" (p. 31).

Chapter 5

1. Raymond E. Callahan, *Education and the Cult of Efficiency* (Chicago: University of Chicago Press, 1962); Ellwood P. Cubberley, *The Portland Survey: A Textbook on City School Administration* (Yonkers-on-Hudson:World Book, 2015).

2. US Department of Education, *A Nation at Risk* (Washington, DC: US Department of Education, 1983).

3. Linda Darling-Hammond, Arthur E. Wise, and Sara R. Pease, "Teacher Evaluation in the Organizational Context: A Review of the Literature," *Review of Educational Research* 53, no. 3 (1983): 285–328; Tom Toch and Robert Rothman, *Rush to Judgment: Teacher Evaluation in Public Education* (Washington, DC: Education Sector, 2008).

4. Sharon Feinman-Nemser, "From Preparation to Practice: Designing a Continuum to Strengthen and Sustain Teaching," *Teachers College Record* 103, no. 6 (2001): 1013–55.

5. Many alternative preparation programs created since 2000 were modeled loosely on the summer institute of Teach for America, which recruited and selected college graduates from liberal arts programs to participate in a summer training program before becoming a teacher of record in a low-income urban or rural school. For example, see our study of five such programs, Susan Moore Johnson et al., *A Difficult Balance: Incentives and Quality Control in Alternative Preparation Programs* (Cambridge, MA: Project on the Next Generation of Teachers, 2005). See also Daniel Humphrey and Marjorie Weschler, *Alternative Certification: A National Study* (Menlo Park, CA: SRI, 2005), https://www.sri.com/work/projects/alternative-certification-national-study.

6. In "A Revolution in One Classroom: The Case of Ms. Oublier," *Educational Evaluation and Policy Analysis* 12, no. 3 (1990), David K. Cohen describes one elementary teacher's unsuccessful efforts to use new pedagogical practices in her mathematics class. In "Shaping Teacher Sensemaking: School Leaders and the Enactment of Reading Policy," *Educational Policy* 19 (2005): 476–509, Cynthia E. Coburn examines how individual and social cognition shape the implementation of reading policy in schools and classrooms. And in "Policy Implementation and Cognition: Reframing and Refocusing Implementation Research," *Review of Educational Research* 72, no. 3, (2002): 387–431, James P. Spillane, Brian J. Reiser, and Todd Reimer explain how "individual cognition," "situated cognition," and "policy stimuli" influence the implementation of new instructional policies.

7. Jonah E. Rockoff, "The Impact of Individual Teachers on Student Achievement: Evidence from Panel Data," *American Economic Review, Papers and Proceedings* 94, no. 2 (2004); Steven G. Rivkin, Eric A. Hanushek, and John F. Kain, "Teachers, Schools, and Academic Achievement," *Econometrica* 73, no. 2 (2005).

8. Eric A. Hanushek, "Teacher Deselection," in *Creating a New Teaching Profession*, ed. Dan Goldhaber and Jane Hanaway (Washington, DC: Urban Institute Press, 2009). Jane Hanaway made a similar proposal in *Testimony Before the District of Columbia City Council on District of Columbia Public Schools Human Capital Initiatives* (Washington, DC: The Urban Institute, 2009).

9. Daniel S. Weisberg et al., *The Widget Effect: Our National Failure to Acknowledge and Act on Differences in Teacher Effectiveness* (Brooklyn, NY: The New Teacher Project, 2009), https://tntp.org/publications/view/the-widget-effect-failure-to-act-on-differences-in-teacher-effectiveness.

10. Evan Thomas et al., "Why We Can't Get Rid of Failing Teachers," *Newsweek*, March 15, 2010, 24–7.

11. John P. Papay, "Refocusing the Debate: Assessing the Purposes and Tools of Teacher Evaluation," *Harvard Educational Review* 82, no. 1 (2012): 123–41.

12. Editors Jason Grissom and Peter Youngs note the "rapid policy diffusion" that followed the announcement of RTTT competition in *Improving Teacher Evaluation Systems: Making the Most of Multiple Measures* (New York: Teachers College Press, 2015), 169. Matthew A. Kraft provides an informative review of the federal government's initiatives to improve teacher quality during the Bush and Obama administrations in "Federal Efforts to Improve Teacher Quality," in *Bush-Obama School Reform: Lessons Learned*, ed. Frederick M. Hess and Michael Q. McShane (Cambridge, MA: Harvard Education Publishing, 2018), 69–85.

13. Ellen Goldring et al., "Make Room Value-Added: Principals' Human Capital Decisions and the Emergence of Teacher Observation Data," *Educational Researcher* 44, no. 2 (2015): 96–104.

14. Charlotte Danielson, *Enhancing Professional Practice: A Framework for Teaching, Second Edition* (Alexandria, VA: Association for Supervision and Curriculum Development, 2013).

15. Liz Griffin, "Charlotte Danielson on Teacher Evaluation and Quality: A School Administrator Interview with the Creator of the Framework for Teaching," *School Administrator* 70, no. 1 (2013): 29.

16. Lauren Sartain, Sara Ray Stoelinga, and Eric R. Brown, *Rethinking Teacher Evaluation in Chicago: Lessons Learned from Classroom Observations, Principal-Teacher Conferences, and District Implementation* (Chicago: Consortium on Chicago School Research, 2011).

17. The New Teacher Project, *Teacher Experience: What Does the Research Say?* (New York: TNTP, 2012), https://tntp.org/assets/documents/TNTP_FactSheet_Teacher Experience_2012.pdf.

18. Bill Gates, "Mosquitos, Malaria, and Education," TED Talk, February 2009, www.ted .com/talks/bill_gates_unplugged/transcript.

19. See, for example, Douglas Harris and Tim R. Sass, "Teacher Training, Teacher Quality, and Student Achievement," *Journal of Public Economics* 95, no. 7–8 (2011): 798–812; John P. Papay and Matthew Kraft, "Productivity Returns to Experience in the Teacher Labor Market: Methodological Challenges and New Evidence on Long-Term Career Improvement," *Journal of Public Economics* 130 (2015): 105–19; Helen F. Ladd and Lucy C. Sorenson, "Returns to Teacher Experience: Student Achievement and Motivation in Middle School," *Education Finance and Policy* 12, no. 2 (2017): 241–279.

20. John P. Papay and Matthew A. Kraft, "The Myth of the Performance Plateau," *Educational Leadership* 73, no. 8 (2016): 37. For more details about this study, see Matthew A. Kraft and John P. Papay, "Can Professional Environments in Schools Promote Teacher Development? Explaining Heterogeneity in Returns to Experience," *Educational Evaluation and Policy Analysis* 36, no. 4 (2014): 476–500.

21. Matthew P. Steinberg and Morgaen L. Donaldson, "The New Educational Accountability: Understanding the Landscape of Teacher Evaluation in the Post-NCLB Era," *Education Finance and Policy* 11, no. 3 (2016): 350.

22. Institute for Educational Science, *State Requirements for Teacher Evaluation Policies Promoted by Race to the Top* (Washington DC: US Department of Education, Institute of Education Sciences, National Center for Education Evaluation and Regional Assistance, 2012), https://ies.ed.gov/ncee/pubs/20144016/.

23. For example, see Michael Lipsky, *Street-Level Bureaucracy: Dilemmas of the Individual in Public Service* (New York: Russell Sage Foundation, 1980); Milbrey W. McLaughlin, "Learning from Experience: Lessons from Policy Implementation," *Educational Evaluation and Policy Analysis* 9, no. 2 (1987): 171–8.

24. Stefanie Reinhorn and Susan Moore Johnson, "Can Teacher Evaluation Provide Both Accountability and Development? Learning from Six Schools' Implementation of Evaluation Policy" (working paper, Project on the Next Generation of Teachers, Harvard Graduate School of Education, Cambridge, MA, 2015), https://bit.ly/2zsRyBP.

25. Walker City School District, "Superintendent's Circular: Performance Evaluation of Teachers," 2010, 1.

26. The responses of teachers at Thoreau illustrate the problems that follow from a lack of trust between administrators and teachers in schools. Anthony S. Bryk and Barbara Schneider, *Trust in Schools: A Core Resource for Improvement* (New York: Russell Sage, 2002).

27. Morgaen L. Donaldson and Sarah Woulfin studied forty-four principals in thirteen Connecticut districts and found that they, too, used considerable discretion in implementing the state's evaluation policy, often adding components to the process. Morgaen L. Donaldson and Sarah Woulfin, "From Tinkering to Going 'Rogue': How Principals Use Agency When Enacting New Teacher Evaluation Systems," *Educational Evaluation and Policy Analysis* 40, no. 4 (2018): 1–26.

28. Morgaen L. Donaldson and Casey D. Cobb, "Implementing Student Learning Objectives and Classroom Observations in Connecticut's Teacher Evaluation System," in *Improving Teacher Evaluation Systems: Making the Most of Multiple Measures*, ed. Jason A. Grissom and Peter Youngs (New York: Teachers College Press, 2015), 131–42.

29. William A. Firestone et al., *New Jersey's Pilot Teacher Evaluation Program: Year 2 Final Report* (New Brunswick, NJ: Rutgers Graduate School of Education, 2014).

30. Timothy A. Drake et al., "Development or Dismissal? Exploring Principals' Use of Teacher Effectiveness Data," in Grissom and Youngs, *Improving Teacher Evaluation Systems*, 116–30. See also Jason A. Grissom et al., "Central Office Supports for Data-Driven Talent Management Decisions: Evidence from the Implementation of New Systems for Measuring Teacher Effectiveness," *Educational Researcher* 46 (2017): 21–32.

31. Lee S. Shulman, "Those Who Understand: Knowledge Growth in Teaching," *Educational Researcher* 15, no. 2 (1986): 4–14.

32. Matthew A. Kraft and Allison F. Gilmour, "Can Principals Promote Teacher Development as Evaluators? A Case Study of Principals' Views and Experiences," *Educational Administration Quarterly* 52, no. 5 (2016): 711–53.

33. Stefanie K. Reinhorn, Susan Moore Johnson, and Nicole S. Simon, "Investing Development: Six High-Performing, High-Poverty Schools Implement the Massachusetts

Teacher Evaluation Policy," *Educational Evaluation and Policy Analysis* 39, no. 3 (2017): 383–406.

34. Morgaen L. Donaldson and Heather G. Peske, *Supporting Effective Teaching Through Teacher Evaluation: A Study of Teacher Evaluation in Five Charter Schools* (Washington, DC: Center for American Progress, 2010).

35. Massachusetts Task Force on the Evaluation of Teachers and Administrators, *Building a Breakthrough Framework for Educator Evaluation in the Commonwealth* (Malden: Massachusetts Department of Elementary and Secondary Education, 2011), 5.

36. Memorandum from Mitchell D. Chester, Massachusetts Commissioner of Education, to the Massachusetts Board of Elementary and Secondary Education, April 16, 2011.

37. Massachusetts Department of Elementary and Secondary Education, *The Massachusetts Model System for Educator Evaluation* (Malden: Massachusetts Department of Elementary and Secondary Education, 2012), http://www.doe.mass.edu/edeval/model/.

38. Donaldson and Woulfin found similar priorities and practices among the Connecticut principals they interviewed, in "From Tinkering to Going 'Rogue.'"

39. See, for example, Steven Kimball and Anthony Milanowski, "Examining Teacher Evaluation Validity and Leadership Decision Making with a Standards-Based Evaluation System," *Educational Administration Quarterly* 45, no. 1 (2009): 34–70.

40. Julie A. Marsh et al., "Evaluating Teachers in the Big Easy: How Organizational Context Shapes Policy Responses in New Orleans," *Educational Evaluation and Policy Analysis* 39, no. 4 (2017): 539–70.

41. Richard R. Halverson, Carolyn Kelly, and Steven Kimball, "Implementing Teacher Evaluation Systems: How Principals Make Sense of Complex Artifacts to Shape Local Instructional Practice," in *Educational Administration, Policy, and Reform: Research and Measurement*, ed. Wayne K. Hoy (Charlotte, NC: Information Age, 2004), 253–88.

42. Susan Moore Johnson et al., *A User's Guide to Peer Assistance and Review* (Cambridge, MA: Project on the Next Generation of Teachers, Harvard Graduate School of Education, 2009), https://www.gse.harvard.edu/~ngt/par/. This website includes detailed examples of policies and practices. See also Susan Moore Johnson et al., *Teacher to Teacher: Realizing the Potential of Peer Assistance and Review* (Washington, DC: Center for American Progress, 2010); Jennifer Goldstein, "Easy to Dance To: Solving the Problems of Teacher Evaluation with Peer Assistance and Review," *American Journal of Education* 113, no. 3 (2007): 479–508.

43. John P. Papay and Susan Moore Johnson, "Is PAR a Good Investment? Understanding the Costs and Benefits of Peer Assistance and Review Programs," *Educational Policy* 26, no. 5 (2012): 696–729.

44. Thomas Bird and Judith Warren Little, "How Schools Organize the Teaching Occupation," *Elementary School Journal* 86, no. 4 (1986): 493–511; Sharon Feiman-Nemser, "Learning to Teach," in *Handbook of Teaching and Policy*, ed. Gary Sykes and Lee S. Shulman (New York: Longman, 1983), 150–70; Judith Warren Little, "Teachers' Accounts of Classroom Experience as a Resource for Professional Learning and Instructional Decision Making," *Yearbook (National Society for the Study of Education)* 106, no. 1 (2007): 217–40.

45. Stefanie K. Reinhorn, Susan Moore Johnson, and Nicole S. Simon, "Peer Observa-
tion: Supporting Professional Learning in Six High-Performing High-Poverty, Urban
Schools" (working paper, Project on the Next Generation of Teachers, Cambridge,
MA, 2015), https://bit.ly/2KzE5g4.

46. W. James Popham, "The Dysfunctional Marriage of Formative and Summative
Teacher Evaluation," *Journal of Personnel Evaluation in Education* 1, no. 3 (1988):
269–73; Anthony T. Milanowski, "Split Roles in Performance Evaluation—A Field
Study Involving New Teachers," *Journal of Personnel Evaluation in Education* 18, no. 3
(2005): 153–69. Brian Yusko and Sharon Feiman-Nemser present an alternative view
in "Embracing Contraries: Combining Assistance and Assessment in New Teacher
Induction," *Teachers College Record* 110, no. 5 (2008): 923–53.

47. We make this argument in Susan Moore Johnson, Stefanie K. Reinhorn, and Nicole
S. Simon, "Reaping Rewards for Students: How Successful Urban School Systemati-
cally Invest in Teachers," in *Teaching in Context: The Social Side of Education Reform*, ed.
Esther Quintero (Cambridge, MA: Harvard Education Press, 2017).

Chapter 6

1. Susan J. Rosenholtz, *Teachers' Workplace: The Social Organization of Schools* (New York:
Longman, 1989); Anthony Bryk et al., *Organizing Schools for Improvement: Lessons from
Chicago* (Chicago: University of Chicago Press, 2010); Anthony S. Bryk and Barbara
Schneider, *Trust in Schools: A Core Resource for School Reform* (New York: Russell Sage,
2004); Judith Warren Little and Milbrey W. McLaughlin, eds., *The Teachers' Work-
place: Individuals, Colleagues, and Contexts* (New York: Teachers College Press, 1993);
Joel Westheimer, *Among Schoolteachers: Community, Autonomy and Ideology in Teachers'
Work* (New York: Teachers College Press, 1998); Milbrey McLaughlin and Joan E.
Talbert, *Professional Communities and the Work of High School Teaching* (Chicago: University of Chicago Press, 2001).

2. Ronald Heifitz, *Leadership Without Easy Answers* (Cambridge, MA: Harvard University
Press, 1998).

3. Ronald Heifitz and Donald L. Laurie, "The Work of Leadership," *Harvard Business
Review* 75, no. 1 (1997): 124.

4. Rosenholtz, *Teachers' Workplace*, 6.

5. Rodney T. Ogawa and Steven T. Bossert, "Leadership as an Organizational Quality,"
Educational Administration Quarterly 31, no. 2 (1995): 224–43.

6. Ogawa and Bossert, "Leadership as an Organizational Quality," 224.

7. Susan Moore Johnson et al., "Ready to Lead, but How? Teachers' Experiences in
High-Poverty Urban Schools," *Teachers College Record* 116, no. 1 (2014): 1–50.

8. James S. Coleman, "Social Capital in the Creation of Human Capital," *American Journal of Sociology* 94 (1988): S95–S120.

9. Jill Harrison Berg provides a valuable insider's perspective on the relationship between
principals and teachers as they lead collaboratively within their schools, in *Leading in
Sync: Teacher Leaders and Principals Working Together for Student Learning* (Alexandria,
VA: ASCD, 2018).

10. Kenwyn K. Smith and David N. Berg, *Paradoxes of Group Life: Understanding Conflict, Paralysis, and Movement in Group Dynamics* (San Francisco: Jossey-Bass, 1997).

11. Smith and Berg, *Paradoxes of Group Life*, 134.

12. Morgaen Donaldson et al., "Angling for Access, Bartering for Change: How Second-Stage Teachers Experience Differentiated Roles in Schools," *Teachers College Record* 110, no. 5 (2008): 1088–1114.

13. Susan Moore Johnson and Morgaen Donaldson, "Overcoming Obstacles to Leadership," *Educational Leadership* 65, no. 1 (2007): 8–13.

14. Susan Moore Johnson et al., *Teacher to Teacher: Realizing the Potential of Peer Assistance and Review* (Washington, DC: Center for American Progress, 2010). These PAR programs and the CTs' roles are described in detail on our website, https://www.gse.harvard.edu/~ngt/par/. See also Jennifer Goldstein, *Peer Review and Teacher Leadership* (New York: Teachers College Press, 2010).

15. For a description of T3, see Celine Coggins, Heather G. Peske, Kate McGovern, eds., *Learning from the Experts: Teacher Leaders on Solving America's Education Challenges* (Cambridge, MA: Harvard Education Press, 2013), 21–38.

16. Richard M. Ingersoll, Philip Sirinides, and Patrick Dougherty, "School Leadership, Teachers' Roles in School Decisionmaking, and Student Achievement" (CPRE Working Paper, Consortium for Policy Research in Education, Philadelphia, 2017), http://www.cpre.org/school-leadership-teachers-roles-school-decisionmaking-and-student-achievement.

Chapter 7

1. OECD, the Organisation for Economic Cooperation and Development, located in Paris, includes thirty-six member countries and is dedicated to economic progress and world trade. See OECD, *Education at a Glance 2017: OECD Indicators* (Paris: OECD, 2017), 388, https://doi.org/10.1787/eag-2017-en. Linda Darling-Hammond reports that, according to the OECD's TALIS survey, US teachers "spend about 27 hours a week teaching students directly, about 50% more than the international average of about 19 hours. By contrast, teachers in Singapore spend about 17 hours a week teaching." Linda Darling-Hammond, *Empowered Educators: How High-Performing Systems Shape Teaching Quality Around the World* (Jossey-Bass: San Francisco, 2017), 113. See also Meg Benner and Lisett Partelow, *Reimagining the School Day* (Washington, DC: Center for American Progress, 2017). The Center for Public Education analyzed data from the OECD's *Education at a Glance 2011* and the Education Commission of the States' "Number of Instructional Days/Hours in the School Year" and found that the data did not support the common belief that US schools require less instructional time than other countries; see Jim Hull and Mandy Newport, "Time in School: How Does the U.S. Compare?" December 2011, http://www.centerforpubliceducation.org/research/time-school-how-does-us-compare.

2. Jonah E. Rockoff, "The Impact of Individual Teachers on Student Achievement: Evidence from Panel Data, *American Economic Review, Papers and Proceedings* 94, no.

2 (2004): 247–52; Steven G. Rivkin, Eric A. Hanushek, and John F. Kain, "Teachers, Schools, and Academic Achievement," *Econometrica* 73, no. 2 (2005): 417–58.

3. Hull and Newport, "Time in School."

4. The American Federation of Teachers, *Quality of Worklife Survey* (Washington, DC: American Federation of Teachers, 2015), 4.

5. OECD, *Education at a Glance 2017*, 388.

6. See examples in Claire Kaplan et al., *Time for Teachers: Leveraging Expanded Time to Strengthen Instruction and Empower Teacher* (Boston: National Center on Time and Learning, 2015), https://www.timeandlearning.org/sites/default/files/resources/time forteachers.pdf.

7. Susan Moore Johnson and James R. Heal, *Investing in Teachers: The Lawrence Public Schools Respond to State Receivership* (Cambridge, MA: Harvard Education Press, 2018), http://hepg.org/hep-home/case/investing-in-teachers.

8. Kaplan et al., *Time for Teachers.*

Chapter 8

1. Kaitlin Mulhere, "These 7 Charts Explain the Fight for Higher Teacher Pay," *Time*, April 11, 2018, http://time.com/money/5228237/teacher-pay-charts/; Madeline Will, "See How Your State's Average Teacher Salary Compares," *Education Week*, April 24, 2018, https://blogs.edweek.org/edweek/teacherbeat/2018/04/teacher_pay_2017.html; Katie Reilly, "Here's Why Oklahoma Teachers Are Striking After Getting a $6100 Pay Raise," *Time*, April 2, 2018, http://time.com/5225514/oklahoma-kentucky-schools -teachers-strike/; Melissa Daniels and Anita Snow, "Seeing Red: Teacher Walkouts Shut Arizona, Colorado Schools," Associated Press, April 26, 2018, https://apnews .com/89a24152327845d1876822a02640d4ca.

2. Carole Feldman and Emily Swanson, "AP-Norc Poll: Amid Strikes, Americans Back Teacher Raises," *US News and World Report*, April 23, 2018, https://www.usnews.com /news/politics/articles/2018-04-23ap-norc-poll-amid-strikes-americans-back-teacher -raises.

3. Paul Krugman, "Opinion: We Don't Need No Education," *New York Times*, April 23, 2018, https://nyti.ms/2Jn268p.

4. Robert Maranto, "Pay Teachers More—but Make Sure They Earn It," *Wall Street Journal*, May 21, 2018, https://on.wsj.com/2KLPzMa.

5. Sylvia Allegretto and Lawrence Mishel, *The Teacher Pay Gap Has Hit a New High* (Washington, DC: Economic Policy Institute, 2018), https://www.epi.org/files/pdf/153196.pdf.

6. Nicole Katz et al., *Low Teacher Salaries 101* (Watertown, MA: Education Resource Strategies, 2018), 3, https://www.erstrategies.org/tap/low_teacher_salaries_101.

7. OECD, *Education at a Glance 2017: OECD Indicators* (Paris: OECD Publishing, 2017), https://doi.org/10.1787/eag-2017-en.

8. Sean P. Corcoran, William N. Evans, and Robert M. Schwab, "Women, the Labor Market, and the Declining Relative Quality of Teachers," *Journal of Policy Analysis and Management* 23, no. 3 (2004): 449–70.

9. Maura Spiegelman, *Teacher Satisfaction with Salary and Current Job* (Washington, DC: Data Point, National Center for Education Statistics, 2018), https://nces.ed.gov/pub search/pubsinfo.asp?pubid=2018116.

10. Edward Liu, Susan Moore Johnson, and Heather G. Peske, "New Teachers and the Massachusetts Signing Bonus: The Limits of Inducements," *Educational Evaluation and Policy Analysis* 26, no. 3 (2004): 217–36; F. Clarke Fowler, "The Massachusetts Signing Bonus Program for New Teachers: A Model of Teacher Preparation Worth Copying?" *Education Policy Analysis Archives* 11, no. 13 (2003), https://epaa.asu.edu/ojs/article /view/241.

11. Jennifer Calfas, "'I Didn't Really Have a Choice.' Meet the Teachers Quitting Their Jobs Due to Low Pay and Dwindling Benefits," *Time*, May 21, 2018, http://time.com /money/longform/teacher-pay/; Katie Reilly, "'I Work Three Jobs and Donate Blood Plasma to Pay the Bills.' This Is What It's Like to Be a Teacher in America," *Time*, September 13, 2018, http://time.com/longform/teaching-in-america/.

12. See, for example, Brandy Bochna Tuck, "I Am a Coal Miner's Daughter and a West Virginia Teacher: Here's Why I'm on Strike," *PBS News Hour*, March 2, 2018, https:// www.pbs.org/newshour/education/opinion-i-am-a-coal-miners-daughter-and-a-west -virginia-teacher-heres-why-im-on-strike.

13. Lucinda Gray, Amy Bittman, and Rebecca Goldring, *Characteristics of Schools, Districts, Teachers, Principals and School Libraries in the United States: 2011–2012 School and Staffing Survey* (Washington, DC: US Department of Education, 2013), 8.

14. Allan R. Odden and Carolyn Kelley provide an informative history of teachers' pay in *Paying Teachers for What They Know and Do: New and Smarter Strategies to Improve Schools*, 2nd Edition (Newbury Park, CA: Corwin Press, 2001).

15. Susan Moore Johnson, "Merit Pay for Teachers: A Poor Prescription for Reform," *Harvard Educational Review* 54, no. 2 (1984): 175–85.

16. Daniel Koretz explains the limitations of relying on standardized tests for school improvement, and the hazards of relying on VAM scores to assess and motivate teachers, in *The Testing Charade: Pretending to Make Schools Better* (Chicago: University of Chicago Press, 2017). See also Henry Braun, "The Value in Value Added Depends on the Ecology," *Educational Researcher* 44, no. 2 (2015): 127–31.

17. Edward E. Lawler III, *Strategic Pay: Aligning Organizational Strategies and Pay Systems* (San Francisco: Jossey-Bass, 1990).

18. Richard Murnane and David K. Cohen, "Why Most Merit Pay Plans Fail and Few Survive," *Harvard Educational Review* 56, no. 1 (1986): 1–18.

19. Susan Moore Johnson, "Will VAMS Reinforce the Walls of the Egg-Crate School?" *Educational Researcher* 44, no. 2 (2015): 117–26.

20. John Papay and Susan Moore Johnson, "Teacher Pay-for-Performance: A Framework for Program Design," in Johnson and Papay, *Redesigning Teacher Pay: A System for the Next Generation of Educators* (Washington, DC: Economic Policy Institute, 2009), 16–21.

21. Jennifer King Rice and Betty Malen track the challenges of implementing merit pay in Prince George's County (MD) 2007–2012. *Performance-Based Pay for Educators: Assessing the Evidence* (New York: Teachers College Press, 2017).

22. The relationships among these three practices are explored in Susan Moore Johnson, Stefanie Reinhorn, and Nicole Simon, "Reaping Rewards for Students: How Successful Urban Schools Systematically Invest in Teachers," in *Teaching in Context: The Social Side of Education Reform*, ed. Esther Quintero (Cambridge, MA: Harvard Education Press, 2017), 37–62.

23. Susan Moore Johnson and John Papay, "Pay and Career Development: A Proposal for a New Generation of Teacher," in Johnson and Papay, *Redesigning Teacher Pay*, 43–77.

24. Richard R. Elmore, *School Reform from the Inside Out: Policy, Practice, and Performance* (Cambridge, MA: Harvard Education Press, 2004); Anthony Bryk et al., *Organizing Schools for Improvement: Lessons from Chicago* (Chicago: University of Chicago Press, 2010); Frederick Newmann et al., *Authentic Achievement: Restructuring Schools for Intellectual Quality* (San Francisco: Jossey-Bass, 1996); Susan J. Rosenholtz, *Teachers' Workplace: The Social Organization of Schools* (New York: Longman, 1989); Anthony S. Bryk and Barbara Schneider, *Trust in Schools: A Core Resource for School Reform* (New York: Russell Sage, 2004).

25. For a description of ProComp, see http://thecommons.dpsk12.org/Page/1551. Detailed accounts of these career ladders and the process by which they were adopted in Baltimore and Lawrence can be found in two teaching cases: Susan Moore Johnson et al., *Career Pathways, Performance Pay, and Peer-Review Promotion in Baltimore City Public Schools* (Cambridge, MA: Harvard Business School Publishing, 2013), https://hbsp.harvard.edu/product/PEL071-PDF-ENG; Susan Moore Johnson and James R. Heal, *Investing in Teachers: The Lawrence Public Schools Respond to State Receivership* (Cambridge, MA: Harvard Education Press, 2018), http://hepg.org/hep-home/case/investing-in-teachers.

Conclusion

1. The strategy also called for linking the teachers' strengths and weaknesses, as identified by evaluations, to individualized training and support and also introducing pay incentives and new leadership roles in order to retain effective teachers. However, RAND found that these practices were minimally implemented. Brian M. Stecher et al., *Improving Teaching Effectiveness: Final Report: The Intensive Partnerships for Effective Teaching Through 2015–2016* (Santa Monica, CA: RAND Corporation, 2018), https://www.rand.org/pubs/research_reports/RR2242.html.

2. Elizabeth McGhee Hassrick, Stephen W. Raudenbush, and Lisa Rosen, *The Ambitious Elementary School: Its Conception, Design, and Implications for Educational Equality* (Chicago: University of Chicago Press, 2017), 7.

3. Based on her study of seventy-nine schools, Susan Rosenholtz characterized schools such as those in the first group as "stuck" and those in the second as "moving." Susan J. Rosenholtz, *Teachers' Workplace: The Social Organization of Schools* (New York: Longman, 1989).

4. Other researchers have reported similar responses among the principals they studied, including Ellen Goldring et al., "Make Room Value-Added: Principals' Human Capital Decisions and the Emergence of Teacher Observation Data," *Educational Researcher*

44, no. 2 (2015): 96–104; Morgaen L. Donaldson and Sarah Woulfin, "From Tinkering to Going 'Rogue': How Principals Use Agency When Enacting New Teacher Evaluation Systems," *Educational Evaluation and Policy Analysis* 40, no. 4 (2018): 1–26; and Julie A. Marsh et al., "Evaluating Teachers in the Big Easy: How Organizational Context Shapes Policy Responses in New Orleans," *Educational Evaluation and Policy Analysis* 39, no. 4 (2017): 539–70. The Gates intervention included goals of both development and accountability for their evaluation process, although RAND evaluators reported that principals in those districts and CMOs also concentrated on teachers' development. Because the reform was intended, in part, to increase dismissals of ineffective teachers, this focus on development was viewed as a shortcoming.

5. Claire Kaplan et al., *Time for Teachers: Leveraging Expanded Time to Strengthen Instruction and Empower Teacher* (Boston: National Center on Time and Learning, 2015), https://www.timeandlearning.org/sites/default/files/resources/timeforteachers.pdf.

6. Theodore Sizer, *Horace's Compromise: The Dilemma of the American High School* (Boston: Houghton Mifflin, 1984).

7. Cynthia E. Coburn, William R. Penuel, and Kimberley E. Geil, *Research-Practice Partnerships: A Strategy for Leveraging Research for Educational Improvement in School Districts* (New York: William T. Grant Foundation, 2013); Paul Cobb et al., *Systems for Instructional Improvement: Creating Coherence from the Classroom to the District Office* (Cambridge, MA: Harvard Education Press, 2018).

8. Superintendent Alonso's approach to "guided autonomy" in Baltimore is described in detail in a teaching case from the Public Education Leadership Program; see Allen Grossman, Susan Moore Johnson, and Elisha Brookover, *Baltimore City Public Schools: Implementing Bounded Autonomy* (Cambridge, MA: Harvard Business School Publishing, 2010), https://hbsp.harvard.edu/product/PEL063-PDF-ENG. It is also described in Susan Moore Johnson et al., *Achieving Coherence in District Improvement: Managing the Relationship Between the District Office and the Schools* (Cambridge, MA: Harvard Education Press, 2014), 51–7.

9. For promising international models, see Linda Darling-Hammond et al., *Empowered Educators: How High-Performing Systems Shape Teaching Quality Around the World* (San Francisco: Jossey-Bass, 2017), 168–82; and Oon-Seng Tan and EE-Ling Low, "Working in Times of Uncertainty to Prepare for the Future: A Study of Singapore's Leaders in Education Program," in *Preparing Teachers to Educate Whole Students: An International Comparative Study*, ed. Fernando M. Reimers and Connie K. Chung (Cambridge, MA: Harvard Education Press, 2018), 221–51.

10. Atul Gawande, *The Checklist Manifesto: How to Get Things Right* (New York: Holt Metropolitan Books, 2009), 160.

11. Anthony S. Bryk et al. explain how the principles of improvement science can be used productively in school improvement in *Learning to Improve: How America's Schools Can Get Better at Getting Better* (Cambridge, MA: Harvard Education Press, 2015).

Acknowledgments

This book would not have been possible without the thoughtful and generous teachers and administrators who agreed to be interviewed for these studies. They found time in their incredibly busy schedules to talk candidly about their goals, their students, their colleagues, and their schools. All that they said illuminated the hopes, practical realities, challenges, disappointments, and successes of their work in ways that no administrative data set ever could. Although I can't thank them personally by name, I've done my best to accurately present their accounts and views so that policy makers, practitioners, researchers, and others who care deeply about public education can learn from them.

I'm indebted to my many students at Harvard over the past thirty-five years who have contributed to this book directly and indirectly with their questions, examples, insights, and clarifications. In class after class, year after year, they continued to teach me while I tried to teach them. The doctoral students who conducted research with me, especially those in the Project on the Next Generation of Teachers, deserve credit for many of the ideas and much of the research reported here. They are an extraordinary group of individuals—curious, astute, principled, skilled, hardworking, productive, kind, generous, and fun—who continue to contribute richly to research, policy, and practice in education.

I've continuously relied on colleagues at Harvard and other institutions as I pursued my career and conducted this and earlier research. Their ideas, articles, assistance, recommendations, and encouragement have motivated, informed, and sustained me. In earlier days, I might have tried to name them all. Now, I realize how impossible that would be. Still, I want to acknowledge their importance and offer my genuine thanks.

I am also very grateful to the Spencer Foundation for generously supporting the SST and Successful Schools studies, and to the Ford Foundation and the Bill & Melinda Gates Foundation for funding the Teachers in Context study. The

Spencer Foundation also supported much of my earlier research on these topics, as well as the research training of many of my doctoral students. In this era of evidence-based everything, funders often prefer quantitative over qualitative studies and clear-cut conclusions over complicated, ambiguous ones, but these foundations generously invest in both.

I also greatly appreciate the support and hard work of many people at Harvard Education Press, led by its director, Doug Clayton. Caroline Chauncey, my editor there, encouraged me to write this book when I had only a glimpse of what it might become. With her magical mix of patience and prodding, she moved me along, responding with spare but spot-on responses to draft after draft. It's now time for me to buy the coffee.

Many of my collaborators at the Project on the Next Generation of Teachers also generously reviewed chapter drafts, often those reporting on studies we had conducted together. Several bravely read the entire draft when it was, in fact, very drafty. They offered their views not only as researchers, but also in their current roles as policy makers, professors, teachers, administrators, consultants, and foundation officers. After our years of working together, they often could see more clearly than I could the point I was trying to make. More than one offered me a piece of advice that I had once given them. With all that in mind, I give my deep thanks for the thoughtful and detailed comments provided by Jill Harrison Berg, Sarah Birkeland, Megin Charner-Laird, Morgaen Donaldson, David Kauffman, Susan Kardos, Cheryl Kirkpatrick, Matt Kraft, Ed Liu, Will Marinell, Mindy Munger, John Papay, Heather Peske, Emily Qazilbash, Stef Reinhorn, Nicole Simon, and Stacy Szczesiul. I'm also beholden to Erika Johnson, who offered candid advice about the draft and crucial assistance with its tables and graphics. When she was a beginning teacher in 1998, she was known as the Project's "favorite data point." Now, twenty years later, she is an accomplished teacher, researcher, and teacher educator in her own right.

My dear friends of many years have been there for me throughout this project with their own special blend of encouragement, reassurance, and entertaining distractions. I've been far more preoccupied than I would like during my recent, extended, self-imposed lockdown, but I'm looking forward to enjoying more of their company soon.

I'm very fortunate to have clever, kind, and generous children by birth and by marriage: Krister Johnson, Erika Johnson, Heather Janoff Johnson, and Leif Asper. Thirty-five years ago in the acknowledgments for my first book, I paid tribute to Krister and Erika's entertaining knock-knock jokes. Now I'm indebted to them and their spouses for their own clever children—Eli and Leah Asper, and Connor and Lola Johnson—who can always make me laugh. Despite living too far away, we manage to stay close.

Finally, I'm grateful to my husband, Glenn, my companion of fifty-five years. While this book was becoming itself, we hiked high and low through Peru, Vietnam, and Tasmania; biked the hills of the Berkshires; stared at the stars while surrounded by music at Tanglewood; watched endless videos; reveled during our grandkids' dance parties; and shared our political anguish. Glenn is a handyman of considerable skill and determination. He can repair espresso machines, replace gutters, reprogram remotes, restore lost documents, realign unyielding margins, and reframe my disappointments. He is my fixer. From past experience, Glenn knows that this process of book writing will eventually end and we will turn the music on again. I'm more than ready.

About the Author

Susan Moore Johnson is the Jerome T. Murphy Research Professor in Education at the Harvard Graduate School of Education, where she served as academic dean from 1993 to 1999. A former high school teacher who served in an administrative role as a teacher leader, Johnson has an ongoing research interest in the work of teachers and the reform of schools and school systems.

Johnson has written four books and many journal articles about teachers and their work. *Teacher Unions in Schools* (1984) focuses on the role of teachers unions in the day-to-day work of schools. *Teachers at Work* (1990) examines the school as a workplace for teachers. *Finders and Keepers: Helping New Teachers Survive and Thrive in Our Schools* (2006), written with colleagues at the Project on the Next Generation of Teachers, centers on the experiences of new teachers. Subsequent research at the Project focuses on teachers' careers, alternative preparation, the role of unions, hiring, induction, performance-based pay, teacher teams, and teacher evaluation. Johnson also is coauthor, with John P. Papay, of *Redesigning Teacher Pay* (2009).

Johnson has also written and consulted widely about educational leadership and management. Her 1996 book, *Leading to Change: Challenges of the New Superintendency*, analyzes the leadership practices of twelve newly appointed superintendents during their first six months in the role. Between 2007 and 2014, Johnson served as cochair of the Public Education Leadership Project (PELP), a collaboration between the Harvard Business School and the Harvard Graduate School of Education, where she and her colleagues wrote *Achieving Coherence in District Improvement* (2015), which examines the management relationship between the central office and schools in five large urban school districts.

Johnson serves on various advisory boards for organizations and publications. She is an inaugural fellow of the American Educational Research Association and a member of the National Academy of Education.

Index